COMPARATIVE LEGISLATURES

PUBLICATIONS OF THE CONSORTIUM
FOR COMPARATIVE LEGISLATIVE STUDIES
Lloyd D. Musolf
General Editor

G. R. Boynton and Chong Lim Kim, Editors, *Legislative Systems in Developing Countries*

Abdo I. Baaklini, *Legislative and Political Development: Lebanon, 1842–1972*

Allan Kornberg and William Mishler, *Influence in Parliament: Canada*

Peter Vanneman, *The Supreme Soviet: Politics and the Legislative Process in the Soviet Political System*

Albert F. Eldridge, Editor, *Legislatures in Plural Societies: The Search for Cohesion in National Development*

Michael L. Mezey, *Comparative Legislatures*

John D. Lees and Malcolm Shaw, Editors, *Committees in Legislatures: A Comparative Analysis*

Joel Smith and Lloyd Musolf, Editors, *Legislatures in Development: Dynamics of Change in New and Old States*

COMPARATIVE LEGISLATURES

Michael L. Mezey

DUKE UNIVERSITY PRESS, DURHAM, NORTH CAROLINA 1979

For my mother and my father,
Regina and Milton Mezey

CONTENTS

FOREWORD

Appropriately, this sixth volume in the series sponsored by the Consortium for Comparative Legislative Studies presents an overview of the burgeoning field. After a decade of close attention to legislatures of every description, the time is ripe to synthesize what has been learned. An astonishing amount of research has been published even since Jean Blondel's brief book with the same title as the present volume was brought out in 1973. The need for updating and synthesizing is acute because of the attention researchers now pay to the legislatures of developing nations along with these researchers' more traditional interests. Compared with legislative research of only a generation ago, a far broader array of legislative phenomena must be noted and assigned significance.

It is one thing to report on diverse changes, another to leave the reader with a sense that the kaleidescopic scene has been viewed sensibly and persuasively. Both tasks have been accomplished remarkably well by Professor Mezey. Added fillips for the reader are jargon-free language, carefully defined terms, and an occasional light touch. Readers from various backgrounds should find themselves edified without enduring pretense or pomposity.

Recognizing that a mere recital of the bewildering diversity of legislatures and the activities in which they engage would be of limited value, Professor Mezey has sought to group legislative phenomena according to the expectations associated with individual legislatures. Is a legislature primarily oriented toward policy making, representation, or system maintenance? These three emphases, Professor Mezey finds, can be correlated with a five-fold typology of legislatures in action (active, vulnerable, reactive, marginal, and minimal). He concludes his comprehensive survey and analysis of the literature on legislatures by predicting that one of the three expectations as-

sociated with legislatures will prove to be more viable in the future
than the other two. As with the rest of this intriguing book, readers
will find his reasoning thoughtful and challenging.

Lloyd D. Musolf

Davis, California
September 1978

PREFACE

Published material on legislatures comes in all shapes and sizes. One finds studies of single legislatures and, less frequently, studies comparing several legislatures. There are short articles in popular and scholarly journals, collections of papers in edited anthologies, and longer monographs. There is work exhibiting deductive theory and sophisticated techniques of data analysis, and there is work that is little more than thinly disguised journalism. Those who produce this literature are equally disparate: modern political scientists attracted by a plethora of things to count and the many opportunities to count them, traditional students of politics attracted by the personalities and drama of daily legislative happenings, itinerant democrats attracted by the confluence of democratic theory and practice, and historians attracted by the vast and relatively accessible record of yesterday's parliaments.

This volume is both a product of and a supplement to the extant literature on legislatures. As its title suggests, its purpose is to discuss legislatures comparatively and, as the reader will discover, no new original data are used in that discussion. Instead, I rely completely on articles, papers, and monographs, most of which focus on individual legislatures. I view this volume as a supplement to that literature because what I've attempted to do in surveying these studies is to generate middle-range theory that underlines those similarities and differences among legislative institutions that are suggested by a cumulative appraisal of the work to date. These generalizations serve as summary statements of what we seem to know at this time as well as useful points of departure for future research, particularly as areas of contradictory or uncertain findings are identified and distinguished from those observations and explanations that have been corroborated at several research sites.

The reader should be warned that this volume trades depth for breadth. It should be read more to find out about legislatures, or about categories of legislatures, and less to find out a great deal about any particular legislature. In making this trade, I have undoubtedly abused the sensibilities of the specialists on particular countries upon whose work I have drawn. I can only ask that they not judge me too harshly. One other caveat involves tenses. I have tried to keep up with the coming and going of legislative institutions in various countries and have altered tenses to reflect the fact that certain legislatures at this writing are no longer functioning. Needless to say, by the time that this book is in the hands of its readers, events will have occurred which will render many of my tenses obsolete. Finally, most of this discussion focuses on the popularly elected lower houses of legislatures; notable exceptions are the Senates of the United States, Chile, and Venezuela.

This book represents the culmination of more than ten years of professional interest and concern with legislative institutions, a period lengthy enough for me to acquire a rather long list of people and institutions to which I am obligated. The most important obligation is to the authors upon whose work I have drawn. Those debts will be immediately apparent in the pages that follow.

During my years as a graduate student at Syracuse University Douglas Price, Frank Munger, and Wayne Francis taught me how to be a political scientist. Doug Price and Steve Koff bear the responsibility for sparking my original interest in legislative behavior. My interest in comparative legislative behavior is something of a fluke. During the winter of 1969, midway through my first year as a member of the faculty at the University of Virginia, I was offered the opportunity to spend some time teaching at Thammasat University in Bangkok. I arrived in Thailand in June 1969, about a week before the National Assembly was to convene for the first time in ten years. Being present at the creation so to speak, I rushed out to investigate that peculiar and usually short-lived legislative institution and by virtue of that act became an instant comparativist. My stay in Thailand and my research on that legislature was made possible by a grant to the University of Virginia from the Rockefeller Foundation's University Development Program.

It was upon my return to the University of Virginia in the winter of 1971 that I first considered the possibility of drawing the literature on the world's legislatures into a coherent whole. Financial support for some preliminary work came from the Rockefeller Foundation and from the University of Virginia. I was assisted at various times by three people who were then graduate students at Virginia and by now have probably forgotten that they had a role in this enterprise. However, I have not forgotten Eve Lubalin, Kathleen McGuinness, and Elizabeth Andrews Hendricks. I benefited as well from conversations with my colleagues David Powell, William Bacchus, and Gerald Heeger, all of whom were quite willing to hear and comment on my early and quite unstructured thoughts about comparative legislative behavior.

In the summer of 1972 I had the good fortune to join the Department of Political Science at the University of Hawaii and to take part in the Comparative Legislative Studies Project, then going forth with financial assistance from the Agency for International Development. These funds purchased such necessities as secretarial and research assistance, unpublished doctoral dissertations, and airline tickets. My debt of gratitude to my colleagues in the Political Science Department would be difficult to overstate. In addition to creating a congenial environment for living and working (in that order) they were people from whom I learned a great deal. The substantive contributions of my friends and associates in comparative legislative studies—Norm Meller, Fred Riggs, and Bob Stauffer—are apparent on many of the following pages. Other members of the Department—Neal Milner, Deane Neubauer, Mike Shapiro, Harry Friedman, Doug Bwy, Glen Paige—made more subtle contributions by talking with me, by being my friends, and by just being there. Among the graduate students with whom I worked several helped me directly with my research while other contributed to my thinking through their own work. In no particular order these good people are Jack Dukesbury, Haing-ja Kim, Jeff Loo, Scott Moore, Mike Shimoda, Jim Schubert, Kathy Higham, Diana Sabater, and Young-chul Paik.

In addition to my colleagues at Hawaii, many people have read and commented on various parts of this manuscript at various stages of its development, among them Richard Fenno, Nelson Polsby, Lloyd Musolf, Dick Sisson, Bob Boynton, and Jerry Loewenberg. The entire manuscript was read by Malcolm Jewell, Allan Kornberg, Kenneth Janda, Chong Lim Kim, and David Mayhew. These people all helped to improve this book and are, of course, absolved from blame for any of the remaining errors.

Most of the manuscript was typed under the direction of Ms. Freda Hellinger of the Social Sciences and Linguistics Institute of the University of Hawaii, a remarkable woman to whom I always shall be grateful.

There is only one person who has been with this project from beginning to end. My wife, Susan Gluck Mezey, by exhortation and by example helped to keep me going when there was no light at the end of the tunnel. More importantly, she did not permit my responsibilities to her and to our children, Jennifer and Jason, to fall victim to this manuscript. One reason why this book took so long to get finished is that my family was not deprived of my active involvement while the work was in progress, and it is to Susan more than anyone else that I owe this appropriate ordering of my priorities.

Michael L. Mezey

Chicago
March 1978

Part I

INTRODUCTION

Chapter 1

DEFINING THE LEGISLATURE: ACTIVITIES AND EXPECTATIONS

What is a legislature? What political institutions should be included in a general analysis of legislatures and what institutions should be excluded? Clearly it is reasonable that we be asked to begin by precisely defining the institution that we are interested in talking about for the remainder of this treatise. Yet, as several colleagues in comparative legislative studies will attest, the easiest way to stymie a conference of legislative scholars is to raise the question of what is a legislature.

Why the difficulty? Strangely, the definitional problem has become more complex as our knowledge about legislatures has become more sophisticated. In the old days, when we assumed that all legislatures everywhere were like the United States Congress, definitions were easy to come by. A legislature was a body elected by the people at relatively frequent intervals, and it made laws.

The complications arose when we discovered that several countries had institutions that were called legislatures but which, even by the most generous standards, could not be considered law-making bodies. Findings like this were not restricted to legislatures in developing or socialist countries. Modern research on western European parliaments demonstrated quite conclusively that the law-making functions of these "established" legislatures had long since passed to executives that controlled disciplined parliamentary majorities, and that legislators in these systems had little or no role in making laws.

Legislative scholars were confronted with a clear choice; either law making had to be abandoned as a functional requirement for an institution called a legislature, or a lot of old parliamentary friends—including the House of Commons itself—might have to be excluded from consideration as a legislature. So law making was dropped as a necessary characteristic of a legislature, and we had to rethink what we meant when we talked about legislatures.

FUNCTIONALISM

A large group of people adopted a functional approach. They argued that law making should never have been considered as the sole or most salient function of a legislature, and suggested that throughout history legislatures had seldom been dominant law-making forces. They argued that the legislature was a functionally adaptable institution that could do a variety of things in a political system (Wheare, 1963; Kornberg, 1970; Loewenberg, 1971b; Mezey, 1973; Riggs, 1973).

In short order studies appeared, or were discovered, indicating that legislatures acted as agencies of political recruitment, that legislators could represent the views of the people to nonlegislative elites in the executive and the bureaucracy, that legislators could educate and inform the public on major political issues, that legislatures could oversee the activities of the bureaucracy, that legislatures were effective instruments for nation building and national integration, and that legislatures could have the effect of mobilizing public support for a regime and thereby legitimizing the political system.

This proliferation of potential functions had the beneficial effect of spurring interest in legislatures, particularly those in developing countries that had previously been ignored because of their apparent lack of policy-making power. However, the long list of functions also increased the definitional confusion. Could any of these several functions be considered peculiarly legislative? Could the presence of one or more of these functions in an institution's functional repertoire qualify that institution as a legislature?

Clearly, most of these functions could be performed by other political institutions, most notably political parties, but also interest groups, the press, and executive leaders. Strong political parties, for example, could recruit elites, represent citizens, educate and inform the public, mobilize regime support, and serve the function of promoting national integration. But just as military juntas that made laws did not qualify as legislatures by virtue of performing that function, political parties did not become legislatures because they performed several of the functions that a legislature could perform. Thus, functionalism widened our legislative horizons but did little to help us define the legislative animal and to separate it from the other beasts in the institutional jungle.

THE A PRIORI APPROACH

To deal with this problem, some scholars turned to what might be called an a priori approach. This involves the positing of a list of words which, taken together, define those characteristics that, in the view of the person doing the talking, an institution must have in order to qualify it as a legislature. For example, Norman Meller (1966) and Gerhard Loewenberg (1971b) suggested that a legislature was both a collegial and a representative body, while Fred Riggs (1973) defined a legislature as a "territorial elective assembly." John Grumm (1973) returned to the law-making concept and argued that anything or anyone that participated in making general rules and policies for a society was part of a legislative system. Nelson Polsby (1975:259–62) has offered the most recent and perhaps the most comprehensive list of structural characteristics associated with legislatures. He suggests that they are assemblies whose members meet, deliberate, and act collectively as formal equals. He says that legislatures are further distinguished by their standing as official rather than private bodies, and by the fact that their formal enactments are officially binding on a population to which they are accountable and from whom their legitimacy emanates.

What this type of exercise involves, of course, is a particular writer telling his readers what he is thinking of when he uses the term "legislature." The only way to demonstrate the validity of these defining characteristics is to see whether or not it fits those institutions that we are accustomed to calling legislatures, or, alternatively, to determine whether it includes institutions which we are unaccustomed to thinking of as legislatures.

For example, is an elective school board (collegial, representative, and territorial) a legislature? How about the House of Lords (collegial, territorial, but nonrepresentative) or the Senate of Thailand circa 1951—half appointed and half elected? Necessarily, any set of words, depending on how they are defined, will exclude certain institutions from the legislative category that someone somewhere has always thought of as a legislature.

The reader who has come this far assuming that I will now provide a solution for this intellectual quandary will be sadly disappointed because I can do nothing more at this point but inform the reader what picture is in my head as I use the term "legislature" throughout this volume. *I think of a legislature as a predominantly elected body of people that acts collegially and that has at least the formal but not necessarily the exclusive power to enact laws binding on all members of a specific geopolitical entity.*

By an elected body of people, I mean people who hold their positions as a result of an election in which all adults are allowed to participate except, for example, those who are insane, imprisoned, illiterate, or who do not meet residence requirements, etc. These elections need not be competitive, but ballots must be cast in secret. When I say "predominantly" elected, I mean that the presence of a small number of appointed members, such as is the case in Tanzania, does not in my view deprive an institution of its status as a legislature, whereas a completely appointed body such as the Canadian Senate is so disqualified. A collegial body is one in which the members are formally equal in status. When I say that the legislature must have a formal law-making power, I mean that the constitution under which the legislature operates must endow it with a law-making capability. When I say that a legislature need not hold that power exclusively, I am recognizing the fact that other institutions in a political system—courts, bureaucracies, presidents—can make laws in the form of judgments, rules, and decrees.

By this definition the House of Lords is not a legislature nor is the military junta that ruled Greece from 1968 to 1974. A school board is not a legislature unless it is elected and unless it can make binding laws; a city council is a legislature and so is the Supreme Soviet, but the Thai Senate of 1951 is not a legislature because half of its members were appointed. The United Nations is not a legislature because it lacks the capacity to make laws that are binding upon a specific geopolitical entity, but the Brazilian Congress is a legislature even though it possesses law-making powers which are inferior to those held by people in executive positions.[1]

LEGISLATIVE ACTIVITIES

Dealing with the definitional problem in the way that we have still leaves us with the question of functions, a question that revolves around the fact that different institutions, all of which conform to our definition of a legislature, may perform quite different functions depending upon the political system in which they are found. A generation of research on legislatures throughout the world has produced a formidable list of these legislative functions. The task of bringing some degree of coherence to this list is difficult because different labels are often stuck onto quite similar activities and because activities are classified as legislative roles, or legislative functions, or legislative behavior in a more or less haphazard manner.

A good deal has been written about what "function" and "role" mean, how the two concepts are related, and how the terms should and should not be used. Without minimizing the importance of these distinctions, they are somewhat beside the point of this discussion. What I will be writing about in the following sections are the activities of legislatures and their members. Whatever their conceptual anchor, with only a modest amount of pushing and shoving these activities can be grouped into three broad categories: policy-making activities, representational activities, and system-maintenance activities.

Policy-making Activities. As we have seen, the invention and enactment of public policy traditionally has been thought of as the essential legislative function. In countries such as the United States, the Philippines, and Chile, legislatures in recent years have actually played this role quite effectively. However, most legislatures have not been quite as active, leading some to conclude, hastily and I think erroneously, that most legislatures have no role to play in the policy-making process.

Many legislatures that play no role in initiating policies and whose approval of policies initiated by others is foreordained still perform what might be called a deliberative function. Bagehot, for example, suggested that the discussion of issues and proposals in the legislature served to teach and inform mass publics as well as political elites (Crick, 1970). One study of three small African countries concludes that the views of parliamentarians, privately and publicly expressed, have on occasion led the government to alter proposals before pushing them through the legislature (Macartney, 1969:98). A recent analysis of parliamentary activity in Uganda demonstrates that parliamentary pressures were quite significant in determining the final shape of important land-reform measures (Ocaya-Lakidi, 1975). Finally, several studies of the British House of Commons have indicated that even though the cabinet can be assured of a parliamentary majority when it wants it, backbench pressures can force changes in government proposals, discourage the government from acting at all, or move it to act with greater dispatch (Lynskey, 1970; Butt, 1969).

What these examples suggest is that legislatures which do not possess the power to initiate or even to compel changes in policy proposals may have a more subtle power of informally setting the parameters within which those with policy-making power actually operate. All government proposals may pass the legislature unopposed and unamended simply because the government refrains from introducing legislation that will provoke substantial legislative opposition. Such a situation illustrates some form of legislative policy-making role, albeit not the type of role that students of American legislatures are accustomed to.

An aspect of policy-making activity found in almost every legislative setting is legislative oversight, or the control function as it is sometimes called (Kornberg, 1970; Agor, 1970; Packenham, 1970; Singhvi, 1970; Lees, 1977). Mill (1958:81) long ago asserted that "to watch and control the Government" is "the proper office" of representative assemblies, in comparison to the governing function for which he thought the legislature to be "radically unfit." Today legislatures have a variety of methods at their disposal for performing oversight activities. In parliamentary systems the question period is used. In both parliamentary and presidential systems legislative committees call administrators to account for their actions, conduct investigations of policies, and make recommendations either to the legislature or to the government. Debate within the legislature may serve to focus public attention on the actions of bureaucrats and thereby encourage them to act more honestly and more efficiently.

Representational Activities. The several activities that we will fit into the representational category share this common characteristic: they involve the connection between the legislative arena and the various publics that comprise the citizenry of a nation. These activities refer directly to one of the defining characteristics of legislatures: the fact that these institutions are comprised of elected officials. This fact carries with it the implication that part of the job of elected officials is to act on behalf of those who have elected them.

One aspect of representational activity is what Walter Bagehot called the "expressive function"—expressing the minds of the people on matters of public concern (Crick, 1970:33). In a similar vein John

Stuart Mill idealized legislatures as the nation's "Congress of Opinions—an arena in which not only the general opinion of the nation, but that of every section of it . . . can produce itself in full light and challenge discussion" (Mill, 1958:82). More recently, as systems theory came to displace political theory, scholars have referred to this activity as "interest articulation" (Agor, 1971b; Blondel, 1973; Packenham, 1970).

A second aspect of representational activities refers to the legislator's role as an intermediary between citizens and government officials. Such activities find legislators involved in lobbying bureaucrats on behalf of constituents, dealing with complaints that citizens might have about bureaucratic inefficiency or corruption and attempting to channel national funds into local improvement projects. Wilder Crane (1962) was one of the first scholars to deal with this activity empirically,—he called it "errand-running"—in his study of Austrian legislators. Since then similar activities have been described and analyzed for legislators in the United States (Olson, 1967, Fiorina, 1977), Great Britain (Barker and Rush, 1970), India (Bailey, 1960), the Philippines (Franzich, 1971), Afghanistan (Weinbaum, 1972), and several other countries.

Jean Blondel suggests that these intermediary activities are a universal function of legislators because "legislators enjoy an access to the central government departments and to members of the government that is unquestionably greater than that of most citizens" (Blondel, 1973:97). Thus it is not surprising that citizens may choose to process grievances through legislators because they perceive legislators to be obligated to them through an electoral connection. Many legislators find satisfaction in such a role. Kornberg (1970:96) reports that Canadian MPs indicate "genuine pleasure over their perceived ability to guide people though the maze of government or to get people a hearing or to help them solve their problems if they have to do with government." Other studies indicate that some legislators feel overwhelmed by their load of particularized demands and think that they should be spending more time on important things (Crane, 1962; Mezey, 1973; Cayrol et. al., 1976).

System Maintenance Activities. System maintenance activities are those legislative activities that contribute toward the stability and survival of the political system—activities which add to the support accruing to the system from mass and attentive publics as well as from relevant political elites.

It has been suggested that one way in which legislatures contribute toward system maintenance is by recruiting and socializing political elites. Robert Stauffer (1970:355) argues that in the case of the Philippines, "the existence of a 'national' legislature long before the nation achieved independence and regular congressional elections throughout the nation greatly contributed to the creation of a political class that was national in geographic spread and integrated in political outlook." Frederick Frey (1965:6) reports that during the dominance of Ataturk's Republican People's Party in Turkey all cabinet members, formal legislative leaders, and top party leaders served apprenticeships in the Grand National Assembly. In Mexico it is common for ambitious young politicians to serve in the legislature at an early point in their careers (Scott, 1964:265).

The role of the legislature in the recruitment and socialization of political elites has direct implications for another system-maintenance activity of legislatures—conflict management. The need for this function rests on the assumption that conflict is unavoidable and even desirable in political systems and that an institutional setting is required within which such conflicts can be adjusted in such a way as to permit the system to meet its responsibilities with minimum disruption and maximum public support (Stauffer, 1970; Jewell and Patterson, 1973). To the extent that legislators come to acquire shared political values and that the members of the legislature are representative of most groups and interests in the nation, the legislature becomes a viable vehicle for conflict management. In a very real sense legislatures domesticate conflict. They are a structural device for keeping conflict within the system and thus within limits acceptable to the policy-making elites. Interactions within the legislature may serve to ventilate grievances, but they also can serve to reveal areas of agreement and promote consensus.

To the extent that legislatures successfully manage conflict, they contribute to the integration of the political system. Jean Grossholtz (1970:94) defines integration "as a process leading to political cohesion and sentiments of loyalty toward central political institutions." One may speak of integration of elites, integration at the mass level, and integration between elite and mass levels.

As we have seen, legislatures, by providing a common national political arena, may serve to integrate national elites. The representation of different segments of the population in the legislature—ethnic groups, regional groups, ideological viewpoints—may serve to create a greater sense of national identification among mass publics. If legislatures perform their representational activities effectively they can serve to strengthen the link between mass publics and political elites, thus further contributing to the integration of the political system.

Lebanon, during more peaceful days, was thought to provide an example of the process. Baaklini (1972:294, 296) reports that through

the electoral process and the sharing of power within the context of the parliamentary system, sectarian conflicts have been reduced and an independent political existence for Lebanon has been guaranteed. . . . In a sense the spatial dimension of a nation was emphasized as a significant political variable while the social and cultural connotations were depoliticized. . . . Members of the Chamber . . . were to act as the link, the brokers . . . linking their people to the central government.

Other system maintenance activities are oriented more toward the government in power rather than toward the nation as a whole. Bagehot said that one function of the British Parliament was to act as an electoral body for the executive branch of government (Crick, 1970), and, in parliamentary systems, a major function of the legislature continues to be the creation and the support of a government.

Legislatures sometimes play more active roles in maintaining regime support. Richard Sisson (1973) has referred to legislatures as a major means for mobilizing support for government policies. As we shall see, in many political systems legislators are specifically required to articulate and defend government policies in their constituencies. More generally the major function of legislative activity can be conceived as that of legitimizing the actions of the regime. Sometimes by providing the semblance if not the reality of popular participation legislative involvement in policy formation can make those policies appear to be popular or democratic. In Brazil Packenham (1970:530) has asserted that "the Congress was a safety-valve or way of letting off steam in a political system where nobody got all he wanted and/or where the government was not willing to let everyone have what he wanted." This legislative involvement in policy making, even if such involvement is in fact a formality, appears to be a general expectation of both domestic and international publics and thereby serves to legitimize the actions of the political elites who really hold the power in the political system.

DIFFERENT ACTIVITIES, DIFFERENT MODELS

Such a long list of possible activities attests to the fact that the legislature is a flexible institution capable of performing several different functions within a political system. It is unlikely that any one legislature performs all of the functions listed. There is rather a package of activities for each legislature.

The contents of a particular legislature's activities package depends in large measure on the attitudes of mass and elite publics toward the legislature. These attitudes may be called expectations and refer to those activities people want the legislature and its members to engage in.

Mass and elite expectations concerning the legislature are conditioned by several environmental variables. The political culture of a nation, its history, the personality and ambitions of its leaders, its level of socioeconomic development, and undoubtedly an array of several other variables all affect the behavior that leaders and citizens alike come to expect of their political institutions and the political actors that people them.

Expectations come in various shapes and sizes. They may be more or less specific; that is, they may refer to a particular task such as passing certain types of laws, or to a more generalized function such as conflict management. They may envision an active role or a passive role for the legislature. Those who hold expectations concerning the legislature may view certain of these expectations as more important or salient than others. Expectations may be more or less consensually shared by members of particular groups, or there may be more or less congruence between the expectations of one segment of society and the expectations of others.

Expectations are manifested in a number of ways. Written constitutions are concrete statements of certain expectations. The political customs and conventions that govern political behavior in a nation are based in part on what people expect from their political institutions. Elites often speak publicly about their expectations in regard to the legislature. Mass expectations can be culled from public opinion polls, but actual behavior, both of masses and elites, are often more reliable guides. That is, the way people act toward the legislature may be an indication of their expectations in regard to that institution.

The specificity or generality of expectations, the degree to which they are consensual and congruent, their relative saliency, and their substantive content will significantly affect such aspects as the nature of the process by which legislators are recruited, the role perceptions of legislators, the functions that legislatures perform, and the stability of the legislative institution in a particular country.

Expectations toward legislatures also take on certain discernible patterns. These patterns may be called legislative models and are distinguished from one another on the basis of the set of legislative activities that are given highest priority in the model. Thus we can identify a policy-making model of the legislature, a representational model, and a system-maintenance model. These models represent constructs in the minds of people that specify what a legislature should be and the activities with which it should be concerned.

The Policy-Making Model. The policy-making model of the legislature is predicated on the assumptions that majorities have the right to decide the laws under which they are governed and that the popular will should become known through the legislature. Thus the legislature, as the supreme governing power, should be an assemblage of the best and brightest in the land, placed there by their constituents to share their views on policy, to negotiate, and to produce legislation that is responsive both to the general public and to the needs of the nation. Representation in the legislature should be calculated to provide all significant segments of the population with a voice in the decision-making process. Through their joint participation in policy making, they should resolve their conflicts among themselves and produce policies that can be supported by the largest possible majorities.

The system-maintenance activities associated with the policy-making model are implicit rather than explicit. The presumption of the model is that policies that emanate from the citizens or their representatives are likely to be supported. Policies that are the product of representative institutions will be perceived as legitimate even if they are not very popular. As Gerhard Loewenberg (1971a:190, 1973:142ff) has suggested, the continuity and salience of parliament affects the durability of public support for the regime which in turn affects regime stability.

The policy-making model has always been most at home in the United States. Legislative power was broadly asserted during the colonial period, primarily because the crown controlled the other organs of government. One historian (Pole, 1966:31) writes that in nearly all the matters that directly touched the people of the colonies, the Assemblies really acted as representatives and really governed. Although colonial taxation was light, the Assemblies laid the taxes, thus establishing their own normal ability to exercise this basic parliamentary power. They received petitions and made laws on innumerable local and provincial issues, session after session, and generation after generation.

Today American legislatures at both the state and national levels continue to exercise significant power over the shape of public policy. Elite expectations continue to support such a role for the legislature. At the national level American presidents have frequently called upon the Congress to act expeditiously to meet national problems and have often taken the opportunity to attack "do nothing Congresses." Leaders of federal bureaucracies maintain close liaison with legislators, particularly those who serve on committees with jurisdiction over their subject areas. In several instances the seeming inability of American legislatures to act swiftly and effectively to deal with policy problems has provoked a literature geared toward reform of legislatures so that they will be better able to execute their policy-making activities and therefore remain "the central institution of the American democratic republic" (de Grazia, 1967:15).

The limited evidence from public opinion polls suggests that the American people expect the Congress to be at least an equal partner with the president in the policy-making process. One study (Parker, 1973) showed that two-thirds of a national sample wanted Congress to exercise equal power with the president while another 20 percent wanted the Congress to have more power than the president. Only 15 percent wanted the president to be more powerful than the Congress.

There is little evidence that the public knows or cares exactly what the Congress is doing with its policy-making power. Several studies have confirmed the observation of one congressman that "people don't care how I vote on foreign aid, federal aid to education, and all these big issues, but they are very much interested in whether I answer their letter and who is going to be the next rural mail carrier or the next postmaster" (Clapp, 1964:58). It appears that the American citizen has and seeks very little information about the way in which their representatives vote or the specific policies under consideration by the Congress. However, there have been indications that the level of popular support for the Congress tends to go up when Congress is perceived to be more active and tends to decline when Congress is thought to be inactive (Davidson, 1970a:171–74).

The Representation Model. The representation model differs from the policy-making model in that it does not assume that policies will emanate from the legislature. Rather it assumes that the legislature will affect public policy though the vigorous performance of its representational activities. The role of the individual legislator is not one of inventing new public policies; instead, the legislator's job is to see to it that the interests of those whom he or she represents are protected in the development and implementation of public policy.

The expectations of mass publics are primarily oriented toward the representation model. This is most apparent when one examines the heavy volume of particularistic demands that come to legislators from their constituencies—demands for information, services, or public outputs that the people making the demand are personally interested in. As we have suggested, these demands tend to reach legislators simply because legislators are elected by constituents and presumably serve at their pleasure. In many political systems legislators may be the only elected public officials and thus the only people that citizens feel that they can turn to when they need assistance in dealing with government agencies. One observer (Vanneman, 1972:243) of the Soviet political system has written that "all recent accounts of the life and duties of deputies stress the red tape cutting, grievance procedure role of the deputies. It is generally agreed that this function was insufficiently attended to in the past."

More generally, constituents tend to expect a particularistic style of representation from their legislators. That is, they expect their MP to elevate constituency interests above national interests and the interests of individual petitioners above more generalized interests. For legislators at the state level this expectation can be intense. F. G. Bailey (1960:123) reports that the citizens of the Indian state of Orissa

see their MLA not as a legislator but as *their* representative who will intercede for them with the Administration. This is meant quite literally. The MLA is an effective broker, who can get a man out of trouble or win a favour for him, or so manipulate matters that the benefits of the Welfare State are diverted away from others towards his own people.

Legislators are expected to bring home to the constituency a sizable portion of the national budget to be spent on various local improvements, and to see to it that the needs of the constituency are accommodated in general public policy. The situation in the Philippines prior to martial law was an extreme example of localism:

In order to meet the requirements of his constituents, the politician needs the resources to provide them with public works projects, jobs, money, and innumerable favors of a personal nature. The search for the wherewithal to meet these requests and the resolution of the conflicts that inevitably arise as politicians compete for government resources occupies the major part of the Filipino politician's time. (Grossholtz, 1964:238)

The same author suggests elsewhere that the Philippine Congress is "the repository of local interests" (Grossholtz, 1969:15).

Such views are not restricted to citizens of non-Western countries. Basil Chubb (1963) reports that the rural farm population of Ireland sees government as a potential source of aid and favors, and looks to parliamentarians as intermediaries between the people and the bureaucracy. Members of the parliament are expected to deliver for their constituency or face electoral defeat.

This style of representation becomes very apparent when the legislator represents a specific, highly visible constituency such as a state (in the case of a federal system), or a tribe, or a distinct geographic region. The representative under these circumstances will be expected to act as the constituency's ambassador to the central government and he will be charged with the duty of defending identifiable constituency interests in the national arena. In Afghanistan, for example, the parliamentary tradition is one that emphasizes the representation of large tribal and ethnic groups. This tradition survives in the behavior of Afghan legislators, or *wakils*; Weinbaum (1977:102) reports that "only a handful of the legislators were directly beholden to the government in Kabul for their victories. The overwhelming number of wakils were to dedicate themselves to the well-being of local, sectarian, and personal interests."

The representational model does not incorporate explicit expectations concerning the policy-making role of the legislature. The presumption is that vigorous articulation of constituency views will produce policy responses from those who have policy-making power. Legislators are expected to gain policy concessions by using their capacity to criticize, embarrass, delay, and obstruct the government. These techniques, combined with the notion that legislators should intervene with bureaucrats on behalf of citizens, means a heavy emphasis in the representation model on oversight activities. Even if the legislature does not make policy, it is expected to act as a "watchdog," guarding the people's interests against those who do make policy and exposing corruption and inefficiency when these are found. The representation model thus looks to the legislature's capacity to generate adverse publicity and encourage public opposition to the government as the means for exercising influence on a policy-making process centered in other political institutions.

The system-maintenance activities of the legislature under the representation model also tend to flow implicitly from the performance of representational activities. If citizens feel that their interests are being represented, then they will be more likely to support government policies and the regime itself. The effective articulation of interests will permit the more expeditious management of conflict and reduce the likelihood of disruption or instability in the political system. At a minimum public articulation of grievances will provide a symbolic hearing for these views, which may serve to decrease their disruptive potential.

The System-Maintenance Model. The system-maintenance model assumes that the best policies emanate from a centralized leadership structure operating outside the legislative arena. The political problem confronting those who make public policies is to generate and maintain support for those policies as well as for their own positions as policy makers. Legislatures are viewed as a vehicle for accomplishing these ends.

The representational activities of legislatures can be construed primarily in system-maintenance terms. For example, it could be said with only some oversimplification that legislatures originally were designed to provide elites with just enough representation to enable them to carry out their policies. One interpretation of the origin of the British Parliament focuses on the throne's need for funds. As one historian (Pasquet, 1967:159–60) has put it,

Edward I . . . was always short of money. The royal demesne was impoverished. The government of the Kingdom was becoming more and more complex and more and more costly. The great undertakings of the reign, the conquest of Wales, the conquest of Scotland, the war with France, were very expensive. The king was thus forced by financial pressure to summon the representatives of his counties and good towns in order to obtain the necessary aids from them; and they used their financial power to diminish the royal prerogative by gaining ever-increasing concessions in matters of legislation and policy.

Since then legislatures have been arenas for the representation of interests that nonlegislative elites wanted represented or were compelled by circumstances to be responsive to.

In some modern political systems legislative seats are distributed as sinecures for the followers of incumbent elites in order to ensure their continued support for the regime. For example, the composition of the Mexican Congress is carefully designed to provide representation for the various wings of the ruling party. Slots are also provided for older politicians who have served the party well in the past and who are in need of a less strenuous but remunerative and honorable position.

In large nations beset by cultural, ethnic, regional, and political diversities elites may look to the legislature as a means of providing a common national focus within which these factions can make their views known. In the case of Lebanon there is evidence that these expectations were held quite explicitly. Michel Cheha, one of the architects of the Lebanese constitution put it this way:

Since it is a country comprising associated minorities of different religious communities, Lebanon cannot last long, politically speaking, without an assembly to be the meeting place and centre of unity for those communities with a view to exercising joint control over the nation's political life. Once you abolish the assembly, you unavoidably transpose debate to the sanctuary or to its shadow, and by so much you slow down the formation of a civic sense. (Quoted in Baaklini, 1972:187)

In bringing together the various factions in a polity, the legislature can provide information for the government, helping it to design policies that will be responsive to popular needs and therefore more easily accepted by those involved. Joseph Stalin stated the concept this way:

In our Soviet country we must evolve a system of government that will permit us with certainty to anticipate all changes, to perceive every thing that is going on among the peasant, the nationals, the non-Russian nations, and the Russians; the system of supreme organs must possess a number of barometers which will anticipate every change, register and forestall all possible storms and ill-fortune. This is the Soviet system of government. (Quoted in Vanneman, 1972:236)

But it is clear that the elites view representational activities as both instrumental and subordinate to the systems maintenance goal. Thus apparently representational expectations may be read quite differently by legislators who are aware of the real priorities of the elite. In March 1969, for example, President Kuanda of Zambia urged Government party backbenchers "to do their homework and produce worthwhile debate so that the peoples' interests could be represented and protected effectively." Yet Helgerson (1970:94–95) reports that few members followed this advice for fear of sanctions that might be invoked against them by the party leadership.

The possible sanctions feared by Zambian MPs suggests that when elites subscribe to a maintenance model of the legislature they expect only minimal and supportive legislative policy-making activities. Opposition and criticism of government proposals may be restricted, or even forbidden altogether. President Julius Nyerere of Tanzania has made it clear on several occasions that members of the Bunge have only a limited right to criticize government proposals once they have been approved by the ruling party's National Executive Committee; these criticisms must focus on matters of detail and may not involve the principles of the legislation. Also the government prefers that critical statements be made in private rather than in public (Hopkins, 1970:704).

Not surprisingly, the maintenance model carries with it unambiguous system-maintenance expectations for legislatures. In addition to supporting the government with their voices and their votes in parliament, members are expected to be the government's ambassadors to the people. They are sent out to the constituencies to explain and defend government policies and to promote compliance. President Jomo Kenyatta of Kenya put it this way:

The Members of Parliament do not simply have a narrow responsibility to their constituents. They have an over-riding duty to the State. Each member is a link, binding the Republic to the people. And in each direction there is an obligation to guide and lead. . . . Members of Parliament have a most important duty in the rural areas, to urge their people to follow the advice of technicians. (Quoted in Stultz, 1970:322)

Sometimes this expectation is coupled with a request that legislators bring citizen complaints to the government's attention. However, there is reason to believe that such activities are not meant to take precedence over activities associated with mobilizing support for the government. One observer of the current situation in Tanzania (Kjekshus, 1974:33) writes that "the role of the constituency members—as seen from Dar es Salaam—does not consist of making effective demands on behalf of the voters, but rather of providing popular support and legitimacy for the Party's policies and helping to implement them in the localities as a leader, as a resident Party activist."

In sum, the maintenance model views legislators as people who will help legitimize government policies by supporting them in parliament and by defending them at the constituency level to the voters upon whom they are imposed. There seems an expectation that legislators will act as buffers, shielding policy-making elites from the discontent of those who have to obey the policies.

These three models are constructs in the minds of people about how legislatures should function, and the difference among these models helps to explain why so many different legislative activities have been suggested and discovered. These models cannot be used to classify legislatures for two reasons: first, it would be nearly impossible to map empirically the legislative expectations of mass and elite publics throughout the world, and, secondly, even if the data problem could be solved, in all probability we would find that not everyone in a political system agrees about what model legislature they have or want to have. As suggested, elites may find a maintenance model of the legislature most suitable to their needs, while mass publics may look toward a representation model and legislators may prefer a policy-making model. The extent to which the models employed by legislators, citizens, and nonlegislative elites are congruent will, as we shall see in Chapter 2, significantly affect the stability of a legislature.

NOTES

1. I realize that this is a "modern" definition of a legislature. The suffrage requirement, for example, excludes the House of Commons prior to the Reform Acts as well as most legislatures in the American South prior to the Voting Rights Acts of 1965. There is nothing intrinsically wrong with this. What I am doing, after all, is stating *my* criteria for deciding what institutions *legitimately* can claim to be legislatures. These criteria are both subjective and relative. If I were doing this study one hundred years ago, my criteria would need to be different from the ones that I've stated here because the universe of legislatures would be different. Given the modern commitment to mass participation, I think that few would quarrel with a decision to exclude an assembly elected by a very limited franchise from the legislative category.

Chapter 2

CLASSIFYING LEGISLATURES

The literature in the field of legislative behavior has been frequently and correctly criticized for its failure to be truly comparative (Loewenberg, 1972). Most research undertakings, with only a few exceptions, have focused on single legislatures. Each researcher has adopted techniques and developed concepts suitable or convenient for a particular legislature under study. Thus while we have been told a great deal about *individual* legislatures, we have been told very little about legislatures.

Hard practical realities are basically responsible for this state of the art. Comparative studies are more expensive and more difficult to execute, especially if they are designed collaboratively with the participation of researchers from several countries. Certain legislatures are studied simply because it is easier to study them; language problems may be acute at one research site and absent at another, while legislators may be open and cooperative in one country and secretive and inaccessible in another. Or it has been argued that detailed knowledge of a country is necessary before you can say anything about its legislature, and thus legislative studies should be done by country experts who, not surprisingly, will write only about that one legislature with which they are familiar.

These practical considerations clearly dictate most research decisions. Once these decisions are taken, they are often justified with elaborate rationalizations. For some period of time it was asserted that any information on any legislature in the world was valuable simply because "so little is known about legislatures." As we came to know more, we were told that studying one particular legislature was worthwhile because that legislature was unique, important, or especially interesting. Or studying a legislature could be defended by asserting that it was "broadly representative" of a nebulous larger class of legislatures, but most researchers who used this rationale did not make the effort to define that larger class clearly or demonstrate how it was related to the legislature in question. Some people, of course, saw no need for rationalization; taking the idiosyncrasies of each country seriously, they proceeded on the assumption that every legislature was entirely different from every other legislature and therefore any attempt at generalization would be both futile and wrong-headed.

Without passing judgment on the good faith with which these claims are made, it is nonetheless clear that there is a sizable segment of the political science discipline that expects more than just a series of studies of single legislatures. If the institutional construct that we have called "legislature" means anything at all, then we must be able to make some general statement about these institutions. If one recognizes that need, then the problems alluded to before must be dealt with: how can we study legislatures comparatively given the constraints of money and the other impediments to cross-national research?

One answer is to exploit the country studies already done. Instead of collecting new data, the findings of previously executed scholarly research can form a data base from which generalizations can be made. While such "library" work is often denigrated in the profession, the fact is that if our colleagues are doing their fieldwork well (and there is no reason to expect that they aren't) then the fruits of their labors can and should be used.

One problem with this method is that it is extremely unlikely that comparable data will be uncovered for a wide range of legislatures. This is especially true if one is dealing with questions of major political moment; the only easily available data for all legislatures are simple constitutional and historical facts (see Blondel, 1973).

The problem can be met in part by developing a classification scheme for legislatures. Such a step is long overdue in comparative legislative research. By taking that step, it then becomes possible to merge information on all legislatures located in the same class and thereby produce categorical statements which can then be compared to yield even more general statements.

There are some obvious drawbacks. All legislatures will not fit neatly into one category or another; undoubtedly there will be some degree of intracategory variation. Also the categories may be defined somewhat arbitrarily. Because classifications depend on concepts, and different concepts produce different categories, one researcher's categories may be inappropriate or unacceptable to other researchers. These quite relevant arguments are countered by the simple fact that there now appears to be no ready alternative short of a massive collection of new, original data that would start us toward generalizations about legislatures. While some may wish to wait for the happy moment of plentiful, representative, and strictly comparable data, others will wish to move tentatively along the road to generalization, comforted by the knowledge that when all the data are in, all of the errors of omission and commission will be corrected.

THE POLICY-MAKING STRENGTH OF LEGISLATURES

The simplest and most common comparative statements about legislatures relate to the strength or weakness of particular legislative institutions. Although not always stated explicitly, such statements usually refer to the importance of the legislature in the policy-making process relative to the importance of nonlegislative institutions, commonly those operating through the executive branch of government.

Although there may well be some disagreement on whether or not a legislature's relative importance in policy making should be the sole criterion for judging its strength (see Mezey, 1975), there seems little doubt that it can be an appropriate criterion for distinguishing legisla- ✓ tures from one another. However, classifying legislatures on the basis of their policy-making importance is not as easy as it may seem to be.

Jean Blondel (1973) has pursued this point in greater depth and with more vigor than most other scholars. He develops a five-point scale that assesses the strength of the legislature compared to that of the executive on the basis of whether or not the right of censure is in the hands of the legislature and whether or not the executive has the power to dissolve the legislature. In addition to these constitutional variations, Blondel discusses the limits on legislative influence in terms of internal and external constraints operating on the institution. Internal constraints subsume several variables relevant to the internal organization of the institution, while external constraints refer to both the strength of the executive and the nature of the constitutional provisions previously included in the five-point scale.

While Blondel's formulation is important, it is of only limited utility for analyzing the involvement of legislatures in the policy-making process. As he suggests, "very strong executives are likely to be found at both ends of the continuum of constitutional powers" (Blondel, 1973:45). Communist systems, for instance, give wide grants of constitutional power to the legislature, yet real power resides in the executive branch. Such anomalies are inevitable when one becomes overly concerned with constitutional provisions rather than with political realities, particularly when dealing with rapidly changing political systems in which written constitutions often obscure more than they reveal.

An earlier formulation of Blondel's gets closer to the problem. Blondel introduces the concept of "viscosity" as an indicator of the legislature's role in law making. Viscosity reflects the degree to which legislatures are "free" or "compliant": "where the legislature is very compliant [government] bills do not merely pass, they pass very easily and . . . the time spent or the number of speakers engaged is very small. As the legislature becomes freer, the time spent increases and amendments are discussed and indeed passed" (Blondel, 1969–70:80).

Nelson Polsby (1975:277) writes in similar terms when he distinguishes between "transformative" and "arena" legislatures, with the former possessing "the independent capacity, frequently exercised, to mold and transform proposals from whatever source into laws," while the latter serve primarily as "formalized settings for the interplay of significant political forces in the life of a political system." Marvin Weinbaum (1975:43) suggests the things that a transformative legislature might do when he says that as evidence of a legislature's "decisional" role, we should look at its capacity "to initiate legislation, to modify, delay, or defeat bills, to influence administration through parliamentary questions, interpellations, and investigations, and to alter departmental budgets, authorizations, and personnel."

These perspectives are useful because they direct our attention to the influence that legislatures have on the policy-making process and suggest a means for classifying legislatures on the basis of the extent of this influence. The key term is Blondel's concept of "constraint," but not, as he says, constraints placed on the legislature that prevent it from influencing the policy-making process, but rather the constraints that the legislature is capable of placing on the policy-related activities of the executive.

In my view a constraint is a limitation that the legislature can place upon the executive branch of government that would not make it—the legislature—directly vulnerable to dissolution, proroguing, or closure. A constraint restricts the action of the executive branch and prevents it from making policy unilaterally. Legislatures will be salient in the policy-making process to the extent that their presence and prerogatives act as a constraint on the executive. If the constraints at the disposal of the legislature are weak, then the institution will be a correspondingly weak element in the policy-making process. The existence of substantive constraints brings with it a salient policy-making role.

It may strike some as prejudging the nature of the legislature's policy-making role to phrase an assessment of that role in negative terms—whether or not the legislature can stop things from happening. However, this conceptualization should not lead to the facile conclusion that legislatures are institutions designed to say no. Rather the argument is that the saliency of the legislature's policy-making role, whether ultimately evaluated as positive or negative, stems at base from its capacity to restrict the process, because that capacity is what compels other institutions to deal with it when they seek to make policy.

The most telling constraint that the legislature can place on the policy-making process is the veto. This means that the legislature can reject any proposal, no matter from which political actor or institution it emanates, without having to face new elections or some other form of disbandment. Constitutionally, almost every legislature in the world has this power, but we are concerned here with real rather than paper powers; a legislature that has a constitutional power to reject that it can never use does not in fact have the power.

A weaker constraint exists when the legislature can exact modifications or compromises in policy proposals even in the absence of a viable power to reject a proposal. Such modifications can be accomplished in a number of ways. Either through private consultation with legislators or through open legislative debate, the executive may become aware of significant criticisms of its proposals and respond to such criticism by agreeing to amendments. Alternatively amendments may be forced upon the government through a voting process. Or the government may respond to legislative demands because the only other alternative would be to dissolve the legislature—a step that the government may not care to take.

Legislatures may be constraining the executive in this manner even in systems where government proposals always are approved by the legislature. Private discussions between the government and its supporters in the legislature may lead the government to modify its proposals before submission to the legislature in order to mollify party dissidents, even though party discipline could be imposed to pass the proposal in its original form. Anticipated opposition in the legislature may lead the government to postpone a potentially controversial proposal until the climate of opinion is more favorable, or it may lead it to phrase its proposals in such a way as to ameliorate anticipated objections. Thus all government proposals appear to pass the legislature unopposed and unamended simply because the government avoids introducing those things which may provoke legislative resistance, or because it has acceded to changes privately.

One observer of the Jordanian Parliament summarized the situation there in these terms:

. . . the executive . . . tries as hard as humanly possible to avoid open clashes with the legislature. Both the legislature and the executive realize they have a share in the maintenance of the status quo and in a stable political order and are aware of the dangers to both from an open clash. Objectionable items are often ironed out before they reach the floor. Key legislators are consulted, cajoled, etc. beforehand. (Jaber, 1975a:17)

This type of constraint is frequently ignored by students of legislators because it is difficult to nail down empirically. One can observe a proposal being rejected or amended on the floor and in public view, but it is difficult to observe a bureaucrat or a president tailoring proposals to meet anticipated opposition in the legislature or privately consulting with Government party MPs before submitting bills. Nonetheless such a legislative constraint can be very significant in systems where executive leaders wish to maintain a legislature but do not care to accord it any substantial policy-making powers.

A legislature can be placed into one of three discrete categories, depending on the constraints at its disposal. Legislatures can be classified as possessing *strong policy-making power* if they can modify and reject executive proposals; legislatures that have no capacity to reject policy proposals but can modify them can be said to possess *modest policy-making power*, while legislatures that can neither modify nor reject policy proposals have *little or no policy-making* power. These three categories constitute one of the two dimensions I will be using to classify legislatures.[1]

SUPPORT

My second dimension for classifying legislatures is the degree of support accruing to the institution. By support I mean a set of attitudes that look to the legislature as a valued and popular political institution. One reason for suggesting support as an additional dimension for distinguishing among legislatures is because it lends a certain degree of predictability to the policy-making dimension that we already have defined.

Taken by itself, the policy-making dimension indicates where a legislature presently is located relative to the other policy-making institutions in a political system, but it offers no guidance to where that legislature might be five or ten years later. Only a casual survey of world events will confirm that the importance and salience of the legislature can be subject to significant change. For example, the Congress of the Philippines was always lionized as one of the most powerful legislatures in the world right up until the time in 1972 when President Marcos suspended the institution, with hardly a murmur of domestic dissent to be heard. Although the Philippine Congress would have been classified with the American Congress as a legislature with strong policy-making power, a carefully constructed support dimension would have distinguished between the two legislatures and indicates that the former was more vulnerable to extraconstitutional attack than the latter.

While it is significant to know how important a legislature is today, it is equally important to know how stable the legislature's position is and therefore how likely it is to continue in that position in the foreseeable future. Such data can affect the roles that the legislators adopt, the recruitment of legislators, the way they behave, and the way in which the legislature itself functions.

Manifest Indicators of Support. There are two ways to infer the level of support for a particular legislature. One way is to interpret the events that occur in a nation and the public statements of significant political actors as indicators of the presence or absence of support.

Another method is to analyze the attitudes toward the legislature extant among mass and elite publics and to attempt to identify a latent structure of attitudes that can be labeled as supportive of the legislature, and, in contrast, an attitude structure that can be labeled as nonsupportive. The latter method, of course, is more sophisticated, but the problems that are encountered in generating appropriate cross-national data are nearly insurmountable.[2] The event-oriented method is more rudimentary, but it still conveys a clear notion of what we mean by legislative support.

One indicator of support is the legislature's institutional continuity. We can ask whether or not coups or other extraconstitutional attacks upon the existence or integrity of the legislature occur in a country. For example, the legislative institution in Thailand was inaugurated in 1932. Since then there have been nine different constitutions, all ushered in by a coup d'etat and each specifying a different format for the legislature. In its 180 years of constitutional history France has been through five republics and three empires, each involving an alteration in the role of the National Assembly. A list of countries in which the legislature has been either suspended or abolished sometime during the last decade would include among others, Greece, Malaysia, Thailand, the Philippines, Indonesia, Pakistan, Bangladesh, Chile, Uruguay, Uganda, Nigeria, and Afghanistan. In addition, legislatures in most of Latin America, in South Korea, in preliberation South Vietnam, and in much of Africa have been subjected to threats against their institutional survival.

We also might investigate the attitudes of government leaders toward the legislature. Do they continually launch verbal attacks against the legislature which question not only the wisdom of legislative actions but the right of the legislature to continue to function? When the Congress of Uruguay was dissolved by a coup d'etat in 1973, the president of the republic explained his actions in the following terms:

Essentially the crisis is institutional. Uruguay requires profound institutional changes; and the parliamentary institution does not function, except for reasons of petty politics. It fails to pass bills which are necessary for the country and prevents the executive from governing. . . . Laws which were favorable to the country were not passed; those which do not coincide with national feelings were. In brief: Parliament did not permit us to govern; it placed itself outside the institutions. . . . (Astiz, 1973a:3)

One of the leaders of the 1958 coup against the Thai legislature spoke in similar terms: "How can representative government function if those who are elected to represent the people in the National Assembly forget the interest of the country as a whole and pursue only their selfish gains" (Darling, 1960:356).

The theme of corruption touched upon in this last statement suggests a third indicator of a low level of support—popular distrust of the legislature coupled with charges of corruption and/or incompetency. Robert Stauffer (1975) discusses at length the very negative portrayals of the Philippine legislator that consistently appeared in the Manila press in the years immediately prior to the Marcos coup. He quotes one journalist's criticism:

Over the years, Congress has fallen into disrepute. . . . The lawmaking body has become an object of scorn, hated and despised. To many Filipinos, Congress stands as a massive symbol of all that is dirty and evil in Philippine politics. To think of the legislature as an assemblage of learned men, many believe, is to be out of one's mind. For one, horseplay and shenanigans are standard fare in congressional deliberations. Absenteeism is prevalent, discipline is sadly lacking, and intellectual bankruptcy characterizes congressional discussions. To some, Congress is virtually a theater of the absurd. (Stauffer, 1975:36–37)

Attitudes like this, of course, are not directed exclusively toward those parliaments in developing political systems. French citizens have been described as "rather indifferent to Parliament as an institution" and "full of distrust for parliamentarians as a collective group." In the early fall of 1958, at the nadir of the Fourth Republic, 88 percent of the French public said "there are too many political parties in Parliament," 75 percent said "parliamentary morality is inadequate," and 44 percent said "Parliament has too much power." As France moved into the Fifth Republic, Parliament's policy-making power was diminished significantly, a change which seemed to be accompanied by a perceptible rise in support for the Parliament (Patterson, Wahlke, Boynton, 1973:309).

Why People Support the Legislature. Assessing the level of support for the legislature by looking at attitudes toward the institution leads us to ask and attempt to answer the question of why people support a legislature.

One possible source of supportive attitudes is policy satisfaction.

Members of a political system may support the legislature because they are pleased with the types of policies that the legislature produces. David Easton (1965:273) has labeled this concept "specific support" and has asserted that it "flows from the favorable attitudes and predispositions stimulated by outputs that are perceived by members to meet their demands as they arise or in anticipation."

This notion of support has been criticized on the grounds that it assumes that citizens have some degree of knowledge about public policies and their utility for them. This assumption, it has been argued, flies in the face of survey data from several nations that show quite conclusively that few voters have specific policy demands, positions, or expectations, few have the knowledge of political structures, processes, and actors that they would need if they had demands to communicate, and that in any event few citizens communicate with their representatives or for that matter have very much interest in the day-to-day functioning of their governmental system.

Because of these data, John Wahlke (1971) has asserted that it is erroneous to conceive of support as deriving from demand-satisfying outputs. Although it seems clear that the supportive attitudes of informed elites may well emanate from policy satisfaction, when it comes to the attitudes of mass publics Wahlke is probably correct in urging the use of a concept of support that is unrelated to the policy-making activities of the government and therefore does not assume that the supportive citizen perceives himself as receiving policy rewards in return for his support.

Wahlke and his colleagues at the University of Iowa have advocated "diffuse support" as such a concept. According to Easton (1965:273), diffuse support

consists of a reserve of support that enables a system to weather the many storms when outputs cannot be balanced off against inputs of demands. It is a kind of support that a system does not have to buy with more or less direct benefits for the obligations and responsibilities the member incurs. If we wish, the outputs here may be considered psychic or symbolic, and in this sense, they may offer the individual immediate benefits strong enough to stimulate a supportive response.

As explicated in the several Iowa studies, the concept when applied to the legislature incorporates such attitudes as a willingness to comply with decisions made by the legislature even if one doesn't agree with those decisions,[3] as well as a prospective resistance to any attempts to dismantle the legislature or to reduce its powers significantly.

While the origins of such supportive attitudes have not been thoroughly investigated, certain inferences can be made. First of all, — diffuse support for the legislature may well be a cultural phenomenon nested within a set of supportive attitudes toward all of the political institutions that make up a political system. As such, it may be considered a part of a more broadly allegiant political culture.

Second, diffuse support, over the long run, is related to specific support. Successful policies, as we have seen, produce specific support; successive successful policies over an extended period of time will produce diffuse support. And, if a regime persists over time, that very fact alone can engender supportive attitudes among citizens. One study of West Germany has shown that the economic successes of the postwar government eventually created allegiant attitudes toward the German Bundestag even among those who did not support specific policies of the government (Boynton and Loewenberg, 1974).

The use of diffuse support is not without problems of its own. For one thing, it appears that diffuse support often exhibits no real political consequences or correlates. For example, one study tested the hypothesis that people whose expectations and perceptions of legislators were congruent would have higher mean legislative support scores than those with incongruent responses. The analysis showed the predicted differences, but these were generally slight and statistically insignificant (Patterson, Boynton, Hedlund, 1969:74–76). In another study an attempt was made to correlate several dimensions of diffuse support for elections with voting turnout. Again, for two of the three support dimensions—approval of the electoral process and the efficacy of elections—the correlation with voting turnout was either small or nonexistent. A modest correlation was found between voting and a third dimension called "voting duty" (Dennis, 1970:833).

One reason why diffuse support measures do not yield high correlations with related attitudes and behavior is that diffuse support is too abstract a concept, too far removed from the behavior and attitudes that the researchers are trying to explain. When the concept of diffuse support is used to study legislatures in developing political systems, an additional problem may arise.

Diffuse support almost by definition develops over time. In new nations legislatures are often new institutions; they will not have had the time to develop a reservoir of diffuse support. Thus measures of diffuse support for legislatures in these systems are of little use and can be quite misleading. In the abstract world of survey research people may indicate a willingness to maintain the legislature and state their distaste for the notion of doing away with the institution. However, when put to the test, these attitudes may yield to less positive views of the legislature based less on abstractions and more on perceptions of current activities by the legislature and its members, no matter how fuzzy or casual these perceptions may be.

At a minimum, if measures of diffuse support for elections cannot predict whether or not someone will vote, it seems extravagant to claim that measures of diffuse support for the legislature will predict how citizens will react when tanks roll toward the parliament building. Clearly what is required is a concept of support that relies on empirical indicators less abstract than those appropriate for measures of diffuse support, yet not so specific as to assume policy knowledge among mass publics. Also, it would be useful to have a support concept that is equally relevant to mass and elite attitudes toward the legislatures. One source of such a concept is the expectations that form the mental constructs, or models that people have about legislatures, and of which we have spoken previously.

Expectations and Support. Expectations, as we have seen, are views about how a legislature should perform—the types of things that legislators should do and the types of functions that the institution should perform. Expectations are more diffuse than the policy-related information relevant to specific support. Thus people can "expect" their legislator to represent them and feel that their expectations are being met even if they are not aware of how he votes on specific issues and of what the consequences of his actions are for their interests.[4]

But expectations are more concrete than the attitudes associated with diffuse support measures because there are empirical and experiential counterparts to expectations. That is, people constantly confront their expectations of the legislature with their perceptions of how the legislature and its members are operating. In contrast, diffuse support concepts measure support in terms of people's reactions to hypothetical situations—for example, how they would respond to attempts to abolish the legislature, or whether they would be willing to disobey a law as long as they don't get caught. For many respondents in many countries, these are abstractions without an empirical anchor. People do not ordinarily contemplate the abolition of their political institutions or the breaking of laws. Survey items probing attitudes toward these acts are not likely to be predictive of how people will act and what they will think when members of parliament are imprisoned or when conditions drive them to consider civil disobedience.

How then are expectations related to support? To the extent that mass, attentive, and elite publics agree on an expectational model of the legislature, and to the extent that legislative behavior is congruent with this model, the legislature will be supported. Lack of agreement, or dissensus, on what constitutes the appropriate legislative model will diminish the level of legislative support. Incongruency between an agreed-upon model and legislative behavior also will diminish support levels.

When a public consensus exists on the appropriate model for a legislative institution, legislative behavior is constrained to conform to that model. For example, if British leaders and British citizens alike believe that something approximating a representation model is most appropriate for the British Parliament, a strong pressure is created on Members of Parliament to construct their roles and behavior accordingly. Few members will view themselves as active creators of policy; few will ignore their representational obligations and view themselves exclusively as legitimators of government policy decisions. A failure to construct legislative roles in this manner likely would result in a sharp decline in support for the Parliament.

Dissensus among the several publics within the political system creates a situation of ambiguity which may provide the legislator with some degree of behavioral latitude. However, it also may create pressures on legislators to choose between satisfying elite expectations, satisfying mass expectations, or seeking something in between. For example, in one-party systems legislators are frequently caught between the system maintenance model of party elites that urges them to mobilize support for often unpopular government programs and the representation model of their constituents that urges them to oppose government programs which they perceive as causing them hardships. In such a context it is likely that no matter what the legislator does, he will violate the expectations of significant segments of the public outside the legislature and thereby jeopardize the support accruing to the legislature.

Other situations may present fewer problems for the legislator. It is possible that the expectations of mass publics toward the legislature will be vague and dissensual, while the expectations of elites will be "crystal clear." In this situation legislators are very likely to tailor their behavior to conform to the expecations of elites, thereby increasing their support from those precincts, while at the same time ignoring the ambiguous and conflictual signals emanating from other sectors of society. The Tanzanian MP might find some support for the representation model among some segments of his constituency, but the clear, forceful, and frequently stated system-maintenance expectations of the president of the country heavily militate in favor of conforming to his particular legislative model.

The Tanzanian illustration suggests that congruence between legislative behavior and elite expectations is more important for legislative support than congruence with mass expectations. Two reasons for this can be adduced. First, elite views tend to be more salient than mass expectations. Elites in the executive branch of government, among the economic leaders of the country, and within the military services tend to deal with legislatures and their members on a continuing basis and so will develop a clearly articulated set of expectations about how that institution should function and how its members should behave. They will make these expectations known and they will also be in a position to accurately assess the extent to which legislative behavior conforms to their expectations.

For the mass public, in contrast, politics is not very salient, expectations tend to be rather diffuse, and perceptions of how political institutions are operating tend to be very vague. Thus, while legislative deviance from their expectations is not likely to go unnoticed by elites, mass expectations can be interpreted in different ways, thus making it difficult to distinguish congruent from incongruent behavior.

The second reason for the greater importance attributed to elite expectations is that elites are likely to have powerful sanctions at their disposal to encourage the conformance of legislative behavior to their expectations and to discourage deviancy. The use of force, or even the threat that it might be used, is frequently an option. While public opinion may or may not applaud such actions, when legislatures are shut down the deed is seldom accomplished by the people. Rather it is the institutional elites resident in the executive branch and the military that send the legislators packing. Aside from force elites often have more attractive, positive inducements to offer legislators in return for conformance to elite expectations: money, patronage, and political influence are three obvious examples.

The point is that if support is to be taken as an indicator of an institution's capacity to survive, then the support of elites is more important to the legislature than the support of mass publics. This is not to imply that the electoral sanctions of mass publics are always inconsequential. In stable democratic political systems, where explicit executive coercion of the legislature is unlikely to occur, the electoral sanctions of mass publics may be as powerful as those at the disposal of elites. However, in these systems it is also likely that elite and mass expectations will be roughly congruent. But in those political systems where incongruence is most likely to occur and where the integrity of the legislature is least certain, the sanctions of the executive are a good deal stronger than the electoral sanctions of the masses.

What all of this suggests is that a continuum of legislative support situations exists. Legislatures located toward the high support end of the continuum will function in a way that does not do violence to the expectations of elites outside the legislature; also, they probably will be acting in approximate conformance to the expectations of mass publics. As one moves down the continuum toward the less supported end, legislative behavior will begin to deviate perceptibly and significantly from elite expectations. The expectations of mass publics may be ambiguous, or they may themselves deviate from the expectations of elites, but the key variable leading to a low level of support is increasing incongruency between the way the legislature operates and the way in which nonlegislative elites expect it to operate.

As I have suggested, there is at least one obvious problem with this explication of the support concept and that is the difficulty in measuring with any degree of precision the support situation of a legislature. What we would need to do that job would be comparable survey data probing the expectations of mass and elite publics toward legislatures as well as precise indicators of the extent to which legislative behavior is congruent or incongruent with these expectations. For now and for the foreseeable future, such data are beyond our reach.

This is not cause for abandoning support as a dimension for classifying legislatures, however. Rather, we can return to the first method that we described for inferring levels of support: that is, looking at the events in a nation and seeking to estimate the extent to which the atmosphere surrounding the legislature is supportive. The imprecision and subjectivity of such an approach literally leaps from the page. One way of dealing with such imprecision is to use a very low level of measurement. About as low as you can get (if I accurately recall my course in research design) is a dichotomized variable. Legislatures are thus divided into two support categories, one labeled "more supported legislatures" and the second labeled "less supported legislatures."

That dichotomized variable may be combined with my previously defined trichotomized division of legislatures according to their role in policy making. Such a cross-tabulation produces the five categories shown in Table 2:1.[5]

TABLE 2.1
A Typology of Legislatures

Policy-Making Power	Less Supported Legislatures	More Supported Legislatures
Strong	Vulnerable Legislatures (Philippines, Uruguay, Chile, Italy, France [Fourth Republic], France [Third Republic], Weimar Germany)	Active Legislatures (U.S. Congress and American state legislatures; Costa Rican Congress)
Modest	Marginal Legislatures (Thailand, Pakistan, S. Vietnam [pre-1975], S. Korea, Kenya, Uganda, Malaysia, Colombia, Peru, Brazil, Afghanistan, Iran, Ethiopia, Syria, Jordan, Zambia, Nigeria, Argentina, Bangladesh, Guatemala, Lebanon)	Reactive Legislatures (United Kingdom, Canada, Australia, New Zealand, India, Israel, Mexico, Norway, Sweden, Denmark, Finland, W. Germany, Belgium, Netherlands, Switzerland, France [Fifth Republic], Austria, Ireland, Japan, Turkey)
Little or none		Minimal Legislatures (Soviet Union, Poland Yugoslavia, Tanzania, Singapore, Tunisia, Taiwan, Ivory Coast, Ghana [Nkrumah])

A TALE OF FIVE LEGISLATURES

In Table 2:1 selected legislatures are divided into five categories labeled active, vulnerable, reactive, marginal, and minimal. The placement of a particular legislature into a specific category depends on my evaluation of that legislature; others who are more expert about a legislature may decide that it should be placed somewhere else. To further illuminate the criteria that I have used in placing legislatures, I will give a capsule description of five legislatures that are prototypical of each category.

An Active Legislature: The United States Congress. For nearly two hundred years, the United States Congress has stood at the center of the American policy-making process. Its capacity to reject, amend, or ignore policy proposals initiated by either the executive or its own members has been attested to and detested by thirty-nine presidents. Even though a decline in the power and authority of the Congress has been announced on several different occasions, it remains today one of the few legislative institutions in the world able and capable of saying no to a popularly elected president and making it stick.

What evidence there is tends to suggest that the American people are supportive of the Congress. Summarizing the existing research on the subject, Roger Davidson (1970a:169) concludes that "citizens hold senators and their representatives in high esteem and would be proud to have their children pursue such a career. When asked to describe the characteristics of a representative, respondents (whose replies were favorable by a 9 to 1 ratio) stress the qualities of service orientation, good personal character, capability, good education, and personality." In regard to its legislative activities Davidson says that "Congress is not usually evaluated directly, but rather through a prism of attitudes to more familiar political objects," such as the goodness or badness of the times, or estimates of how well the president is performing. However, there also seems to be some evidence that support for the Congress tends to increase when it is being perceived as acting quickly and efficiently on legislation (Davidson, 1970a:171–72).

Although presidents and bureaucrats may chafe against the active policy-making role of the Congress, in comparative perspective they have shown little inclination to challenge the legitimacy of the legislature. Among modern presidents Richard Nixon seemed to go the furthest in the direction of challenging the Congress's constitutional prerogatives and we all know how he made out.

Vulnerable Legislatures: The Congress of the Philippines (1946–72). During the first twenty-six years of its independence from the

United States the Republic of the Philippines had one of the strongest legislatures in the developing world. Jean Grossholtz (1964:117) writes that despite a strong presidency, the Congress "often refused to pass administration bills or so weakened them with amendments as to destroy their aim. This has been the common fate of land reform measures." Robert Stauffer (1970:351) reports that when the president wanted things passed by the Congress he had to negotiate with the legislators: " . . . bargaining goes on constantly before and during a session of Congress between the President and the legislative leaders over what will be passed and what will have to be paid by the chief executive for congressional cooperation." Although this bargaining resulted in mutual legislative-executive control, "Congress imposed a recognized set of parameters on where and how public resources [were] to be allocated and [had] an important voice in any changes in established patterns" (Stauffer, 1970:351).

As the reader will note, this description of the Philippine Congress was altered from the present to the past tense because in 1972 President Ferdinand Marcos decided that he no longer cared to negotiate with the legislators, suspended the constitution, imprisoned some legislative leaders, and sent the rest home. These events occurred with almost no public dissent; Stauffer (1975:6) reports that the "government's precautionary move of calling out an elite unit of the Philippine Constabulary to put down any demonstrations that might occur . . . was wasted effort; resistance to martial law was not to be occasioned by regret over the closing of Congress." Stauffer suggests that it was commonplace in the Philippines to think of legislators as corrupt people bent on enriching themselves as a part of their duties. Steven Franzich (1971:404) observes that "the Philippine Congress is one of the most criticized institutions in Philippine society."

It is not clear that such behavior on the part of legislators seriously conflicted with the expectations of mass publics, for whom such activity, in the view of some observers, constituted a cultural norm. Grossholtz (1964:163) says this about the Filipino political culture: "Those who have power are expected to use it to promote their own interests and that of their family. There is no moral contempt for those who benefit from their power. It is as it should be, and a man would be a fool to ignore his opportunities."

But it does appear that legislators did violate the expectations of President Marcos and other Philippine elites. Stauffer (1975:50–55) suggests that prior to the coup, the Philippine Congress was pursuing a representational model with traditional local elites as the focus of representation. This behavior came to be increasingly incongruent with the models employed by the new technocratic elites in the cities, thus provoking the 1972 coup.

A Reactive Legislature: The British House of Commons. Every veteran of a western European politics course knows that British politics is dominated by the prime minister and his cabinet who, working through a disciplined majority party in Parliament, can regularly produce a majority vote in the House and pass its programs. A defeat of the government by the House of Commons could be interpreted as a vote of no confidence and the government likely would dissolve Parliament and call for new elections. Bernard Crick (1970:51–52) writes that "all important legislation is government legislation and, with very few exceptions, goes through without substantial amendment—outright defeat is politically inconceivable and withdrawal phenomenally rare."

While it is clear that the House of Commons does not have the effective power to say no to the government, it seems equally clear that the House does set certain parameters within which the government must act and thereby discourages the government from introducing legislation that will cause a row in Parliament. Dissent from government backbenchers particularly may convince the government to modify legislation before submission to the Parliament. One writer concludes a careful analysis of backbench influence on government policy during the 1945–57 period with the following statement:

The role of the government backbenchers in the decision-making process is a substantial one. Neither their constituents nor their leaders can claim them as puppets who respond only to the pull of a string. The members of both parties were quite often responsible for serious policy changes. . . . Furthermore, backbench pressure on the leadership was not by any means limited to a small backbench cabal. On the contrary, it has been noted that in each party there was an impressively large number of members who were energetically involved in disagreements with government leaders over issues which were of great concern to them. (Lynskey, 1970:347)

Another analysis of the 1968–69 parliamentary session comes to a similar conclusion. While few opposition and backbench amendments were accepted by the government, many others were indirectly incorporated or accommodated by the government into its legislation (Herman, 1972).

The results of national opinion polls in Great Britain indicate that the Parliament is a highly supported institution. In one poll, 85 percent of the respondents indicated that they thought that "what goes on in the House of Commons is important." However, the same polls indicate some discontent with individual members of Parliament, particularly in regard to what many feel to be the MP's overly subservient role in regard to his party and the consequent distance this subservience creates between the member and his constituency (Patterson, Wahlke, Boynton, 1973:308).

In my terminology these data indicate that legislators in Great Britain are shaping their behavior to meet the expectations of party elites rather than the expectations of mass publics. This dominance of legislative behavior by party elites is a common characteristic of the reactive legislature, and is even more pronounced in the one-party dominant political systems in this category. In these countries mass expectations are unlikely to be either salient or very clear, whereas the expectations of the party elites will be quite unmistakable.

This is not to suggest that reactive legislatures are the objects of mass alienation. There is no evidence at all that mass expectations have been frustrated to the extent of threatening the institutional stability of either the Parent of Parliaments, or of its several offspring throughout the Western caucasian world.

A Marginal Legislature: The National Assembly of Pakistan (1962–69). The legislature created by the 1962 Pakistani Constitution was designed to be subordinate to the president, with no real power to reject government proposals. During the 1962–65 period, the government introduced forty bills, of which thirty-nine were passed (Sayeed, 1967:107). In addition, presidential ordinances promulgated while the legislature was not in session were routinely approved when the Assembly reconvened (Ahmad, 1970:218). Finally, the Assembly's budgetary power was constitutionally restricted to new items; it could neither consider nor vote on continuing expenditures.

However, the Assembly did exercise the power to amend legislation. According to Rashiduzzaman (1969–70:492), from 1962 to 1968 eleven major government proposals were "extensively amended" by the Assembly. The Security Act of 1965, for example, was amended in the Assembly to require the government to communicate its grounds for detention within fifteen days, to produce detainees before a board that included a Supreme Court judge, and to empower the board to prevent a detention from exceeding two months (Ahmad, 1970:244). Public debate within the legislature often created a climate of opinion that encouraged the government to act. Ahmad (1970:244) reports that the Political Detenus Amendment Bill and the Political Parties Bill of 1962, though officially sponsored, "were the direct outcome of the demand inside the House backed by popular support outside."

Government acquiesence to legislative pressures was most likely to occur without a vote or in the privacy of committee rooms. Although such activity was not always visible, it nonetheless seems clear that even though the National Assembly could not reject government proposals outright, the legislature was capable of modifying such proposals and thereby participated in setting the parameters within which the government operated.

During the twenty-eight years of its independence Pakistan has been through two periods of martial law during which the Parliament was suspended. Such occurrences stem from conflict between the behavior of legislators and elite expectations about the role the legislature should play. While government leaders perceived the legislature largely in integrative, system-maintenance terms, legislators looked at the legislature in representative terms. General Ayub Khan explained the reasons for the 1958 coup this way: "The army could not remain unaffected by the conditions around it, nor was it conceivable that officers and men would not react to all the political chicanery, intrigue, corruption, and inefficiency manifested in every sphere of life" (Ahmad, 1970:176).

Apparently the 1969 imposition of martial law was welcomed by several segments of the population. It has been suggested that the corruption of the Parliament and the Ayub regime generally, as well as the lack of responsiveness to demands for greater regional autonomy, directly contributed to the reimposition of martial law. All of this indicates that the legislative institution in Pakistan has been incapable of fulfilling the expectation of either the political elites with whom it must work or the mass publics whom it ostensibly represents (Maniruzzaman, 1971:234–37; Wheeler, 1970:276ff).

The support that elites give to legislatures in this category can best be described as tentative and that is why we have called these legislatures marginal. The elites create these legislatures and allow them a restricted but perceptible policy-making role. They do so because their control over their political systems is nonhegemonous and thus an elite consensus concerning the legislature does not exist. This is attributable in large measure to the weakness or in some instances complete absence of political parties in marginal systems. The legislature exists because of these intraelite cleavages; when these cleavages shift or are reduced, the legislature must be either changed or eliminated. Mass expectations may provide some transient support for this leadership faction or that, but they count for very little when the inevitable institutional alterations are made.

A Minimal Legislature: The Supreme Soviet (1917–   ). That the Supreme Soviet can neither reject nor amend policy proposals put before it by the government is beyond dispute. Also, it seems clear that the legislature does not constrain those who do make policy even through the more informal, parameter-setting process. Such a constraint depends at a minimum on either an ability to criticize publicly or a capacity to oppose privately in a manner sufficiently strenuous to increase intolerably the cost to the government of pushing the proposal through. There is certainly no capacity in the Supreme Soviet to oppose publicly. The capacity to oppose privately within the parliamentary commissions seems to exist on a limited basis but does not appear to be potent enough to discourage the government from doing what it wants to do (Vanneman, 1972:288–90; 300; 305–6; 310).

Support is difficult to assess in the Soviet Union. Nonetheless it is reasonable to say that sixty years after the revolution, the major elements of the Soviet political system, including the Supreme Soviet, are generally accepted political institutions, supported by most Soviet citizens. The Supreme Soviet is an instrument of the political elite in that country and so their support for the legislature is a given. If that support were not there, the institution would not be there at all.

This points to a distinction between the marginal legislature category and the minimal legislature category and also indicates the reason why there is no sixth category of less-supported legislatures with little or no policy-making power.

Marginal legislatures have, while they exist, the tentative support of nonlegislative elites; minimal legislatures have a more permanent and continuing commitment from elites. If, by definition, this commitment involves only the most minimal policy-making role, then the expectations of nonlegislative elites must be oriented toward either the representation or the system-maintenance model, or toward some hybrid of the two.

The modest policy-making role of the marginal legislature derives in part from significant elite cleavages; we assume that similar cleavages are either nonexistent or have no legislative consequences in minimal systems, and thus elite consensus exists, at least to the extent of agreement that the legislature should have no policy-making role. An elite consensus strong enough to ban the legislature from any significant policy-making activities is strong enough to impose a different expectational model upon legislators *and* exact conformance to that model. By this reasoning, a nonsupported legislature with no policy-making role becomes a logical impossibility.

These five categories of legislatures will provide the framework for our discussion in the remaining chapters of this book. I am under no illusions about these categories and the reader should have no illusions either. As we move through the substantive topics of legislative behavior, there will be countless instances of intracategory variation. There will not always be differences among the categories; on certain comparative dimensions some categories of legislatures will look very much like others. In some instances, the categories will have nothing at all to do with observed interlegislative variation.

These categories, rough as they may be, will provide us with a mechanism for bringing some degree of order to the disparate data that we have on legislatures and legislative behavior all over the world. The categories will enable us to begin the arduous process of seeking out similarities and differences so that some day in the future we can honestly speak of a discipline of comparative legislative behavior.

NOTES

1. This classification may strike some as being incomplete because the fourth possible combination—power to reject but not to modify—is missing. It is missing simply because it seems to me inconceivable that a legislature could have the power to reject proposed legislation but not have the power to modify it.

2. The one notable exception to this generalization is the ongoing research being conducted by the Comparative Legislative Research Center at the University of Iowa. At this writing the Center has succeeded in administering parallel questionnaires to mass publics, legislators, and elite publics in six countries: Kenya, South Korea, Turkey, Switzerland, Belgium, and Italy. A preliminary report of some of their findings may be found in Loewenberg and Kim (1976).

3. It should be noted that there have been questions raised about the validity of the compliance dimension as a measure of diffuse support for the legislature. Easton (1975) and Mezey (1976) have discussed several reasons why compliance with the law need not imply diffuse support for the legislature and even the Iowa researchers themselves have voiced some doubts (Patterson and Boynton, 1974).

4. The view that supportive attitudes might emanate from the interface between expectations and perceptions has been discussed by Easton (1975), Muller (1970), and Mezey (1976). See Mezey (1977) for a complete review of this question and others concerning support for legislative institutions.

5. The entries in Table 2:1 should be taken as illustrative rather than inclusive. The absence of a particular country from the table means that I haven't the faintest idea where it should go and that I am not including the country in the analysis. The absence of a sixth cell in the table (lower left corner) will be discussed at the end of this chapter.

Part II

POLICY MAKING

Chapter 3

LEGISLATURES AND POLICY MAKING

The classification system developed in the last chapter deals in part with the extent of legislative involvement in policy making. I said there that a legislature's policy-making role is a function of the degree to which it can constrain the actions of executive-centered elites. Thus active and vulnerable legislatures are substantially involved in the policy-making process by virtue of the fact that they are capable of vetoing any policy-making initiatives taken by nonlegislative elites. Reactive and marginal legislatures, in comparison, are only modestly involved in the policy-making process because they usually cannot prevent executive elites from doing what they want to do; rather they can modify, delay, or publicly oppose their actions and thereby set definite parameters on the scope of executive policy-making activities. Minimal legislatures are so-called because they can place only very weak constraints on the policy-making prerogatives of executive-centered elites, and therefore have very little role to play in the policy-making process.

Clearly this simple ordinal classification of legislatures does not tell us all there is to know about the policy impact of legislatures. In the chapters that follow, I will attempt a more detailed assessment of the way in which the five legislative types are involved in policy making. This comparative analysis will be organized about two concepts: policy-making *phases* and policy-making *arenas*.

POLICY-MAKING PHASES

Simply, but essentially, the activities associated with policy making may be divided into three phases. The first phase is *formulation*;

relevant activities here include the identification of demands in need of responses, the drawing of preliminary policy proposals, fact-finding procedures that generate relevant information, and consultations among concerned publics at the mass, attentive, and elite levels. The formulation phase culminates in a formal proposal submitted to those with the constitutional and political power to make final decisions for the polity.

The second phase of the policy-making process is called *deliberation*. During this phase the merits of alternative proposals are discussed and debated. Amendments to formal government proposals may be considered, compromise positions may be sought and discovered, and majority coalitions may be formed or reinforced around a particular policy alternative. The deliberative phase concludes with a decision in favor of or against a particular proposal.

The final stage of the policy-making process is *oversight*. During this phase, policies are evaluated to determine how well they are working, how well they are being administered, and whether or not they are in need of modification, reversal, or enlargement. In a sense this "last" phase of the policy-making process is the origin of a new policy, because effective oversight activity can create new demands for which new policies must be formulated, deliberated, and decided upon.

POLICY-MAKING ARENAS

These different phases of the policy-making process are acted out in various *arenas*. A policy-making arena is a physical setting within which policy-makers interact; for our purposes arenas can be identified and classified by the extent to which they involve legislators. Specifically, we can ask what percentage of the participants in a particular policy-making arena are legislators, and what percentage of the legislature's membership is eligible to participate in that arena. The answers to these two questions produce the typology shown in Figure 3.1.

The arenas located in the bottom half of Figure 3.1 are labeled as *extraparliamentary*. Some legislators may participate in some of these arenas but they usually do so at the invitation of nonlegislators rather than by right, and they always constitute a minority of the total participants. These arenas are normally removed from the physical surroundings of the legislature. In Thailand (1969–71), for example,

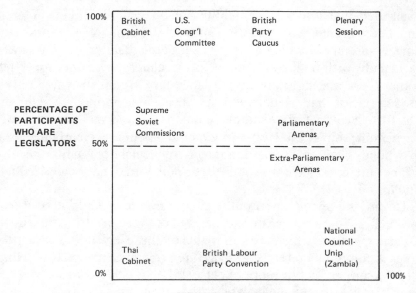

FIGURE 3.1   A Classification of Policy-Making Arenas

members of the cabinet could not be members of Parliament; cabinet meetings—held at Government House and not at the Parliament building—sometimes were attended by a few selected legislators, but the policy-making activities were clearly not going forth in a parliamentary arena. In all countries bureaucratic policy making takes place in similar extraparliamentary arenas.

As one moves to the right along the base of Figure 3.1 arenas such as general party meetings are encountered which may be attended by legislators who are party members and by other party leaders or workers who are not in the legislature but who constitute a majority of those at the meeting. The annual convention of the British Labour party is an example of such an arena. At the lower right corner one would find a party meeting in a one-party state in which all legislators are party members. All legislators therefore may participate in the party meeting but they will comprise only a small percentage of those attending the meeting. The National Council of the UNIP—the ruling party of Zambia—is an example of such a policy-making arena (Saidi, 1976).

Several kinds of *parliamentary arenas* are found in the top half of

Figure 3.1. Just above the center line and on the far left of the diagram one finds arenas such as the subcommissions of the Supreme Soviet—arenas in which a very small percentage of the legislators participate with a similar number of bureaucrats. In the upper left corner there are more purely parliamentary arenas in which only a few legislators may participate but as the major or only participants. The British cabinet, for example, contains only a small percentage of the membership of the House of Commons, but it is clearly a legislative policy-making arena dominated by legislators who are also cabinet members. We may call these policy-making locales *leadership arenas*.

Toward the upper center of the diagram we have legislative arenas in which a somewhat greater percentage of the legislators are eligible to participate and which are dominated by these legislators. One such arena is commonly referred to as a *committee*; it is less exclusive than a leadership arena but more exclusive than a *party caucus* which is open to all legislators who are party members. Finally, a *plenary session* of a legislature is an arena located at the upper right corner of Figure 3.1; this is an arena in which almost all participants are legislators and in which all legislators may participate.

In addition to the two dimensions shown in Figure 3.1 that define the scope of legislative involvement, policy-making arenas have two other relevant characteristics. First, arenas can be arrayed on a *public-private* continuum. In all countries certain policy-making arenas are more open and more public than others. Extraparliamentary arenas located toward the lower left corner of Figure 3.1 are probably the most private arenas, followed closely by the leadership arenas in the upper left corner of the diagram. As one moves to the right on Figure 3.1, the arenas tend to become more public because there are more people involved and because in all systems there is a general expectation that the larger the meeting the more likely that it will be open.

Policy-making arenas also can be differentiated on the basis of their degree of *specialization*. Specialized arenas deal with a specific policy area and have the capacity to bring expert knowledge to bear upon the issues under consideration. In contrast, policy issues may be dealt with in generalized arenas; on each issue that comes up it can be expected that only a few participants will have relevant expert information, while most will know very little.

Arenas that are both private and specialized are likely to have the greatest influence on the shape of public policy. Those who work in private arenas are able to hammer out policies in an environment that is insulated from many of the pressures that impinge upon actors in public arenas. Sensitive information, often essential to effective policy making, is more likely to be available in private than in public arenas. Policy makers working in private will say what they think secure in the knowledge that what they are saying will be confidential. Also, private retreats from established positions are less embarrassing to make than public retreats and therefore compromises are more likely to emerge from private discussions. Thus when policy proposals emerge from private arenas, they are usually in the form of an entire package which will be difficult for those outside these arenas to untie. At a minimum they provide the starting point for further public discussion.

In regard to specialization it is a truism that as policy becomes more technical and complex, policy-making power will gravitate almost inevitably to specialized as opposed to generalized policy-making arenas. Only in the former will there exist a capacity to understand the issues at hand. The experts who work in specialized arenas are likely to have both physical and intellectual access to the relevant information. This information monopoly means that the experts not only provide the answers to all of the questions but will often be the only ones who know what questions should be asked. Even if those who operate in specialized arenas are forced to do so in public, there will be comparatively few people who understand enough to effectively control them.

The preceding remarks are not intended as a brief for the desirability of private and specialized policy-making arenas; rather, it is a simple assertion of where power has come increasingly to reside. It should go without saying that there is a particularly severe price to be paid for such a policy-making style in democratic nations that purport to value the concept of popular rule. Popular control of policy making is difficult to achieve when the process is dominated by experts who deal in languages and symbols which are alien to most other people in the political system. Popular control is impossible when these experts operate privately, away from public view. Under such circumstances, power can be abused and policy may be nonresponsive, because those who make decisions cannot be held accountable for them.

ASSESSING POLICY-MAKING ARENAS

The Bureaucracy. Bureaucratic policy-making arenas are extra-parliamentary, highly specialized, and relatively private. From what has been said already, it should be obvious that because of these characteristics they have a most substantial impact on public policy making in every political system in the world. Karl Bracher attributes the dominance of bureaucracy primarily to the increased size and complexity of state activity in the latter part of the twentieth century. He suggests that "lawgiving is transferred to the apparatus of the administration and parliament loses its authority to a quasi-dictatorship of the executive. Finally, the will of the experts triumphs over the parliamentary act of submitting technical decisions to political decisions and control; the decisions have already been made" (Bracher, 1968:424). Bureaucracies are likely to have their greatest impact on policy formulation, and this is an extension of their control over policy administration. Because they are charged with the responsibility of implementing the ongoing policies of the state, they are seen as being in the best position to evaluate the effectiveness of these programs and to assess the need for new policies or for changes in existing policies. The people who know the most about these policy areas are often in the employ of the bureaucracy and are often the ones who are asked to design new policy proposals. Because they are *the* experts, it is often difficult to find other experts who are capable of assessing the accuracy of their evaluations or the desirability of the new policies that they are proposing. It is also difficult to find people outside the bureaucracy who know enough to determine whether or not the bureaucracy is successfully implementing current policy. Such is the stuff of which the administrative state is made, and in our terminology its foundation is the private, highly specialized policy-making arenas that characterize bureaucracies.

Control by Political Executives. The traditional theories of government have it that bureaucratic abuses are prevented because the bureaucracy is a subordinate arm of the political executives of the states in which they function. Presidents, prime ministers, and their cabinets, under this model, exercise control over the bureaucracy, provide direction for their policy initiatives, and prevent abuses of power.

The first thing to be said about such an argument is that the policy-making arenas dominated by these executive elites often share the same penchant for privacy as the bureaucracy, and thus have very little to gain by bringing bureaucratic abuses to public light (King, 1975:174). The second thing to say is that these arenas, unlike the bureaucracy, are generalized rather than specialized. Consequently they are at a clear disadvantage when they seek to control the specialists under their command. One of the foremost students of the American presidency suggests that the president's ability to command the bureaucracy to action is severely limited and in fact what a successful president must do is "bargain" with the bureaucrats who are presumably under his control (Neustadt, 1960). When it comes to policy formulation, it is not at all clear who is in charge. According to Rourke (1969:49) "apparent presidential hegemony over the legislative process masks the fact that much of what ultimately comes to be regarded as the President's legislative program stems in the first instance from the advice of bureaucrats in the executive establishment." Parliamentary executives, composed of legislators serving in cabinet positions, are also not very successful in controlling bureaucracies. The Italian bureaucracy, for example, has been described as

a source of advice and information on the basis of which administrative decrees are issued and legislative proposals prepared. Insofar as the government and the legislature become dependent on the information that the bureaucracy husbands, organizes, and communicates, the bureaucracy becomes an intimate and important—sometimes dominant—factor in the rule-making process. (LaPalombara, 1964:121)

An assessment of the effectiveness of the British cabinet's control over the British bureaucracy reaches a similar conclusion:

though politicians may dislike the advice given to them, though they may ignore it, procrastinate, argue against it, the one thing they are rarely able to do, without expert assistance, is to question the analysis on which advice to them is based. Where in the existing executive system is such assistance to originate, except with the civil service which monopolizes it and which, moreover, vigilantly chokes the flow of information to outsiders. (Gordon, 1971:42)

What all of this suggests is that there exists in every country an amalgam, or complex, which we will refer to by the cumbersome but descriptive term "executive-centered elites." This complex consists of the bureaucracy operating in specialized and private arenas, and the political executive operating in parliamentary or extraparliamentary arenas only slightly less private but much more generalized than bureaucratic arenas.[1] The evidence is that there is at best an uneasy balance between the bureaucratic and political components of this complex with the latter usually endowed with formal constitutional control and the former endowed with informal control deriving from its monopoly of policy expertise.

Legislative Arenas and Control of Executive-Centered Elites. The policy-making activities of legislative arenas other than leadership arenas are inhibited by the fact that they are less specialized than the arenas dominated by executive-centered elites. A minimal prerequisite, then, for effective policy participation within legislative arenas is a source of legislative expertise comparable to that which is present in the bureaucracy. In many legislatures that expertise is provided by a committee system. By dividing the work of the legislature into substantive policy areas and by placing a committee in charge of each area a structure is created that can generate legislative specialization across the full array of policy areas.

Of course the mere existence of a committee system is no guarantee of legislative specialization. Committees with no fixed jurisdictions or committees with very broad mandates are unlikely to develop any degree of expertise. Even committees with stable and manageable jurisdictions will not become specialized unless legislators are willing to remain on the committees and devote their energies to mastering the policy area under the committee's jurisdiction. Rapid turnover rates among legislators, either in terms of membership in the legislature or in terms of tenure on the committees, will retard specialization and thereby reduce the policy-making role of committees.

Given some degree of specialization, committees can be effective participants in all three phases of the policy-making process. Their expertise will enable them to participate with executive-centered elites in policy formulation, or at least to effectively evaluate the policies that they propose. The fact that committees are relatively small bodies means that they have a capacity for privacy which should, in turn, facilitate bargaining and increase their deliberative capabilities. Specialization is a prerequisite to an effective oversight capacity; it is obvious that administrators can be overseen only by those who have some degree of understanding about what the administrators are supposed to be doing.

Plenary arenas are both general and public, and are therefore at some disadvantage as effective participants in the policy-making process.[2] In terms of policy formulation, plenary arenas must rely on public statements made during its sessions as instruments for identifying demands and suggesting possible solutions to those who will actually formulate the policies. Individual legislators also may introduce their own policy proposals in the form of a private member bill. While such proposals sometimes succeed, their primary purpose is usually to encourage those in other more efficacious arenas to move in a certain policy direction.

More informally, individual legislators may seek to consult with bureaucrats, cabinet ministers, committee chairmen, or others charged with the primary responsibility for drawing up policy proposals in an attempt to have their views incorporated in the drafts of these policies. Those doing the policy formulation will be responsive to such advances if they are concerned with minimizing conflict during the policy deliberation phase.

It is during the deliberation phase that plenary arenas are most effective. Public discussions of proposals emanating from private arenas may bring pressures to bear that had previously been avoided. In some legislatures an adverse vote may be a real possibility and the deliberative activities of plenary arenas may be important in determining whether or not such a vote will take place. The effectiveness of plenary deliberation is limited by two factors. First, public rather than private deliberations may make it more difficult to reach decisions. It has been argued that "visibility hampers responsible behavior, instigates image-selling and demagogy, intensifies conflicts, [and] leads to decisional paralysis" (Sartori, 1975:155). Secondly, deliberative activities are largely reactive rather than creative. By this I mean that when a legislature deliberates, it is reacting to a specific proposal put before it and its options in regard to that proposals are limited. It may amend it, defeat it, or pass it, but it really can't create a new proposal. So, while the public deliberation that goes on in a plenary session may affect the general shape of public policy, it is unlikely to affect its substantive core.

Oversight activities conducted in plenary sessions may expose responsible ministers to public criticism and often severe embarrassment, but the administrators still have the advantage of their specialized knowledge as against the more general knowledge of individual legislators. Again, the purpose is to bring public light and therefore public pressures to bear upon policies originally determined in private arenas.

One other legislative arena with a policy-making potential is the caucus. Like the plenary arena, the caucus is general, but unlike the plenum it is somewhat less public. Thus, while it is usually unable to bring specialized knowledge to bear upon proposals emanating from executive-centered elites, the caucus of government supporters is often able to get these elites to offer franker explanations for their actions in the relative privacy of the caucus than they would be prepared to offer in public plenary sessions. Because governments must rely on the support of their followers in the legislature to secure ultimate approval for their proposals, they have some incentive to confer with them prior to formal submission of the proposal to the legislature. Such consultation may well affect the shape of the policy ultimately submitted and therefore gives the caucus some role in the formulation process. This role can be increased by the formation of party committees within caucuses that, like general legislative committees, divide policy into substantive areas and seek to provide the caucus with some independent specialized knowledge.

Caucus committees can further assist the caucus in its deliberative capacities. Once bills are formally submitted, it is practice in many legislatures for them to be discussed in the government caucus before they are discussed on the floor. Without caucus committees, such discussions are usually dominated by the party leaders who have submitted the proposals. But caucus committees provide an independent source of information that may cause the government's proposals to be subjected to more severe criticism within caucus, criticism which may lead to modifications before the proposal goes to the plenary session.

Caucus arenas play only a minimal role in overseeing executive-centered elites. In some countries where government supporters are not permitted to participate in plenary oversight activities such as the question period, government leaders will respond to legislators' questions in the caucus. But because the major goal of oversight is to bring private abuses to public light, and because caucuses usually convene in private, the effectiveness of caucus oversight activities is questionable.

EXPECTATIONS

From what we already know about the five types of legislatures that we have been dealing with, we can articulate certain expectations about the nature of the policy-making process that we expect a more detailed analysis to reveal.

Active and vulnerable legislatures can be expected to be involved in all three phases of the policy-making process. As a prerequisite to such involvement, these legislatures will have highly developed committee arenas. Plenary arenas are more likely to be involved in deliberative than in formulation or oversight activities, simply because the latter two phases place the greatest premiums on specialized knowledge. Caucus deliberation will take place in those vulnerable legislatures that have relatively strong legislative party systems.

The differences between active and vulnerable legislatures stem from the lower level of elite support accruing to the latter. Because the policy-making involvement of vulnerable legislative arenas is neither accepted nor supported by the executive-centered elites of those systems, there is a great deal of tension and competition between legislative and nonlegislative policy-making arenas. Executive-centered elites will seek to usurp or impede the policy-making prerogatives of legislative arenas. They will also try to keep as much policy-making activities as possible in private rather than public arenas. While the executive-centered elites in countries with active legislatures are not exactly sanguine about the broad policy making prerogatives resident in legislative arenas, they nonetheless accept the principle of such authority. They, too, have a taste for private as opposed to public arenas, but active legislatures are more successful in bringing the policy-making activities of executive-centered elites to public view than are vulnerable legislatures.

Reactive legislatures have a less influential policy-making role than active or vulnerable legislatures, particularly during the formulation phase. Consequently, a good deal of the policy-making activities in these political systems goes forth in extraparliamentary or leadership arenas. However, the deliberative and oversight activities of reactive legislatures do serve to restrict the actions of executive-centered elites. These constraints are more likely to be imposed in caucus and plenary arenas than in committee arenas. Most reactive systems are controlled by relatively strong governing parties that resist the establishment of independent sources of legislative expertise. As a result, committee systems are weaker than they are in active and vulnerable legislatures, while party caucuses are normally stronger. Also, much of the oversight activities that take place in the committee systems of active and vulnerable legislatures will take place in the plenary sessions of reactive legislatures. In sum, legislative arenas in reactive systems are generally subordinate to executive-centered elites, but still possess the means to constrain if not control the activities of those elites. And because reactive legislatures are highly supported, their policy-making involvement is accepted by those who control extra-parliamentary and leadership arenas.

Marginal legislatures, like reactive legislatures, are dominated by executive-centered elites, but unlike reactive legislatures, these elites usually are not partisan; also, they do not accept with equanimity the constraining activities that take place in legislative arenas. Most policy making takes place in extraparliamentary arenas or, occasionally, in leadership arenas; committee and caucus arenas are generally weak and therefore whatever legislative constraints that exist are exercised in plenary sessions, and only occasionally in smaller arenas. The fact that the plenary session is the least specialized policy-making arena ensures the ineffectiveness of the deliberation and oversight activities that go forth there, and further guarantees the subordinate role of these legislatures. The low level of support that accrues to these legislatures means that even the modest constraints that these legislatures seek to impose will be resisted, sometimes forcibly, by the executive-centered elites who run these systems.

Minimal legislatures are completely dominated by executive-centered elites and have only the most peripheral role to play in the formulation and deliberation of public policy. Some oversight of executive activities takes place in minimal legislatures, primarily in committee arenas. This is not because these arenas are particularly specialized, but because these arenas are more private than caucus or plenary arenas. The elites who run minimal legislative systems are more willing to accept criticism and even mild dissent in private rather than in public arenas. Because these legislatures exist by the grace of these elites, these legislators keep their activities within permissible bounds. Within that very restricted framework minimal legislatures are able to exert some policy-making influence.

NOTES

1. Anthony King (1975:182) has noted that the executive branch consists "not of a single structure or class of structures but of a wide variety of structures, including . . . monarchs, presidents, cabinets, central staffs, operating agencies, regulatory commissions, administrative tribunals, armed forces, investigatory commissions, advisory bodies, and publicly owned enterprises. Legislatures and judicatures are, so to speak, firms that specialize. Executives are conglomerates." Elsewhere, King (1976) has some important things to say about the artificiality of the term "legislative-executive" relations, observing quite correctly that in many legislatures the important conflict is between the executive and part of the legislature.

2. For a discussion of some of these same points, see Shaw (1978).

Chapter 4

ACTIVE AND VULNERABLE LEGISLATURES: POLICY MAKING THROUGH COMMITTEES

This chapter will deal with active and vulnerable legislatures—the two legislative types characterized by substantial policy-making roles. Data for the former category come from studies of the United States Congress and the Costa Rican National Assembly. Among the vulnerable legislatures that will be discussed are the now-suspended Congresses of the Philippines, Chile, and Uruguay, and the Parliaments of Italy and the French Fourth Republic.

POLICY FORMULATION

Executive Domination. It is not at all clear whether executive-centered elites dominate active and vulnerable legislatures during the formulation phase of policy making, or if the legislature has at least an equal and possibly a dominant role. It has often been asserted that the United States Congress simply reacts to the policy initiatives of American presidents. One student of the contemporary American presidency writes that since the Truman Administration,

the President has been expected to present an annual legislative agenda in every area of legislative action and to send bill drafts to Congress under his own name. . . . Public debate will be concerned largely with the issues with which he is concerned. Because he will have initiated that debate, it will occur on his terms. He can arrange to present his ideas in their most favorable light, taking full advantage of his unique capacity to gain publicity and public attention in order to inform and influence the ensuing debate. (James, 1974:198–99)

Another observer of the presidency suggests that "when it comes to the passage of major legislation about which there has been great political controversy . . . it takes the President as catalyst to pull together all the supporting forces in Congress and the country for the most innovative actions" (Hargrove, 1974:232).

However, available data suggest that these statements somewhat underestimate the policy-initiating role of the Congress. The classic study was done by Lawrence Chamberlain who surveyed ninety major laws enacted by the American Congress between the late nineteenth century and the beginning of the twentieth century and concluded that no less than seventy-seven of these acts "trace their ancestry directly to bills which originally had been introduced without administration sponsorship" (Chamberlain, 1946:446). An updating of this study covering the period from 1940 to 1967 suggests that for approximately 50 percent of the legislation considered by the Congress, the Congress was the major contributor to the legislation, and that a further 25 percent was attributable to joint efforts involving both the Congress and the president (Moe and Teel, 1971). Finally, during recent periods when the Republicans have controlled the presidency and the Democrats have constituted the congressional majority, there is evidence that a great deal of important legislation was initiated by the Congress (Orfield, 1975).

Data from Costa Rica show a somewhat less impressive legislative record. One study of a sample of two hundred bills passed by the Costa Rican Assembly during the 1958–70 period found that 56 percent had originated in the legislature. However, when these bills were divided into "national" and "local" categories—on the assumption that the former were more important than the latter—the executive was found to have initiated 63 percent of the national bills while 79 percent of the local bills originated in the legislature (Hughes and Mijeski, 1973:37).

The data from vulnerable legislatures are closer to the Costa Rican than to the American findings. Studies of the Philippine Congress have concluded that the more important business considered by the legislature is initiated by the executive (Grossholtz, 1964:121; Dodd, 1973:140–42). In Chile 91 percent of all legislation introduced and 82 percent of the legislation characterized as important was initiated by legislators. Every year, however, extraordinary sessions of the legislature were convoked by the president and all bills considered in these sessions had to be either initiated by the president or approved by him before they were introduced. In those sessions 59 percent of all bills and 66 percent of the important bills were initiated by the executive. In addition, during regular sessions the Congress played only a minor role in submitting budgetary legislation. Thus, "while Congress introduced a greater quantity of bills, it is the executive that submitted the important ones" (Hughes and Mijeski, 1973:12–13).

In the parliamentary systems in the vulnerable category executive domination was even more pronounced. During the Fourth French Republic "more than 70%" of the bills passed by the National Assembly were of government origin (Williams, 1964:259) while in Italy, 75 percent of the laws enacted by Parliament between 1948 and 1966 were government bills (Di Palma, 1977:44–45).

What these data indicate then is that while a great number of the policies enacted by these legislatures are formally initiated by the executive in each political system a significant number of policy enactments are formulated in legislative arenas. In the case of the United States, the data suggest that the Congress and the president have a nearly equal role in policy initiation.

TABLE 4.1
Success Rates for Private Member Bills in Three Legislatures

Legislature	Time Span	Introduced	Passed	Success Rate
United States[a] (Polsby, 1971:90)	1967–68	24,786	2,419	9.8%
Italy (Di Palma, 1977: 44–45)	1948–68	11,991	1,992	16.6%
Philippines (Stauffer, 1975:18)	1954	2,786	229	8.2%
Philippines (Stauffer, 1975:18)	1962	3,578	64	1.8%
Philippines (Stauffer, 1975:18)	1970	3,149	52	1.7%

a. In the United States, all bills are private member bills because no bills may be introduced by the Executive. Therefore, the American figures refer to all bills introduced during the 1967–1968 period rather than to bills introduced without executive sponsorship as is the case for the other countries discussed in this section. Finally, "private member" bills should be distinguished from "private" bills which are introduced for the benefit or relief of specific individuals. These are not included in this discussion.

Private Member Bills. In all of these legislatures, members are free to introduce their own legislation without government endorsement. Because very few of these private member bills clear all legislative hurdles and become law, such efforts are often discounted as ineffectual. Data on the success rate for private member bills in three legislatures are compiled in Table 4:1.

These low approval rates may be, in part, a reflection of the large volume of private member bills introduced. Thus, in Italy during the 1963–68 Parliament, only 17.5 percent of the private member bills introduced were passed, but these bills accounted for 38.3 percent of the total parliamentary output. In explaining these findings, Di Palma suggests that many of these bills duplicated each other and therefore the percentage of proposed bills passed is not really an indicator of the success rate for these proposals (Di Palma, 1977:45–46).

Of course, all of these bills are not viewed by those who introduce them as destined for the law books; in Italy, for example, "many private bills are presented for propoganda purposes or as a gesture to please local and special interests, with little intent to press for their approval" (Di Palma, 1977:46). Some private member bills may be designed as instruments for attracting publicity for a particular policy cause, or they may serve as a focal point for diverse groups interested in that area, or they may be a means of encouraging others to formulate policies responsive to the need addressed by the bill. During the Fourth Republic 4,800 private member bills were introduced in the first Parliament and 4,000 in the second, and, while they accounted for about a quarter of the acts passed by these two Parliaments, their more significant role, according to Williams (1964:261), was as a source of pressure that stimulated policy proposals from the government.

This last point is important because it suggests the real influence that the individual member of the active or vulnerable legislature, operating in the plenary session, has on policy formulation. Because these legislatures are capable of placing great constraints upon the activities of executive-centered elites, these elites are naturally solicitous of the interests and concerns of legislators. Speeches by legislators, points raised in informal discussions with administrators, and the introduction of legislation are all instruments through which legislators can prod administrators, cabinet members, and even presidents into initiating policies that speak to the problem that legislators perceive, and formulating these policies in terms which are acceptable to the legislators.

Committee Arenas. As suggested in the last chapter, active and vulnerable legislatures have highly developed committee systems which enable them to divide the legislative labor in such a way that a degree of legislative expertise is generated in most policy areas. Such expertise is particularly important if legislators are to have an impact on policy formulation, because this policy stage requires at least an understanding of the existing policies.

One factor that fosters such expertise is stability of committee membership. In the United States Congress committee membership has been highly stable because of the operation of the seniority system—a practice that ensures that the power and perquisites of a committee are monopolized by those who have served the longest on the committee. While the influence of the seniority system has been eroded somewhat by recent reforms (Ornstein and Rhode, 1976, Hinckley, 1976), it has encouraged members to remain on committees rather than switch from one to another, and this has been especially true for the most important committees of the Congress. Thus many American legislators acquire detailed knowledge of the subject area under the jurisdiction of the committees on which they serve and committee leaders almost always possess such specialized knowledge.

In Costa Rica there is more fluidity in committee membership than there is in the American Congress; however, one study found that

within each committee there were two or three individuals at any given time who could bring a certain amount of expertise to bear upon matters before the committee. These individuals led most of the substantive discussion. . . . Although it was the eleven or twelve members of the committee who re-solved the questions, they did so under the guidance of a few individuals who were well versed in the general subject matter at hand. (Baker, 1971:87)

Committees in vulnerable legislatures are more like the Costa Rican than the American committees. In the Philippine House of Representatives, for example, the committee chairmen selected in 1970 averaged slightly over three years of prior service on their respective committees and almost ten years of House experience.

However, the chairmen of the most important committees had a much longer period of prior service on their committees than the chairmen of the less important committees. (Dodd, 1973:63–67). Similarly, in Chile the Finance Committee and the Committee on the Constitution, Legislation, Justice, and Rules were the two most important committees in the Senate. Data collected for the period from 1894 to 1965 show that of the five members of each committee at least two and usually three or four continued on the committee from one legislative period to the next (Agor, 1971a:87–88). During the Fourth Republic, membership on the major parliamentary committees tended to be continuous while membership on the lesser committees was quite fluid and attendance highly irregular (Williams, 1964:249). However, even on these lesser committees, there was always a working nucleus of members who were particularly concerned with the legislative area under the committee's jurisdiction (Harrision, 1958).

The pattern that emerges from these legislatures then is one in which for each policy area a certain number of legislators operating in the committee arenas possess more specialized knowledge than the rest of their colleagues. Whether or not that knowledge rivals that of their bureaucratic counterparts is difficult to say. However, it does seem clear that much of the legislative influence on policy formulation is held by these expert committee personnel.

In the United States executive-centered elites will consult with senior committee personnel as part of the process of drawing up legislation that they intend to propose. Suggestions from members of the relevant committee are more likely to be heeded than suggestions from legislators who are not on the committee that will consider the legislation. When legislation is formulated in the legislature, members of the committee with jurisdiction in that area are likely to be among the authors. Similarly, in France during the Fourth Republic private member legislation was likely to be introduced by one of the specialists on the committee that would consider the legislation (Williams, 1964:258).

Frequently, the oversight activities of legislative committees reveal areas in which new legislation is needed. Questions or comments directed by committee members to responsible administrators are more likely to evoke relevant policy responses than random comments in plenary arenas. One scholar has described this subtle process in the following terms:

What matters here is not that an administrator is forced by a vote or an overt instruction of a legislative committee to initiate a particular policy. . . . More important is an administrative assessment of the given ecology within which he must take his policy decisions. For efficacious policy initiation, he must attempt to perceive and anticipate the behavior of legislative committees and the environment reflected by them. (Boyer, 1964:42)

Partisan Arenas. In the United States, Costa Rica, the Philippines, and Uruguay, party organizations have played very little role in policy formulation. In these countries parties have provided convenient labels for legislative groups as well as occasional guidance on votes taken in the legislature, but these parties have had very little influence on policy formulation, either through their extraparliamentary organizations or through their parliamentary party caucuses.

In Italy, France, and Chile the situation is different. In these countries parties have been more ideological and more highly organized, with the result that party organizations have often influenced policy at the formulation stage. In Italy, for example, the parties, although they initiate far fewer policy proposals than the bureaucracy, "stimulate the introduction of a goodly share of the broader and more controversial bills of general application" (Zariski, 1972:266). However, the capacity of the Italian parties, as well as the parties in France and Chile, to impose their will upon their parliamentary deputies is, as we shall see, subject to a great deal of variation.

DELIBERATION

While a good deal of policy formulation takes place in extraparliamentary arenas, the deliberation of policy proposals is preeminently a legislative prerogative in countries with active and vulnerable legislatures. While policy proposals may be designed outside these legislatures, they are discussed, amended, and often rejected in legislative arenas.

In Italy and in France the first deliberative stage within a legislative arena is in what we have called leadership arenas. Cabinets in these countries include legislators who are leaders of the parties that compose the government coalition. These coalitions are frequently depicted as weak and ineffectual, and certainly their deliberations are heavily influenced by the wishes of external party organizations as well as by the wishes of their members in the legislature. Nonetheless cabinet members, as leaders of their fellow partisans in the legislature, have a significant role in conciliating policy differences within the government coalition. Policies proposed by the bureaucracy or instigated by one part of the governing coalition will be discussed in cabinet before transmittal to other legislative arenas. The outcomes at this initial deliberative level will determine whether or not a proposal is to be forwarded to other parliamentary bodies and, if it is to be forwarded, in what form it will arrive.

Committees. Once a policy proposal is formally submitted to the legislature—either by those in leadership arenas, or by those in extraparliamentary arenas, or by individual legislators—the primary arena for legislative deliberation is the committee. Active and vulnerable legislatures follow procedural rules that mandate committee referral of all legislative proposals immediately after they are introduced, and then require some form of committee action before the proposal may be considered by the legislature sitting in plenary session. Thus, committees get first crack at all legislative proposals and, except for extraordinary situations, a favorable committee report must be in hand before the proposal may be sent to the plenary session for final disposition. Conversely, a negative committee view of the legislation usually means that the bill will have no chance to be considered by the legislature as a whole.

After bills are sent to the committee, and after the committee has agreed that it wishes to consider the legislation, hearings are held during which government officials and private citizens may give testimony. With that testimony in hand, committee members will discuss the merits of the proposals, often amend it, and otherwise seek compromises that will pacify significant groups inside and outside the legislature. Sometimes a committee confronted with several different proposals all dealing with the same topic will write an entirely new bill incorporating provisions from the various bills originally submitted.

The parliamentary committees in France under the Fourth Republic pursued these deliberating prerogatives with something of a vengeance. They frequently altered private member bills so that they bore little resemblance to their original form (Harrison, 1958:178). They could and usually did redraft government measures (Williams, 1964:245). So thorough was the redrafting done in committees that "the bill which came up for discussion in the full Assembly [was] the committee's bill" (Bromhead, 1957:146). The current Italian committee system operates in a similar manner: "committees usually employ drafting subcommittees which include the opposition, collect government and other proposals relative to the same subject matter, and prepare new drafts for committee discussion. The new draft reflects in various degrees a negotiated balance of the various proposals" (Di Palma, 1977:194–95).

In the United States data from the Appropriations Committee of the House of Representatives can be used to indicate the extent to which legislation is modified in congressional committees. Between 1947 and 1962 the Committee made 575 decisions on the budgetary requests of thirty-six federal bureaus. In 106 instances (18.4 percent), the committee recommended that the agency receive exactly the amount it requested. In 228 decisions (52.2 percent) the committee reduced the request by 10 percent or less, and in thirty-nine more cases (6.7 percent) there was an increase of less than 10 percent (Fenno, 1966:354). Thus 77 percent of all the committee decisions were within 10 percent of the original agency request. Whether these amendments are slight or substantial is a matter of interpretation, but the point is that they constituted somewhat less than a drastic revision of what had been proposed by the executive branch. However, most proposals were modified—either significantly or marginally—and it seems obvious that just about every major piece of legislation that eventually passes through the American committee system is altered somewhat from the form in which it is introduced.

This does not seem to be the case in other committee systems in these two legislative categories. An analysis of 146 bills reported by the committees of the Costa Rican Assembly shows that two-thirds were either completely unchanged or only slightly modified from the form in which they were originally introduced (Hughes and Mijeski, 1973:32–33). In the Philippines administration measures were usually reported out of committee without amendment, but sometimes several bills would be consolidated or an entirely new bill reported out, combining elements of several different proposals (Grossholtz, 1964:122). Philippine Senators, however, seemed to feel that their committees were more independent of presidential control than House committees (Jackson, 1971:59).

More important than the power of committees to amend legislation is their power to pigeon-hole proposals to which they object, thus preventing them from being deliberated on the floor of the legislature.

In the United States Congress, for example, 93.6 percent of the bills introduced in the House of Representatives between 1967 and 1968 and 66.6 percent of those introduced in the Senate died in committee. (Polsby, 1971:90). During the Fourth Republic, French committees killed seven out of eight private member bills without debate (Williams, 1964:262). In the Philippines, a "large part of the legislation referred to committees is pigeon-holed and very little emerges for floor consideration" (Grossholtz, 1964:122).

The power of committees to pigeon-hole proposals and the great influence of their affirmative recommendations on the chances for ultimate passage of a proposal has led to the frequent observation that these committees monopolize the deliberative activities of the legislature and are, in effect, exercising an autonomous influence on the policy-making process.

Committee expertise makes some degree of autonomy from the parent body inevitable. As the expertise of the committee increases, legislators who are not members of the committee and presumably not specialists in the policy area under the committee's purview will find it difficult to challenge the findings of the committee on substantive issues. Legislators tend to defer to the judgment of their colleagues both because they respect their expertise and also because they want their own expertise to be respected when their committees make recommendations to the legislature.

The deference of the full legislature to committee decisions is most clearly demonstrated in regard to negative decisions—committee refusals to report legislation to the floor. From 1949 to 1965 there were only fifteen occasions when the United States House or Senate discharged one of its committees from consideration of legislation and then ultimately passed the proposal (Goodwin, 1970:237–38). In a study of a sample of bills considered by the Costa Rican Assembly during the 1958–70 period the only bills accepted by the Assembly "were those that received affirmative committee reports" (Hughes and Mijeski, 1973:40). Jackson's informants in the Philippines reported only one instance in twenty years when a bill had been discharged from a committee of the Philippine Congress (Jackson, 1971:68). In Fourth Republic France the government had the power to extract bills from dilatory committees but seldom exercised it, apparently because they feared that the committee in response might severely amend their proposals (Williams, 1964:258). And in Italy

deadlines for reporting legislation are either not imposed on committees or when imposed are unenforced or easily postponed (Di Palma,
1977:195).

It is important to note in this context that the refusal of a committee
to report a proposal to the floor does not necessarily mean that the
committee is acting in conflict with the wishes and the interests of the
general membership. First, every bill that a legislator introduces is not
destined in his or her eyes to become law. It may instead be a response
to constituency pressures: "French committees rejected private
member bills with the knowledge and even complicity of sponsors
who had often meant them for the local newspapers or election
addresses rather than the statute books" (Williams, 1964:262). A staff
member of a committee of the Chilean Senate commented that many
proposed amendments to major pieces of legislation were rejected at
the committee stage, but he added that many of the amendments "are
submitted to meet district or pressure group demands. But imagine,
the same senator will take them out in committee" (Agor, 1971a:55).
In the Philippines as well, much of the load of private member bills
dealt with particularistic constituency problems, and the mortality
rate for such bills in committee was very high (Stauffer, 1975:13–14).
Legislators may feel free to engage in such publicity-seeking, secure
in the knowledge that their hyperbole will be buried in the anonymity
of the committee room.

Second, committees may be acting at the behest of party leaders
and sometimes of the membership at large when they pigeon-hole bills
in committee. Sometimes bills are so controversial or sometimes the
degree of public support for them is so much greater than their
wisdom that it would be embarrassing for members to have to stand
up and be counted during a vote in plenary session. In such situations,
it is easier for the legislative majority to defeat the proposal in the less
public committee arena. In Italy, for example, the governing Christian
Democrats have used the committee to bottle up popular legislation
that they didn't want to oppose publicly on the floor of the Chamber
(Zariski, 1972:246). Committees in the Chilean Senate often delayed
presidential proposals until the Senate majority was able to exact
concessions from the executive; once the compromise was reached
and the bill was reported to the floor, it went through very quickly
(Agor, 1971b:10–14).

This information suggests that members of active and vulnerable
legislatures exploit the privacy of committee arenas to quietly bury

legislation that they aren't very serious about, or that is too popular to be rejected publicly, or too politically charged to allow on the floor. Thus committees, in this respect at least, are not acting autonomously; they are simply providing a private arena in which the legislature may work its will, when the more traditional public arenas are less attractive.

Another aspect of autonomy involves the relationship between committees and partisan arenas. For the two active legislations—the United States Congress and the Costa Rican Assembly—committees are quite independent of party influence, but for most of the vulnerable legislatures partisan influence on committee deliberations is a more significant variable.

The Philippine Congress probably has the weakest party structure of all the vulnerable legislatures. Nonetheless, almost half of the legislators responding to a questionnaire indicated that at least to some degree they felt strongly obliged to follow party policy in their committee work, and more than two-thirds considered the party caucus important in determining policy stands on committees (Jackson, 1971:61–63).

In Chile party influence at first glance seems to be much stronger than in the Philippines, but closer analysis reveals more similarities than difference. Chilean parties issued orders as to how members of the Senate should vote on important issues and senators were expelled from party membership for failure to follow the party line. But the parties, with the exception of the Communists, did not issue party orders frequently. As one Senator said: "I think orders serve a useful purpose, but they should be used prudently, not habitually" (Agor, 1971a:42). Also, the party, when arriving at its positions, tended to rely quite heavily on the advice of its members serving on the relevant committee because "their knowledge gained through committee study enabled them to explain the bill and its articles and to warn about details to watch out for" (Agor, 1971a:125). Finally, although party discipline was likely to prevail at the voting stage in committee, members usually could get permission to vote against party orders when these orders conflicted with their constituency interests or with their own personal views. In the privacy of the committee arenas, party loyalties tended to yield to mutually shared expertise of committee members; this was particularly true for highly technical bills where "committee norms of expertise and specialized study seemed to predominate" (Agor, 1971a:55).

This theme of diminished partisanship in committee arenas is re-peated in studies of the Italian and French committee systems. In Italy the level of partisanship and passion appears to be significantly lower in committees than on the floor. A very high percentage of bills passed *in sede deliberante* (see below) are approved unanimously or receive no more than two negative votes (Zariski, 1972:279). Di Palma's analysis of a sample of laws introduced by either Christian Democratic deputies or by the government and passed by the Parlia-ment finds that Communist deputies supported 77 percent of the laws that were approved by committee procedures, but only 41 percent of those passed in plenary sessions, leading him to the conclusion that committees "tend to adopt more balanced roles and to relax partisan and ideological distinctions" because their meetings are not open to the public, their decisions usually aren't reached through formal votes, and because "their style of operation is more informal and collegial than the floor's" (Di Palma, 1977:57, 195).

In Fourth Republic France the allocation of committee seats was made in proportion to the strength of the party in the Chamber, but the personal interests and expertise of the members was the major crite-rion in selecting the person who would actually sit on the committee. As a result, "considerations of party discipline [did] not appear to play a substantial part in the allocation of places. Committee seats [were not] given as rewards for faithfulness to party leaders, or withheld as a penalty for voting against the rest of the party" (Bromhead, 1957:141). Thus, as in Italy, committee work

was less partisan than debate in the Assembly. . . . The club atmosphere moderated passions and allowed opposition members to work usefully with their colleagues. It was in committee that Gaullists and even Poujadists grew accustomed to bargains and compromises with the System and the Com-munists themselves frequently made genuine concessions to achieve una-nimity (Williams, 1964:255).

One additional and more reliable indicator of committee autonomy is the success that committees have in getting their affirmative rec-ommendations approved in plenary arenas. Perhaps the extreme of committee autonomy in this respect is the Italian system in which committees have the power to approve certain types of legislation and send it directly to the executive without first sending it to the floor for a final vote. This power cannot be exercised in regard to certain classes of legislation and in the remainder there are safeguards which enable the bill to be brought to the floor if the government or a sufficient number of deputies request it. Nonetheless between 1948 and 1958 approximately three out of every four bills approved in either house of the Italian Parliament were approved by committees *in sede deliberante* (Adams and Barile, 1966:66). It is argued that the procedure is used only for "unimportant" legislation or for highly technical legislation, while all of the "major" legislation comes to the floor for the debate. But, as LaPalombara (1964:221) points out, such technical matters often involve important economic interests, such as export and import regulations, the governance of state-owned industries, tariffs, and similar measures.

Although the committees in other legislatures in these categories cannot enact legislation in the manner of the Italian committees, some have a nearly equivalent power because their recommendations are regularly accepted in plenary sessions. In Costa Rica, for example, aggregate figures for the Assembly's five standing committees for the 1966–70 period show that 82.6 percent of the committee reports were passed without amendment, 13.2 percent were approved with amendments, 2.5 percent were returned to committees, and 1.6 percent were rejected (Baker, 1971:110). In the case of the Chilean Senate, it is reported that committee recommendations are accepted approximately 90 percent of the time. In a poll of Philippine legislators 95 percent of the senators and 68 percent of the representatives indicated that committee reports were always or usually accepted (Jackson, 1971:68).

The regularity with which positive committee reports will be supported in the American Congress tends to vary from committee to committee, with the more prestigious committees enjoying higher success rates than the less prestigious committees. Data for four committees are assembled in Table 4.2.

Again, the question arises as to whether these relatively high success rates indicate committee autonomy or if they simply mean that committees are conforming to the expectations of the legislature at large. Studies of the Appropriations Committees and the Ways and Means Committee of the American Congress come to the latter conclusion (Fenno, 1966:1–78; Manley, 1970:246). In Costa Rica plenary and committee arenas appear to be dominated by a small group of influential members and the evidence is that they generally work together rather than independently toward the accomplishment of mutual goals (Baker, 1971:97–100).

It is clear that in some legislatures committee reports are not handled quite as respectfully as they are in the Philippines, Chile, Costa Rica, and the United States. In France and in Italy amendments to committee recommendations are frequent occurrences. During the Fourth Republic committees sometimes escaped the control of the government, thus compelling it to defeat or amend committee proposals on the floor. According to Williams (1964:255) "a determined Cabinet could almost always persuade the house to disavow a recalcitrant committee." In Italy amendments to committee reports are attributable to either of two factors: differing views in the Senate which compel changes to be made in the Chamber, or divisions within the Christian Democratic party which surface on the floor (Zariski, 1972:289–95). The latter point is illustrated by Di Palma's data showing that while only 14 percent of all amendments proposed on the floor are accepted, 83 percent of those proposed by Christian Democratic deputies are accepted (Di Palma, 1977:62).

Caucus Deliberations. In the active legislatures caucus deliberations are very informal and have only minimal influence on legislative outcomes. At caucuses of the majority National Liberation Party of Costa Rica discussions focus on specific bills that already have been assigned to committees. These discussions are occasions for (1) examining the socioeconomic and political implications of the bill and (2) determining what strategy should be followed in order to provide effective support or opposition for the bill (Baker, 971:93). In the

TABLE 4.2
**Acceptance of Committee Reports in the
United States Congress: Four Committees**

Committee	Period	Finding
House Appropriations	1947–62	89.9% of recommendations accepted without amendment (Fenno, 1966:450).
Senate Appropriations	1947–62	88.5% of recommendations accepted without amendment (Fenno, 1966:597).
House Ways and Means	1947–65	90.6% of recommendations accepted without amendment (Manley, 1970:221).
House Education and Labor	1955–66	59% of bills reported were passed, most in amended form (Fenno, 1973:235).

United States Congress party caucuses are just as informal and seem to have the same general purposes as those held in Costa Rica: to mobilize support for positions which seem to have majority support within the party. As we shall see, no one is really coerced in this process and, most importantly, the caucus does not abridge the specialized work of the standing committees. Party members who occupy leadership positions within committees view party-centered deliberations as a threat to the prerogatives of their committees. And because all party members are also committee members, all members will feel that they have something to lose by allowing deliberative activities to shift to party arenas. Thus the deliberative role of caucuses in these legislatures remains informal and quite secondary to the deliberative activities that go on in committee and plenary arenas.

In the vulnerable legislatures the situation is quite different. In most of these systems significant deliberative activity frequently goes on in party caucuses and these more private discussions affect the nature of the deliberations and the decisions reached in public plenary sessions.

In the Philippines party membership tends to be rather fluid at the beginning of the legislative session. However, a majority coalition is eventually hammered out and once that happens the caucus becomes an important arena for policy deliberations (Stauffer, 1970:361). Grossholtz (1964:124) reports that "much of the crucial negotiation on these [important] matters has taken place in the majority party caucus. Apparently there have been real debates in which many points of view were expressed, but these are not made public. The replacement of the legislature with the majority caucus as a forum for discussion . . . [means] that the legislature does not debate these matters publicly. . . . "

Similarly, in the Chilean Senate the party caucus seems to be a key deliberative arena, usually operating at the point between committee deliberation and the discussion of the matter on the floor: "In some instances national party orders have been issued, and the floor leaders simply explain the position to be taken on the floor and answer any questions that arise. But party orders do not accompany most legislation and so open discussion ensues in the caucus. Here the merits of the bill and certain articles will be reviewed" (Agor, 1971a:125).

In Italy there is evidence that Italian deputies view themselves primarily as delegates of their parties and quite readily accept the fact that their policy-making activities are constrained by the positions that their parties adopt (Di Palma, 1977:159–63). It also appears that much of the deliberative activities that go into developing these party positions take place in extraparliamentary arenas. It has been argued that executive bureaus of the parties (*partitocrazia*) "have effectively usurped the parliamentarians' powers and have become the locus of all top decision-making. It is in the executive bureaus that the major policy issues are fought out, decided, or postponed" (Kogan, 1962:56). In France party policies are regularly articulated and deliberated within the executive committees of the parties after which attempts are made to gain the support of parliamentarians for these policies.

Plenary Arenas. In all of these legislatures plenary deliberations, although heavily influenced by prior deliberations in arenas dominated by executive-centered elites, as well as in legislative arenas such as committees and caucuses, still can have a significant impact upon the shape of policy outcomes. While policy is not really made on the floor, arrangements carefully designed to meet the needs of partisan, committee, and executive personnel may be blown to pieces by the hostile reactions of rank and file members, if their wishes have not been adequately considered. Alternatively, speeches extolling the merits of the proposal may increase the popularity and comprehendibility of the proposal, thereby making it easier to implement after formal approval by the legislature.

Such potential power in the hands of the general membership of the legislature will lead wise committee and party leaders to at least pursue informal consultations with the general membership before moving controversial legislation out of the relative privacy of committee and caucus arenas into the highly public plenary arena. Often the threat of significant verbal opposition to a policy proposal will be enough to convince the government or a committee to withdraw or modify its proposal. In the Philippine Congress privileged speeches served as a vehicle for mobilizing public opposition to legislative proposals and this, in the view of one observer of that legislature, was its "most effective instrument for influencing policy emanating from the executive branch" (Stauffer, 1970:352).

The purpose of debate is not really to work out or decide major policy issues. At their best they provide an opportunity for the airing of opposing views, a process which can serve to educate both mass and elite publics concerning the intent of the legislation. This beneficial effect of debate is somewhat limited by the generalized nature of the plenary arena; many will be commenting who know very little about the policy area in question, and the wisdom and accuracy of their remarks may be highly questionable. Also, because the plenary session is public, debate will be aimed as much at scoring political points outside the legislature as at elucidating the merits and demerits of policy proposals. Finally, because there is a feeling in these legislatures that all the big questions have already been dealt with in committee, plenary sessions often suffer from lack of attendance.

Many a member of the United States House of Representatives has delivered an erudite speech to a group of thirty or forty colleagues, most of whom weren't listening. Debate in the Italian Parliament has been characterized as ideological, abstractly philosophical, ill-informed, badly attended, and better suited to campaign addresses than to policy making (Zariski, 1972:277–78). During the Fourth Republic the French National Assembly was frequently accused of assiduously avoiding the really important issues (Leites, 1959:122) while in the Philippines, the rate of legislative absenteeism was so high that it was embarrassing for the Congress and helped cause the low level of esteem in which most Filipinos held their legislature (Stauffer, 1975:22–23).

Discipline. It has been argued that in many legislatures deliberation in plenary arenas is a pointless exercise because the final outcome of the votes taken on the floor have been determined by party leaders who simply impose discipline on their members in the legislature. Thus, no matter how the debate goes, or what the merits of the issue might be, legislators follow the instructions of their party leaders.

This generalization does not appear to apply to the two active legislatures that we have been considering, but it is a somewhat more accurate description of the vulnerable legislatures. Even in that category, however, there is substantial interparty variation concerning, first, the degree to which discipline is imposed and, second, whether party instructions emanate from extraparliamentary party leaders or from party leaders who are also legislators. In the latter case legislators may be said to be imposing discipline on themselves, whereas in the former discipline is being imposed from outside the legislature.

While "roll call votes in the United States Congress follow party lines more often than they follow other alignments" (Jewell and Patterson, 1973:451), it is very seldom that the parties are unanimous on a contested roll-call and even when such unanimity is approached it is not because the party has imposed it upon its membership. The party unity that does exist in the Congress comes from ideological and issue consensus among members rather than from the imposition of discipline by the party leadership. Several studies have attested to the fact that effective party leadership in the American Congress must be based on bargaining rather than on command (Huitt, 1961; Ripley, 1967).

In Costa Rica the data are similar. A two-thirds vote in the caucuses of any of the major parties in the Assembly can bind the party members to vote for the supported position. However, in those cases where a party line was voted members of the majority National Liberation party were allowed to vote against the party-line position if they could explain to the caucus why it would be unwise or difficult for them to publicly support the party. For the opposition Republican Party, party positions were infrequently taken and when they were, they were applied to the membership in a flexible manner. And members of the opposition National Union Party claimed that they did not believe in forcing a position on anyone; rather, they asserted that freedom of choice for the individual was of paramount importance within their group (Baker, 1971:93–96).

In the Philippines, although party members were expected to vote with the party once a party position had been determined, some freedom was allowed on issues that did not involve leadership choices or the power position of the party as an organization: "Party positions are decided in caucus, with the party leadership playing an important role in guiding discussion and decisions. Caucuses are not binding, but a party member is expected to publicly register his plan to oppose a party stand at the time of the caucus" (Franzich, 1971:166–67). In a survey of the attitudes of Philippine legislators, just under two-thirds said that if a bill was important for the party's record, a member should vote with the party even if it costs him some support in his district (Franzich, 1971:271). However, the point should be made that these party policies are determined primarily by legislative leaders rather than by extraparliamentary party organizations. In the case of his party the president has a great deal to say about these policies, but he is the only nonlegislative actor involved. And the nature of party politics in the Philippines means that legislators are as likely to be influenced by local party elites as by the president and his followers in Manila.

In Chile the expectation that senators will support national party orders was more than balanced by the view, articulated by one senator, that "Senators are mature men and can make up their own minds. . . . My view is that there should be orders only on key issues, and then only in the form of recommendations. Senators are elected by the people, not the party" (Agor, 1971a:42). There also was consensus among the Chilean senators that the degree of party discipline varied significantly across parties, the Communists being the most disciplined of the party groupings. Sometimes party orders dictated a general stance on the bill but left the member free to decide for himself on specific sections. And, even "if orders are issued for both stages of a key bill, senators may ask for and normally are granted freedom to vote as they wish for constituency or conscience reasons" (Agor, 1971a:43–44). As was the case with the Philippines, party positions, although influenced strongly by external party organizations, are ultimately decided and enforced by legislators themselves.

The situation during the French Fourth Republic varied among parties as the party cohesion scores calculated by Wilson and Wiste (1976:469) and replicated in Table 4:3 demonstrate. Communist deputies clearly were the most disciplined. Their parliamentary salaries were paid to the party which in turn paid them a much smaller allowance. Communist deputies signed blank letters of resignation and filed them with the party so that they might be submitted by the party when and if the member broke party discipline. Deputies were shifted from one constituency to another so that they could not gather the personal popularity that would enable them to act independently of the party. And, finally, those who rose to power in the party would place themselves in parliamentary positions, thus assuring the supremacy of the party over the individual deputy (Duverger, 1954:197–202).

TABLE 4.3
Indices of Party Cohesion in the French National
Assembly During the Fourth Republic

Parties	1946–51	1951–56	1956–58
Communists	99.8	99.9	99.9
Socialists	97.9	98.7	96.4
Radical Socialists	79.6	79.3	68.6
Popular Republican Movement	93.7	89.4	94.6

In the Socialist party, the party executive frequently clashed with deputies and on several occasions the deputies successfully defied party instructions. The fact that twenty of the forty-five members of the party executive were parliamentarians suggests that party directives, when they came, were likely to reflect the views of the deputies, and the relatively high cohesion scores indicate agreement among the deputies themselves (Williams, 1964:93).

An uneven record of discipline characterized the centrist Popular Republican Movement and the Radical Socialists. In these parties parliamentarians tended to dominate the external party organization, and therefore instructions were seldom issued. In the case of the Radical party, deputies "agreed only in defence of their personal independence of judgement and decision." Thus in the second National Assembly three of the four Radical premiers were overthrown with members of their own party voting against them (Williams, 1964:121).

The strongest and most consistent party discipline among vulnerable legislatures is exercised by the Italian parties. "In all Italian parties, breaches of party discipline are often—but not always— punished by suspension or expulsion from the party" (Zariski, 1972:151). The qualifications that should be added to this statement concern those instances when the external party leadership itself is split, a situation which, according to Kogan (1962:57) can lead to breakdowns in discipline. Zariski (1972:152–53) suggests that the threat of a revolt from the rank and file, particularly in the case of the Christian Democrats, may cause the party to retreat from a potentially divisive policy in order to maintain the facade of unity. Finally, in Italy, there is another unique feature—secret balloting—which provides members of all parties with the opportunity to vote against the party leadership and have such deviations go undetected if they wish.

Another aspect of discipline is the capacity of executive-centered elites to control policy outcomes. In none of these legislative systems can these elites command unquestioned support for their proposals from legislative majorities. Between 1954 and 1974 American presidents had only 46 percent of their proposals approved by both houses of the Congress; that figure was as low as 20 percent for Richard Nixon's 1971 proposals and as high as 69 percent for Lyndon Johnson's 1965 Great Society proposals. (Schwarz and Shaw, 1976:223). Legislative proposals of Costa Rican presidents fare somewhat better; they are approved 62 percent of the time (Hughes and Mijeski, 1973:36).

Comparable figures are not available for vulnerable legislatures, but studies suggest that the presidents of the Philippines and of Chile often had to struggle to get what they wanted. Philippine presidents eventually got most of their legislative program passed, but only after hard bargaining with legislators, primarily involving exchanges of public works programs under presidential control for voting support in the legislature. (Franzich, 1971:193–98). In Chile, "a higher percentage of presidential than congressional proposals are enacted" (Hughes and Mijeski, 1973:16). Nonetheless Chilean presidents were required constantly to negotiate with legislators and to accept modifications to their proposals as conditions for their passage. Otherwise, presidential bills would be delayed for nearly interminable periods of time.

In Italy and France, the right of the government to rule is predicated on its command of a majority in the Parliament. Those majorities have been constantly tested and, as the very brief average life spans of French and Italian cabinets attest, these majorities are frequently found wanting. The immobilism that characterized Fourth Republic politics and continues to plague Italy is in no small part attributable to the inability of cabinets to deal with major problems because they cannot get their policies through the Parliament. The first Assembly of the Fourth Republic passed about 60 percent of the bills that the government introduced, while the second Assembly passed just over half (Williams, 1964:259). Although the Italian governments seemed to perform more effectively—passing 84.7 percent of their proposals during the 1948–68 period—in fact, most of this legislation concerned "limited matters for the simple reason that Parliament cannot form the necessary agreement on the important ones" (Di Palma, 1977:45, 70).

OVERSIGHT

Committees. The committee is the primary parliamentary arena for the exercise of oversight activities in both active and vulnerable legislatures, with some additional oversight activities carried on in the plenary arenas of vulnerable legislatures.

The reason for committee dominance of oversight should be obvious: committees are specialized arenas and effective oversight assumes that those who are doing the overseeing possess knowledge comparable to those they are supervising. Also, these committees are the main deliberative arenas of these legislatures and therefore it makes sense that they should have the responsibility for overseeing the way in which the laws that they have been instrumental in enacting are implemented.

In the case of the American Congress, the Legislative Reorganization Act of 1946 realigned committee jurisdictions so that they paralleled the structure of executive agencies and would thereby be more effective oversight bodies. The act specifically charged the committees with the responsibility of exercising "continued watchfulness" over executive agency activities and authorized the hiring of professional staff members to help the committees to do this (Galloway, 1954). Committee oversight mandates were further strengthened by the Legislative Reorganization Act of 1970 and the Congressional Budget and Impoundment Control Act of 1974 (Knezo and Oleszek, 1976). During the postwar period congressional committees have pursued countless investigations of the executive branch, instituted such controversial procedures as the committee and legislative veto (see Saloma, 1969:139–45) and, through annual authorization and appropriation processes, attempted to hold executive branch actors continuously accountable for both their fiscal and substantive policy performance.

The committees of vulnerable legislatures also have a key role in oversight activities. Jackson's poll of Philippine legislators found general agreement among them that oversight should be an important role of the committees:

Almost all respondents in both houses considered that committees should scrutinize government Departments, and approximately half of them agreed that this was being done. However, in the Senate a fairly large group—30 percent—responded that while they favored committees scrutinizing the executive, they did not believe that the committees were doing a very good job of it. As for the fiscalizing role, approximately half of each house thought that committees played an important role in routing out graft and corruption in government. Only about 10 percent in each house thought that they did not. (Jackson, 1971:70)

Adams and Barile (1966:64) suggest that investigatory committees in Italy have not been "particularly active or useful." Committees have been set up to study such matters as unemployment and industrial working conditions. Although their work was competent and the committees were led by respected and specialized individuals, their recommendations were ignored by the Parliament.

In France, in contrast,

The committees were the most effective instrument of scrutiny. Ministers were often asked to appear, especially before those like Foreign Affairs and Defence which were more concerned with checking administration than with legislating. Others like Finance, were active in both. The government gradually gained new powers to issue decrees applying budgetary bills, but Parliament required consultation with the finance committees of both houses and sometimes the consent of the Assembly's committee; after 1956 a new budgetary procedure extended and formalized this practice. Some aspects of administration were supervised by statutory sub-committees representing several standing committees. . . . Special committees of inquiry might be useful on administrative questions, but not for probing political scandals. (Williams, 1964:223)

Plenary Arenas. In each of the presidential systems in the active and vulnerable categories, plenary session time is provided for speeches criticizing the administration or calling attention to failures in policies or policy implementation. The United States Senate has a morning hour. In the Philippines the privileged speech, which takes place during the first hour of every legislative session, is used as an opportunity for "fiscalizing"—for exposing incidents of graft, corruption, and inefficiency in the bureaucracy. This type of floor activity, incidentally, was becoming increasingly popular among legislators at the time that the Congress was dissolved by President Marcos (Stauffer, 1975:21). In the Chilean Senate, the *hora de incidentes* (hour of incidental matters) was used by senators to "call attention to administrative bottlenecks." During this period, senators were free to bring up or debate whatever matters they deemed to be in "the public interest" (Agor, 1971b:15–17).

The effectiveness of these techniques is questionable. First, responsible ministers are not present when these speeches are made and because they are not members of the legislature, they cannot be compelled to respond directly to the criticism being voiced. Agencies may respond, of course, but do so at their discretion and in whatever depth or brevity they wish. Most importantly, the plenary arena is a generalized arena; there is no guarantee that the member voicing the criticism will have any degree of expertise about the issue at hand.

In the parliamentary systems in this category legislators have the full repertoire of oversight weapons that comes with a system in which the executive simultaneously sit as members of parliament. Italian and French deputies may ask questions, interpellate the government, and offer motions to censure the government or to vote no confidence. In Italy between 1948 and 1958 there were an average of 5,545 questions (*interrogazioni*) per year, 1,855 *interpellanze*, and 235 motions. From 1958 to 1968 there was a significant increase in the number of interrogazioni and interpellanze (Adams and Barile. 1966:69).

In Fourth Republic France, written questions were numerous but relatively unimportant in controlling the civil service. "Oral questions were really short debates limited to five-minute speeches by the minister and then the questioner." The interpellation was a more potent instrument, because of its capacity to lead directly to a vote of no confidence in the government. "Nearly half the governments overthrown by the Chamber of Deputies were beaten on interpellations." The Second National Assembly held full debates on 316 interpellations and brief debates on 220 more out of a total of 1,549 submitted (Williams, 1964:223–24).

Both legislatures have freely used their ability to vote no confidence in the government and have thus been able to make and "un-make" governments at will. In Italy, it should be mentioned, the consensus of opinion is that governments are not really un-made by votes of no confidence in the Assembly, because such votes are dictated by the party bureaucracies that really make such decisions. (Kogan, 1962:100). In France, however, members often voted against their own party's ministers in order to force a change in governments.

Limitations on the Effectiveness of Oversight Activities. There are several factors that limit the effectiveness of legislative oversight in both active and vulnerable legislatures. First, legislative oversight, like most other legislative activities, will be pursued most vigorously when the legislator has compelling reasons to do so. The most compelling reason, of course, usually involves the legislator's chances for reelection. Seymour Scher (1963) found that in the United States Congress committee oversight of federal regulatory agencies was infrequent and ineffectual unless the constituency interests of the legislator was directly involved. In the Philippines the privileged speeches tended to focus heavily on local themes (Stauffer, 1975) while Leites (1959:15) observes that in the Fourth Republic "too many matters of local interest intrude" upon budgetary oversight activities. In the parliamentary systems as well, a large percentage of the questions asked were provoked by local constituency interests.

In the United States several studies have suggested that a close working relationship develops between senior legislative committee members and the bureaucrats whom they are supposed to be supervising; this relationship torpedoes any possibility of effective oversight because administrators learn to anticipate the actions of their legislative overseers and act accordingly (Freeman, 1955:34, Wildavsky, 1964:74; Davidson, 1976).

Third, even the relatively high degree of specialized legislative knowledge generated by committee systems in these legislatures may fail to cope with the expertise and information in the hands of the bureaucracy and with the increased complexity of public policy making in the modern world. One study of the oversight activities of the American Congress suggests that "no amount of congressional dedication and energy, no conceivable increase in the size of committee staffs, and no extraordinary boost in committee budgets will enable the Congress to carry out its oversight obligations in a comprehensive and systematic manner. The job is too large for any combination of members and staff to master completely" (Ogul, 1976:5). One of the problems is that legislators in many instances may have to depend on the bureaucrats that they are monitoring for the information essential to effective oversight. This is particularly true for budgetary matters where the mass of information is so great that legislatures have a difficult time coming to grips with it. Both the United States Congress and the Costa Rican Assembly have a Comptroller-General's office responsible to the legislature and charged with the responsibility of auditing government expenditures (Baker, 1971:72). More recently the United States Congress has created budget committees in each house to consolidate and coordinate congressional consideration of the budget. The new staff of the Congressional Budget Office is now, for the first time, providing a congressionally dominated staff of budgetary experts capable of rivaling the budgetary expertise in the hands of the president's Office of Management and Budgeting (Ellwood and Thurber, 1976). Needless to say, other legislatures in these categories are much less well equipped.

In Chile and the Philippines the most formidable barrier to effective legislative oversight was the power of the president. Chilean presidents possessed the unilateral power to impose certain types of legislation by decree. In 1966, 1967, and 1968 the number of executive decrees exceeded legislative actions by ratios of 24, 28, and 15 to 1. (Hughes and Mijeski, 1973:19). In the Philippines the president lacked decree power, but he could "certify measures he deems important for immediate congressional action, bypassing normal procedures; he alone can call a special session and designate the agenda for it; he has considerable independence in budgetary matters and what appears to be policy-making power in certain fields" (Grossholtz, 1964:112). When Jackson asked his sample of Philippine legislators to assess the effectiveness of committee activities in various areas, 2.8 percent of the representatives and 5 percent of the senators said that the committees were effective "in everything" but 52.8 percent of the representatives and 50 percent of the senators qualified that by saying, "in everything not controlled by the President." In response to a subsequent question about whether or not the president could control the Congress, two-thirds of the representatives and 60 percent of the senators said that the president did indeed dominate Congress. The remaining 40 percent of the senators said the president dominated the House only (Jackson, 1971:71–73).

This information suggests that effective oversight in active and vulnerable legislatures, just like the effective formulation and deliberation of policy, is most likely to occur in committee arenas. General overviews of policies cannot be developed in generalized arenas such as the plenum or the caucus, but require instead the smaller, more private, and more specialized committee arena. It is only in committees that the legislature can hope to match or even approximate the expertise resident in the bureaucracy.

The only plenary technique that achieves any effectiveness in oversight is the parliamentary question and interpellation. The strength of this technique lies in the ability of the rank and file legislator to confront a responsible minister in a public forum and compel him or her to justify and explain the government's actions. Its effectiveness is limited, however, by the inability of the questioner to compel the responsible minister to alter his or her official actions.

Chapter 5

REACTIVE LEGISLATURES: POLICY MAKING AND POLITICAL PARTIES

Reactive legislatures are usually depicted as subordinate to executive-centered elites who, operating through disciplined majority parties, are able to minimize the legislature's policy-making role. In this chapter I will demonstrate that this assertion is oversimplified and that executive-centered elites are in fact constrained in a significant manner by policy-making activities in the parliamentary arenas of reactive legislatures. My data come from the major Western European parliamentary systems (United Kingdom, West Germany, Fifth Republic France, Switzerland, the Scandinavian countries), from several countries influenced by the Westminster model (Australia, Canada, India, Ireland, Israel, New Zealand), and from Japan and Mexico.

POLICY FORMULATION

Executive Domination. Many studies have suggested that reactive legislatures are dominated by executive-centered elites during the formulation phase of the policy-making process. In West Germany, for example, Loewenberg identifies the federal ministries, the *Land* ministries, representatives of national organized interest groups, and the chancellor as the four major actors in the bill-drafting process. He goes on to note that Members of the Bundestag, aside from those who are in the Cabinet, "are conspicuously absent" from the formulation process (Loewenberg, 1967:282, 288). During the Fifth French Republic "top ranking bureaucrats have prepared important policy decisions in every detail without consulting parliament or other elective bodies" (Ehrmann, 1971:263).

These generalizations appear to be supported by the available aggregate data. First, opportunities for initiating legislation are relatively rare for members of reactive legislatures. The government controls the legislative agenda and therefore most business is government business. During its 1957–58 session the British House of Commons devoted 6.4 percent of its sitting days to private members' bills (Crick, 1968:51), and in India, the comparable figure for the Third Lok Sabha (1962–66) was 3.2 percent (Singhvi, 1970:218). The 1966–69 British Labour Government increased the number of days for private members' bills from ten to sixteen, but in 1970 the new Conservative Government cut the allocation back to twelve days (Leonard, 1972:137).

Even if a private member's bill is introduced, its chances of passage

TABLE 5.1
Private Members' Bills vs. Government-Sponsored Bills
in Six Legislatures

Country (Source)	Time Period	Percent of Government Bills Passed	Percent of Private Members' Bills Passed	Government Bills as a Percentage of all Bills Approved
Great Britain (Schwarz and Shaw, 1976:199)	1957–69	96	27	77
West Germany (Loewenberg, 1967:270)	1949–69	88	39	76
Japan (Kuroda, 1975:29)	1947–69	81	24	85
Israel (Edelman and Zelniker, 1973:199)	1957–69	47	9	90
France (Schwarz and Shaw, 1976:199)	1961–66	81	4	93
Canada (Hyson, 1974:265–66)	1958–62 1963–65 1968–72	87	2	95

are quite slim compared with the likelihood that a government-sponsored bill will pass. Data from six reactive legislatures on the relative success rates of private members' bills and executive-sponsored bills are assembled in Table 5.1. In all of these countries government-sponsored legislation stood a much better chance of being approved than private members' legislation and government legislation also accounted for the bulk of all legislation ultimately approved by these parliaments.

It seems clear, therefore, that while in all of these countries members have the right to initiate their own legislation, they have no right to expect that such bills will be favorably acted upon. This suggests that such bills are introduced in these legislatures, as they were in active and vulnerable legislatures, for a variety of reasons, perhaps the least of which is their possibility of enactment. In Canada, where private members' bills account for more than two-thirds of the legislation proposed, but for less than 6 percent of the legislation passed, they are a means for the MP to express his or her opinion "either criticizing the Government's programs or publicizing new proposals" (Hyson, 1974:272). In West Germany private members' bills exert a subtle influence on the policy-formulation process. They are "usually the product of interest groups for which Members in the governing parties act as spokesmen. They are used for tactical purposes to influence the details of Government bills, or to press the Cabinet for action. Rarely do their proponents expect them to pass. . ." (Loewenberg, 1967:267). Deputies in Mexico are also said to introduce bills at the behest of the various groups that they represent in order to encourage some kind of executive action (de la Garza, 1972:59).

Private members' bills do not appear to be vehicles for protecting constituency interests in reactive legislatures as they were in active and vulnerable legislatures. This may be because constituency interests are more effectively and visibly represented in reactive legislatures through the question period or through private negotiations with government leaders than through the futile process of introducing bills that have little or no chance of success. During the Fourth Republic French deputies introduced an average of eight hundred private members' bills a year, many designed to satisfy particularistic constituency concerns. After the Constitution of the Fifth Republic made it very unlikely that such bills could be approved, the number introduced dropped to approximately two hundred per year

(Williams, 1968:57). In systems such as the British and Canadian the chance to discuss one's private member bill comes so rarely that MPs who get that opportunity may be reluctant to squander it on something of particularly narrow constituency concern.

Caucus Consultation. There is a danger in taking this evidence of executive domination too literally. While it certainly indicates that legislative involvement in policy formulation is unlikely to take the form of drafting and passing a private member's bill, it does not necessarily indicate the absence of a legislative role in policy formulation. For example, there is ample evidence that certain legislators who are members of the government party are consulted by executive-centered elites on a regular basis prior to the formal submission of bills to Parliament. In Japan, for example, policies are initially formulated in bureaucratic arenas, but are then passed on through the various policy levels of the governing Liberal Democratic party, including levels where parliamentarians are involved (Kuroda, 1975:20). At all stages in policy formulation, there is "close interaction between party functionaries and agents of the concerned bureaucratic organs" (Pempel, 1974:653).

Similar reports come from France, West Germany, and Mexico. In France members of the Council of Ministers make "a real effort to minimize difficulties by consulting the party, or at least those members interested in the subject, in advance of legislation." Members of the governing UNR have brought "successful pressures to bear for bills to be introduced, like the amnesty for political offenders which the minister refused in November 1964 and presented in December" (Williams, 1968:105, 109). In West Germany "leaders of the governing parties in the Bundestag have been consulted on legislation controversial within their ranks, especially in the fields of social and economic policy where it is necessary to negotiate with interest groups within these parties" (Loewenberg, 1967:289). And in Mexico one deputy from the governing Institutional Revolutionary party (PRI) described the process in these terms: "If the president is going to present a law, before he does so he engages in extra-chamber consultations. This is done without publicity. He then decides whether to accept the view given him. So, when the law comes to the Chamber, the concerned committees are already familiar with it" (de la Garza, 1972:54).

Other Forms of Plenary Action. In many reactive legislatures individual members are permitted time to offer and discuss private member motions. Such motions usually constitute requests that the government initiate legislation on a particular subject. In Switzerland a further distinction is made between a motion, which "demands" government action, and a postulate, which "requests" such action. While executive action in response to either a motion or a postulate is not mandatory either in Switzerland or in other reactive systems, they are nonetheless useful instruments for drawing public attention to a perceived need for legislation. Thus, they are often "the parents of laws, and set in motion the procedure of drafting legislation" (Hughes, 1962:121).

Plenary arena practices such as question period and debate on adjournment motions, although classified in this analysis as oversight instruments, also have a role in the formulation process. Questions may suggest the need for remedial legislation in a particular policy area; a government consistently embarrassed by a point raised in adjournment debates may respond by introducing appropriate legislation.

Committee Arenas. The major departure from the active and vulnerable legislative model in the reactive legislature is the reduced importance of committee arenas, especially in regard to the formulation of policy. As a general rule the strength of executive-centered partisan elites is inversely related to the strength of committees and thus committees in reactive legislatures possess comparatively little autonomy (Shaw, 1978:49–51). There are exceptions, particularly in West Germany and Israel, but most of these committee systems get to consider legislation only after it has been approved in principle by the government and by the legislature on second reading. They seldom have the option to bury legislation or to thoroughly rewrite bills that have been consigned to them, although they often do have ample room to reach compromises and approve amendments. Thus, committees in reactive legislatures tend to be more important as deliberative than as initiating bodies.

Again, a possible formulating power that might be considered committee-centered lies at the borderline between oversight and formulation. Effective legislative oversight through committees can provoke the government to act to rectify a situation. Crick (1968:98) reports that in the nineteenth century much important legislation in Britain was a direct result of reports of select committees. Although the importance of select committees has declined somewhat in this century, their reports can, but need not necessarily provoke a government response. In Canada it is estimated that committees spend about 25 percent of their time collecting information and preparing reports on particular problems. The government permits the committees a relatively free hand in these matters because the reports, though submitted to the House, are not normally debated and therefore the government is free to ignore any policy recommendations that emanate from them. (Kornberg and Mishler, 1976:33).

DELIBERATION

Reactive legislatures are preeminently deliberative bodies. While executive-centered elites certainly influence the process, their actions are frequently constrained and often severely so by the reactions of private members working in caucus, committee, or plenary arenas.

The deliberative influence of the government stems in the first instance from its activities in policy formulation already discussed. Because the government drafts or supervises the drafting of most of the major legislation that will be considered, it is able to phrase the questions with which the legislature will deal. It provides the legislature with specific policy initiatives on the tacit understanding that deliberation and possible alterations proceed from those government proposals. Second, the government controls the legislature's time and therefore determines what the legislature will deal with and for how long. Finally, the government in reactive systems has presumptive control of a majority of the votes in the legislature and therefore can negotiate with those who oppose its proposals from a position of strength. Given such an impressive arsenal for control, it is understandable that the deliberative effect of other legislative policy-making arenas is so easily underestimated.

Caucus. The first such arena with which the government must contend is the caucus of the majority party or the caucuses of the various parties that form the majority coalition. As we have noted, selected members of the government party are usually consulted during the formulation phase of the process. After the drafting is completed government proposals ordinarily are presented to the party caucus before they are formally discussed at plenary sessions of the legislature. Such a procedure on the government's part can be easily discounted as "going through the motions"—appearing to consult without any genuine intention of responding to partisan demands. A more realistic interpretation is that majority party support is not always assured; rather, the government must work to secure it, perhaps not on every piece of legislation, but on many, and certainly on the most important items.

In Germany the government's ability to marshall support in the majority party caucus is made difficult by the structural separation of the cabinet from the legislative party. As a result, "rarely do parliamentary leaders participate in Cabinet decisions and, in turn, ministers participate in the parliamentary party as influential outsiders rather than as its accepted leaders. Both sides will still cherish their traditional independence of each other. This organizational separation imposes obstacles to the Government's ability to mobilize its parliamentary majority" (Loewenberg, 1967:379). Even in situations where cabinet leaders are also parliamentary party leaders, the backing of the caucus cannot be taken for granted. Interviews with a sample of Canadian MPs show that 51 percent of the members of the government party believed that caucus deliberations provided them with the opportunity to influence policy. Moreover, "although caucus may facilitate party discipline and thus the Government's control of the House . . . it can be argued . . . that this discipline is voluntary and achieved as a consequence of discussion and concession and not imposed upon a passive backbench by an authoritarian group of cabinet ministers" (Kornberg and Mishler, 1976:174–81).

Deliberations in caucus take the form of free discussion, sometimes preceded or accompanied by discussions within party committees set up to consider specific policy areas. Caucus committees are in use in many reactive legislatures and can be seen as an attempt to bring specialized knowledge to the deliberations of the normally generalized caucus arenas. Although caucus committees are not official bodies in the British parties, they meet regularly, they occupy a great deal of the time of the backbencher, and they have an effect upon the policies that are ultimately embraced by those in leadership positions. The committees "tend to form the focal points of systematic dissent both within the Government, and the Opposition Party" (Crick, 1968:101).

Similar party groups have operated within the Union for the New Republic (UNR) during the Fifth Republic. Although some groups have been more effective than others, "the half-dozen active subject groups kept in regular contact with the major interests in the field, invited their spokesmen for hearings, questioned ministers on their proposals, and sometimes promoted bills of their own. . . . The negative role of the subject groups was at least equally important, for they could mobilize party opinion against a measure as well as for one" (Williams, 1968:106–7). In addition to the United Kingdom and France, similar party working groups function in Canada (Jackson and Atkinson, 1974:69), West Germany (Loewenberg, 1967:306), and India (Berry, 1971:244–45).

Some of the government's aims in caucus deliberations are fairly obvious. Given the fact that its policies are formulated largely outside parliamentary arenas, the caucus is the arena within which the average parliamentarian first learns about the specifics of the proposal. The government uses the private caucus arena to explain its proposals to those who will have to support them in public plenary sessions. Negative reactions in the private caucus arena are less embarrassing to the government and can be dealt with more readily than negative reactions that are publicly voiced. Interactions of this sort permit executive-centered elites to gather information and to gauge the degree of opposition that may be expected from within the ranks of government supporters. The threat of an actual revolt within its party may even discourage the government from pursuing certain policies, or it may affect significant alterations in proposed policies (King, 1976:15).

It would be wrong to suggest that backbench revolts of a serious nature are everyday or even probable occurrences in the British parties, but the evidence is that when they do occur, they are likely to achieve at least some degree of success. The most intensive study of backbench revolts in the House of Commons identified fifty-seven such revolts from 1945 to 1957. In twenty-one of these cases (37 percent) the backbenchers were completely successful in achieving their goals; in another fourteen cases (24 percent) they were partially successful, and they failed completely in twenty-two instances (39 percent) (Lynskey, 1966:73, 90). A more recent analysis arrives at a similar conclusion. During the 1966–70 period, backbench rebels in the British Labour Party forced "the Government into open retreat from specific consensus policies aimed at 'reforming' the trade unions and the House of Lords, and probably succeeded in toughening the stand of the Government vis-a-vis the Smith regime in Rhodesia and in weakening Government controls on wages; the concessions failed to alter the basic pattern of consensus politics" (Piper, 1974:394). Similarly, in France it is at the private meetings between cabinet members and deputies allied with the government coalition in the National Assembly that amendments to government bills were agreed to (Goguel, 1971:89).

The influence of the backbench members is greatest when the cabinet itself is divided on an issue. In Canada the caucus meetings provide an opportunity "to demonstrate to the Prime Minister that divisions exist in the Cabinet, and individual ministers may employ it to illustrate that support exists for their pet projects" (Jackson and Atkinson, 1974:69). In the caucuses of the French UNR "some radical members of the government . . . mobilized support for their proposed reforms against the resistance of their colleagues or their civil servants" (Williams, 1968:106).

On those issues where the government isn't divided and on which it does not want to accede to backbench demands, or on which it does not feel it necessary to make any changes, the party discussions still serve a useful purpose. Sensitive areas vulnerable to opposition attack may be identified and rebuttal arguments prepared for use in plenary debate. At a minimum the discussions assist in maintaining party unity by leaving legislators with the impression that their leaders care about their opinions. One observer of the Indian Parliament concludes that general meetings of the Congress party's Parliamentary Group have the "related function of allowing for free and open discussion and individual catharsis" or blowing off of steam, a process that "contributes to party unity and to a public image of party cohesion" (Berry, 1971:244).

In sum, the caucus is a constraining influence on the government. Generally, the government's view prevails, but in most of these systems the view of the governing group is far from monolithic. Divisions within the government will be reflected and often magnified in caucuses of the party's legislative supporters, and this heterogeneity of opinion will have its greatest impact when the government produces controversial legislation that is relevant to these internal divisions. This conclusion is supported by Lynskey's data that show that backbench rebels in the House of Commons enjoyed complete success on 52 percent of the issues that he classified as being of major importance, while they were successful on only one-quarter of the issues that he classified as being of intermediate or minor importance (Lynskey, 1966:73, 90). What all of this suggests is that the government's aim in caucus is to take the necessary steps in private to ensure party unity when the policy proposals reach the more public plenary arena, because the price for party disunity is much higher in public than in private arenas. There may even be instances when the government will not offer a particular proposal because it does not think that it can mobilize enough party support behind it, or instances in which the government withdraws proposals that have received widespread negative reactions in caucus. Thus, what might appear to be strong cabinet control of the deliberative process may simply be an indication that the government is avoiding those issues that might threaten its control.

Committees. The effectiveness and autonomy of committees as deliberative arenas is directly related to the degree to which committees are specialized (Shaw, 1978:27–8). Strong governing parties therefore are likely to resist the development of specialized knowledge in committee arenas because such expertise may ultimately threaten their control of the legislature. Thus, committees in reactive legislatures are less effective deliberative arenas than their counterparts in active and vulnerable legislatures. There is, however, some variation across the legislatures in this category, with weaker committee systems in Japan, Britain, Canada, and Mexico and somewhat stronger committee systems in Israel, West Germany, and France.

Despite the fact that they have permanent jurisdictions, committees in the Japanese Diet are dominated by the government and are never permitted to amend legislation. The best study of these committees arrives at the following conclusion: "Since decisions by parties are accepted as binding by their respective members in committees, the degree of influence which committeemen qua committeemen exert on the substance of legislation is very much limited. This is compounded by the actual high turnover rate in the committee membership" (Kim, 1975:83).

Committees in the British House of Commons usually have been evaluated in similar terms: they are notoriously weak, have "little real chance of influencing legislation, and no compensatory possibility of discussing the broad subject" (Crick, 1968:88). The committees are not specialized in their subject focus and are, in fact, not really "standing" committees: "the chairman, the Members, and the clerks are all appointed only during consideration of a particular bill; and the Bills themselves allocated to any one standing committee bear no necessary relationship to each other" (Koester, 1968:66). However, even with these problems, it appears that the British committees, though generally dominated by the government, have, on occasion, been an arena for a government defeat. Such defeats occurred at the rate of four a year during the 1959–70 period, and at the rate of six a year in the 1971–74 period. It has been suggested that majority members are more likely to vote against the government in committee than on the floor because the consequences of a government defeat in committee are less severe. For one thing, it is less public; for another, the government can seek to reverse an adverse committee decision on the floor. However, there is also evidence that about half the time the government accepts its defeats in committees by incorporating the dissenting views into its own bill (Norton, 1976). But the point still remains that these pressures on the government are not generated from independent sources of committee expertise; rather, individual dissenters within the governing party may use the committee arena to articulate personal views, or the views of dissenting interests from outside Parliament or from within the party caucus. The committee stage is essentially a private arena within which the government can acquiesce to these forces, if it chooses to do so, with a minimum of public embarrassment.

Committees in Canada appear to be similar in strength to those in Britain. Although there have been some instances in which important legislation has been altered by committee action, even the most prestigious committees are characterized by poor attendance, non-participation of those who do attend, and high-turnover rates of committee membership (Kornberg, 1970:101–3). Therefore, little in the way of expertise has developed on Canadian committees (Mallory, 1963:4–5). Thus, as in Britain, the occasionally demonstrated capacity of the committees to affect significantly the shape of public policy stems from the presence of divisions within the governing party on an issue. In that context the committee provides another arena, in addition to caucus, for such divisions to be manifested and for them to affect the substance of policy (Jackson and Atkinson, 1974:84, 126, 129), a conclusion supported by data from a small sample of MPs that show government party members participating more extensively in committee debates than they do in plenary sessions (Kornberg and Mishler, 1976:156).

The private nature of the committee arena is responsible for any importance that it has in the Mexican Congress: "PRI deputies can be expected to amend bills in the secrecy of committee hearings, but they would be unlikely to attempt to do so in public because this might be taken as an indication of a party split and affect their own careers" (de la Garza, 1972:48). Amendments in committee are not frequent occurrences; approximately 7 percent of all legislation is amended in committee, but there is some evidence that such amendments take place on the more important and more controversial measures (de la Garza, 1972:52, 56).

The committee systems in Germany, Israel, and France are in a quite different category than the four systems just discussed. In the German Bundestag committees receive legislation after a perfunctory first reading on the floor and have the authority to amend legislation before it returns to the floor. Almost all bills are extensively amended in committees, and as a result committee deliberations draw the serious attention of national and *Land* ministries and representatives of interest groups affected by the legislative proposals. The influence of the committees is based on the high degree of expertise that their members develop in the committee's area of substantive concern. This expertise leads to a sense of cohesion and group identification among committee members that frequently transcends party lines. Thus, even though the governing parties possess a majority proportionate to their strength in the House, "their view does not necessarily prevail. The corporate sense within the committees softens party differences and substitutes others." (Loewenberg, 1967:334) When the committees are through with their deliberations, their decisions are usually accepted by the party caucuses and then on the floor of the Bundestag. Only in extreme cases do parties challenge their experts on the committees; "they are particularly reluctant to vote down in public what they have negotiated in private" (Loewenberg, 1967:352).

Committees in the Israeli Knesset seem to have a similar degree of effectiveness. As in Mexico, it appears that members of the governing party are permitted more freedom to dissent in the privacy of the committee room than they are allowed in the public forum of the plenary session. Unlike Mexico, the result of this is that government legislation is frequently and often extensively amended in committee, or else it is delayed until the government is willing to accept changes. In some Knesset sessions, the average length of time that bills have stayed in committee has been about one hundred days. Bills referred to the Committee on Law have averaged nearly half a year in committee (Edelman and Zelniker, 1973:16–27).

As we have seen, committees in the Fourth French Republic were extremely important deliberative bodies and the erosion of their power was a major goal of the Gaullist reforms. Their attempts to weaken the committee system were only partially successful, however; while party discipline is invoked to hold government positions on certain issues, on other issues the committee has become the instigator and mobilizer of opposition to government proposals (Williams, 1968:64). The government, in turn, has developed a more tolerant attitude toward the committees and apparently, like the governments in Mexico, Germany, and Israel, it is "ready to make in committee concessions which it would refuse on the floor" (Williams, 1968:79).

For all of these committee systems then, the pattern that emerges is one of general dominance by the government, modified to some degree by its willingness or the necessity to concede in private committee arenas what it would be unwilling or unable to concede in public plenary arenas. Government backbenchers are consequently emboldened in committee arenas and are willing to do and say things there that they would not or could not attempt on the floor. In this sense, the committee is a supplement to the party caucus—an additional arena within which majority party divisions can be manifested, but an arena that is unlikely to be significant in the face of a unified majority party.

Plenary Arenas. The nature of plenary arena deliberations is determined in large measure by the nature of prior deliberations in caucus and committee arenas. Effective deliberative activities in caucus arenas can reduce intraparty cleavages, while effective deliberation in committee arenas can reduce cleavages both within the majority party and between it and the opposition parties. Thus, if deliberative activities have been performed effectively in both arenas, deliberations in plenary arenas will tend to be formalistic, often perfunctory, and generally ineffectual. Alternatively, if serious backbench discontent persists after caucus or committee deliberations, it may well surface during debates in plenary sessions. Or, if committee deliberations are dominated by the government to the exclusion of opposition views, then the opposition is likely to provide an enthusiastic plenary arena debate.

Working from these premises, it is not surprising that the least effective plenary deliberations take place in the German Bundestag—a legislature characterized by very effective committee deliberations and sufficient caucus deliberations. During the fourth term of the Bundestag (1961–65) 260 of the 429 bills enacted were not debated at all. Of those debated, 41 were debated for less than ten minutes and only 25 were debated for more than three hours on the floor. Furthermore, the evidence is that relatively few members of the Bundestag participate in debates; during that same term 44 percent of the speeches in debate were given by 10 percent of the members (Hennis, 1971:75, 78). The dominance of the committees and the importance of party views also means that very few amendments are successfully offered on the floor.

In contrast, in systems where work in the committees does not approach the level of specialization and bipartisanship exhibited by the committees in the Bundestag, floor debate is likely to be more significant. In France the government during the Fifth Republic is much more firmly in control of debate than it was during the Fourth. The most important instrument for control is the government's right to call for a "single vote" on its draft proposal, forcing the Parliament to either accept or reject the entire package and thereby protecting itself from debilitating amendments. In addition, budgetary amendments can be ruled out of order. However, despite the availability of these powers amendments are still passed on the floor. In the first Parliament each House passed about half the budgetary amendments offered on the floor and about two-thirds of those put forth by the rapporteur-general of the finance committee. Generally UNR deputies and their Conservative allies were able to win acceptance of more than half of their amendments and even the Communists had 28 percent of their proposed amendments accepted (Williams, 1968:79). A detailed examination of the power of the National Assembly in regard to the Government of the Fifth Republic concludes that parliamentary debates "imposed controls on executive legislation, despite the existence of a Gaullist majority in the Assembly throughout the period. Clearly, if parliament had been less Gaullist it would have been more inclined to give greater effect to the control mechanisms available to it. Parliament was relatively restrained, not by necessity but by choice, not by oppression but by common interest and general accord with the executive" (Andrews, 1975:29).

In systems with strong governing parties and weak committee systems, debate in the plenary arena is the major way in which the opposition participates in the deliberative process. If effective deliberations take place in extraparliamentary, leadership, and caucus arenas—arenas from which the opposition is largely excluded—it follows that the main purpose of debate is to allow the opposition to make its points and compel the government to defend its positions. That this is the case in Canada is demonstrated by an analysis of floor speeches delivered during the first two years of the 28th Parliament which concludes that

opposition MPs made approximately two-thirds of the speeches and used almost two-thirds of the House's time. . . . 22 of the 31 nonspeakers in Session I and 29 of the 35 nonspeakers in Session II were Liberal [i.e., Government] backbenchers. The several Liberal committee chairmen were almost as quiet as the backbenchers. Even the cabinet ministers, including the prime minister, spoke considerably less often and for much less time than the leaders of the opposition parties. The government leaders spoke, it would appear, only when it was necessary to defend their policies or to make a public record (Kornberg and Mishler, 1976:132).

Similarly, in the British House of Commons, the Opposition questions and debates government policy when the government proposes legislation, after the government proposes its agenda in the Queen's Speech, during adjournment debates, and on the less frequent debates of confidence in the government. The effect of such debates is difficult to assess. One view is that the government will use such debates as a means of finding out what the more difficult points of its proposal are and will make appropriate modifications by accepting amendments either on the floor or in committee. In some situations the government will be compelled to give an explicit "undertaking" to the House and thus to the country specifying how it interprets a part of the legislation and how it proposes to administer it once it is passed. Generally the government agrees to very few Opposition amendments on the floor. During the 1968–69 Parliament, the Labour Government accepted twelve of 225 Conservative and Liberal amendments moved, all of which were of a minor or technical nature. However, the government itself moved 533 amendments, all of which were accepted, and in addition it accepted two of ten amendments moved by its own backbenchers, again both of which were minor or technical (Herman, 1972:149). These data must be qualified. It is very probable that many of the amendments moved by the government were in direct response to backbench pressures (Lynskey, 1973–74), while others may well have been in response to Opposition demands. The government is loath to admit its failings by accepting an Opposition amendment on the floor, but there is nothing to prevent it from adopting the Opposition amendment in slightly reworded form and presenting it as its own. Thus, deliberation in the plenary session of the House of Commons is more than a minor part of the total deliberative process in that legislature; it has some effect on the final shape of policies ultimately adopted, but not as much effect as the deliberative activities in caucus and plenary arenas have.

Discipline. The general rule in reactive legislatures is that at the formal and final stages of policy action party discipline prevails. In Germany there is an extremely high degree of party unity among members of the SPD, with a slightly lower level of discipline in the CDU. The CDU situation is attributable to the divisions among the broad coalition of interests that make up that party, divisions more likely to be displayed on domestic measures than on foreign policy measures (Rueckert and Crane, 1962; Schwartz & Shaw, 1976:124). Generally, dissent within the parties may be manifested by abstentions from voting and, much less frequently, voting against the party. Also, it should be indicated that leadership in the case of both parties is in the hands of the parliamentary wing of the party so there is no question of policy being dictated by extraparliamentary party organizations (Loewenberg, 1967:175, 355–57).

The French, Canadian, and British situations appear to be similar to the German. In these countries, party discipline is strong without being oppressive. Abstentions and even an occasional antiparty vote are permitted, provided that they do not threaten the ability of the government to continue in power. In France "individual abstentions were not uncommon, though large-scale defections were rare. Sanctions were applied only rarely, reluctantly, and on great occasions" (Williams, 1968:194–95).

Nonetheless party unity, as measured by cohesion scores, has been demonstrably greater during the Fifth Republic than it was during the Fourth. Although the scores are generally high for all parties some degree of interparty variation persists, with left-wing parties being the most disciplined, centrist parties the least disciplined, and Gaullists somewhere in between (Wilson and Wiste, 1976). However, French deputies still appear to be committed to a philosophy of individualism. When members of the National Assembly were asked how a deputy should resolve a conflict between his own conscience and the views of his party, 54 percent said that the deputy should follow his conscience. Sixty-two percent said it was legitimate for a deputy to vote against his party while only 14 percent (70 percent of the Communist deputies, however) were willing to unconditionally endorse rigid discipline (Cayrol et al., 1976:77–79).

In Britain intraparty dissent in different forms and at various levels of intensity has been permitted within both parties. Furthermore, according to one analysis, "opposition to government policy does not by any means preclude members from consideration for ministerial positions" (Lynskey, 1970:347). In other systems in this category— Japan and India, for example—party discipline appears to be a good deal stronger. In Japan "every member of the LDP without exception follows the decision of the party with regard to all bills presented in the Diet, as do members of the Opposition" (Kuroda, 1975:21).

If one had to generalize then about party discipline in these systems, the clearest point to make is that discipline at least sufficient to maintain the stability of the government is a given. Returning to our original classification scheme, these legislatures are highly supported, and that is partially attributable to their efficient and consistent performance of policy-making activities, which in turn is predicated on the stability of the government. Governmental stability in such systems is contingent on a level of cohesion among the government's legislative supporters sufficient to permit it to govern.

OVERSIGHT

The involvement of reactive legislatures in oversight activities is continuous and highly structured. Opposition elements are largely excluded from the formulation and deliberation phases of policymaking and backbench government supporters, while not excluded, tend to be more peripheral participants than those in leadership positions. However, during the oversight phase, opposition and backbench members are allowed a much greater opportunity to participate and as a result the structures for such participation are more precisely articulated.

Committees. While the deliberative role of committee systems in reactive legislatures is constrained by leadership and party decisions, the oversight role of these committees tends to be more autonomous. Oversight functions can be performed by either select committees or by standing committees; in reactive legislatures the most important in the last category are the budgetary and the public accounts committees. The former is generally charged with reviewing the estimates before they are presented to the full legislature, while the latter is usually the auditing arm of the legislature, charged with determining whether or not expenditures have been made according to the law and to the intent of the legislature.

In the House of Commons select committees may be established to scrutinize the executive's handling of a particular matter, to supervise a particular governmental activity—such as nationalized industries or science and technology (Palmer, 1972)—or to investigate specific matters referred to it by the House. These committees may take oral evidence from citizens, civil servants, and ministers; they may send for persons and papers; and they may at their discretion publish or otherwise publicize their activities. (Boyd-Carpenter, 1971:101) While most observers agree that these committees are useful in their sphere, there is some dissatisfaction with the restriction of their power to discussions after the fact and with their inability to discuss policies and programs (Crick, 1968:98–100).

Select committees are regularly used in the British Parliament because of that legislature's peculiar practice of having no fixed jurisdictions for its so-called standing committees. In all other legislatures in this category there are standing committees with continuous and well-defined jurisdictions, and in such legislatures select committees are seldom established. In France, for example, the creation of special committees has been resisted by standing committees jealous of their jurisdictions and by ministers who were afraid of their unpredictability. As a result, few of these committees have been established during the Fifth Republic and those that have seldom deal with major legislation (Williams, 1968:64).

The existence of standing committees is no assurance of legislative control of government activity. In Canada, despite recent attempts at reform, committees have not been very effective instruments of legislative oversight (Mallory, 1971:255). In Japan, the committee system is designed to parallel the structure of the national bureaucracy, but the committees are frequently criticized for being too subservient to the government agencies that they were supposedly designed to control (Tsuneishi, 1966:94). The only exception is the Budget Committee, which, presumably in the absence of effective oversight activity from the other committees, has "become the forum for the questioning of Cabinet Ministers on all matters of policy regardless of whether these queries are in any way related to an item in the Budget" (Baerwald, 1974:90).

Not surprisingly, the vigorous committees in the German Bundestag exercise effective oversight of several areas of governmental activity. In the case of the Defense Committee oversight is encouraged because each committee member has a specialty corresponding to the jurisdiction of a subdivision of the Defense Department (Loewenberg, 1967:332–33).

Often standing committees exist that are charged only with oversight responsibilities. In Sweden the standing committee on the Constitution may ask for the minutes of the Council of Ministers at any time so that the ministers are made to account collectively and individually for the advice which they give as well as for their policy actions (Elder, 1970:156–58). In Switzerland the entire oversight process, called *gestion*, is handled in the first instance by standing committees on *gestion* that function in both houses of the legislature. The reports of the committees structure the *gestion* debate and provide a source of information for other members of the legislature (Hughes, 1962:131–33).

India has at least three special oversight committees aside from those that deal with financial matters. A Standing Committee on Government Assurances exists to oversee the implementation of various promises and assurances given by ministers on the floor of the Lok Sabha (Jain, 1975:37). A Committee on Subordinate Legislation is charged with verifying that the government has not exceeded the powers delegated to it by parliament. In performing this task, it may call for witnesses and papers from the bureaucracy and it "pursues the matter until some action on its recommendations is taken by the Government" (Bharadvaja, 1972–73). In addition, a system of informal consultative committees composed of members of all parties is in operation in the Lok Sabha. Their purpose is to bring concerned members of the Parliament together with various ministers and senior government officials for informal discussions of the principles and problems of government policies and the workings of the administrative departments. They appear to siphon off some of the questions that might ordinarily be raised on the floor (Maheshewari, 1968).

In reactive legislatures, the most important component of the oversight process takes place in regard to budgetary and other financial matters. Legislatures influenced by the British parliamentary tradition usually have an estimates committee to deal with the budget submitted by the government and a public accounts committee to oversee the expenditure of funds. Of these two committees, the estimates committees have usually had the greatest difficulty. Because they are concerned with current budgetary figures, they must consider the policies behind such estimates and to the extent that they do this, they encounter conflicts with the government departments responsible for those policies. They are usually short of staff, restricted in the time that they may spend on the budget, and dominated in their decisions by the government (Boyd-Carpenter, 1971:103; Crick, 1968:90–1).

Public Accounts Committees, in contrast, generally perform more effectively as auditors of government expenditures. In Britain, its members are among the most respected and experienced members of the House, and, more importantly, it has the resources of the Exchequer and the Audit Department to assist it in its activities. In addition, its chairman is a member of the Opposition (Crick, 1968:90). In India the Public Accounts Committee's influence "is largely the product of the prestige attached to its published reports." Conventionally, if not legally, the minister of finance "is obliged to implement its recommendations as far as possible and to report to the committee on any other actions he may have taken" (Harrison and Douglas, 1972:100). In New Zealand the Estimates Committee and the Public Accounts Committee have been merged into one Committee on Public Expenditures, the most effective activities of which are in the oversight area. Its subcommittees, each usually chaired by an Opposition member, may carry out inquiries on the spot and often arrive unannounced in government offices demanding information from startled bureaucrats. Official policy is that Departments must accept or respond to committee recommendations (Mitchell, 1966:79).

In those countries which aren't of the Westminster tradition, other financial procedures are used. Germany uses an Appropriations Committee that functions in a manner similar to the Appropriations Committees in the United States Congress. It reviews proposed estimates and supervises the auditing of government expenditures. Its work is facilitated by a subcommittee structure which generates specialized knowledge, and it is thus a widely respected committee whose recommendations are usually followed by the Bundestag. And, traditionally, it has been chaired by a member of the Opposition party (Loewenberg, 1967:374–77). Sweden uses a system of parliamentary auditors; they are twelve members of the Riksdag elected by the legislature and charged with inspecting the government, management, and condition of the administration, the Bank of Sweden, and the National Debt Office, and searching out evidence of wasteful expenditures and making suggestions for economies. They can make suggestions either to the Parliament or directly to the government, and their suggestions are usually followed (Elder, 1970:160–65).

Plenary Arenas. The plenary sessions of reactive legislatures possess a full range of parliamentary techniques for overseeing the actions of governments. Debate is free, questions can be asked, interpellations can be moved in many of these bodies, motions of censure and of no confidence can be moved, and in all of these systems save Switzerland and Mexico, the government may be forced from office by adverse votes in the legislature.

The most well-known of these techniques is the question period. In Britain there have been as many as twenty-four thousand questions posed in a session of Parliament, more than half requesting oral as opposed to written responses (Rose, 1972:106–7). In India there have been as many as fifteen thousand questions submitted in a six-week session of the Lok Sabha (Shakdher, 1967:134), in Canada more than ten thousand questions per session (Kornberg and Mishler, 1976:142–44), and in Germany twelve thousand a year (Loewenberg, 1967:412).

The governments of these countries treat questions with varying degrees of interest and concern. French ministers, for instance, are often obstructive: "While they showed no particular zeal for replying quickly to questions they did not like, most of their delays were doubtless due to simple inertia" (Williams, 1968:48). Similarly, Canadian MPs feel that ministers "denigrate question period by refusing to supply direct answers" (Jackson and Atkinson, 1974:92), and therefore it is not surprising that only 7 percent of the MPs questioned in one study cited question period as a means of influencing policy in the House of Commons (Kornberg and Mishler, 1976:175). In Britain, in contrast, all indications are that ministers take their obligation to deal with questions most seriously.

Questions often involve issues of general government policy, but more frequently they are concerned with matters of relevance to local constituents. In Ireland, for example, "about half of all questions are clearly and explicitly personal or local and many more have some bearing on a local interest of the questioner" (Chubb, 1963:280). In Britain the relatively heavy load of questions directed at the ministers of Transport, Housing, and Social Services attests to the "local" influences on question period (Rose, 1972:106–7), and in West Germany, "the largest proportion [of questions] continues to be parochial in nature, directed heavily . . . to the ministries of Transport, Finance, and Interior" (Loewenberg, 1967:412).

Although question time is generally thought of as opposition time, government supporters are also permitted to participate. In Britain and Canada the bulk of the queries come from the Opposition (Kornberg and Mishler, 1976:143–44), but in France, there have been accusations of ministerial favoritism in responding to questions from government supporters in the Assembly (Williams, 1968:48).

The use of questions appears to be inversely related to the strength of committee systems. In countries such as Germany, where committees function effectively both as deliberative and oversight arenas, question period is a less important oversight instrument than it is in Great Britain where committees are not as effective (Johnson, 1963:26). Similarly, there is evidence that an increase in the use of questions in the postwar Norwegian Störting coincided with a decline in the importance of the committee system (Storing, 1963:88, 92).

The value of question time is difficult to assess in a general manner. Certainly it provides an unparalleled opportunity for backbench members of these legislatures to gain public attention for a particular issue or viewpoint that might otherwise go unheard. The evidence is mixed with regard to whether or not ministers take these questions seriously and attempt to respond. There is more suspicion than evidence that questions are the source of major changes in government policies or the seeds of new policies.

One of the deficiencies of question period is that it normally does not provide the opportunity for prolonged debate on the subjects raised by the question. In the British Parliament supplementary questions require a minister to expand upon his response or enable a backbencher to score a debating point, but the Speaker soon hurries the discussion on to the next question. In most reactive legislatures there are vehicles for pursuing questions that either have not been adequately dealt with by the government or that merit greater attention than can be provided in the context of a question and answer format.

In legislatures modeled after Westminster, the adjournment debate provides one vehicle for achieving these goals. British adjournment debates provide the Opposition with an opportunity to question the merits of government policies at length and in a debating format; they also provide the government with an opportunity to explain and defend what it is that they are doing or to respond favorably to the points raised during the debates, particularly in regard to specific policy applications at the constituency level. One study demonstrates that ministers respond positively to points raised in adjournment debates 21 percent of the time, negatively 53 percent of the time, and in some intermediate manner the remainder of the time (Herman, 1972).

In the Indian Lok Sabha adjournment motions involve debates which may ultimately lead to censure of the government. As a result, the process for admitting them is very difficult and very few—an average of one a session are ever debated. However, the Lok Sabha member has several other instruments to use that expand upon the question period. Calling Attention Notices provide a vehicle for small debates on matters of urgent public importance, and recent Parliaments have spent approximately 6 percent of their time on such discussions. A member may request that an answer to a particular question be followed by a half-an-hour discussion at the end of the day; such discussions have occupied about 4 percent of the time of recent Parliaments. Members may also request short discussions on matters of urgent public importance. Unlike adjournment motions, such discussions lead to no vote, but simply provide an opportunity for airing out a particular issue. Such discussions occupied approximately 4 percent of the time of the Fourth Lok Sabha. Altogether the Fourth Lok Sabha devoted 14 percent of its time to these types of discussions, which, combined with the 16 percent of its time it devoted to Questions, means that approximately one third of the time of that Parliament was devoted to general backbench oversight activities (Jain, 1975:50–61).

In parliaments on the European continent the interpellation is the time-honored method of forcing debate on a matter of public urgency.

So effective was this device in the Third and Fourth Republics that the architects of the Fifth Republic abolished it, substituting in its stead a debate on censure of the government—a practice which has taken place eighteen times between 1959 and 1972. Only one motion of censure carried the National Assembly during that period (Pickles, 1972:64).

The interpellation survives, however, in other European countries. In Finland it is rarely used—seven times between 1957 and 1960, for example—but, it is argued, such infrequent use means that it is taken more seriously by both the government and the opposition. Two of the seven interpellations in the 1957–60 period led to a no confidence vote and the resignation of the cabinet (Nousiainen, 1971:205–6). In Sweden and in Switzerland the process is a bit more benign because the interpellation does not lead to a vote of confidence. In Sweden the ministers are not even obligated to respond but "almost always do so" (Elder, 1970:165; Hughes, 1962:121).

Limitations. The effectiveness of the oversight activities of reactive legislatures tends to be limited by some of the same factors that we noted in discussing active and vulnerable legislatures. These legislators, like their colleagues elsewhere, can seldom match the information and expertise resident in the bureaucracy and thus at the disposal of the government. The staff and expert advice available to legislators, particularly to members of the opposition, are seldom on the scale of that available to the leaders of the government. As a result, ministers have the advantage not just of advance notice in dealing with questions, but also the advantage of assistance from the bureaucracy. Thus, in summarizing the oversight activities of committees in the Canadian Parliament, Jackson and Atkinson (1974:89) conclude that while committees "provide a forum where members may be educated by the bureaucracy in the operations of particular departments, they lack a permanent staff and there is an absence of the specialization necessary to launch detailed investigations."

The more important factor to consider, however, in regard to the reactive legislature is the effect of the parliamentary system on oversight activities. This is at once the strength and the weakness of oversight in reactive legislatures. It is its strength because the parliamentary system forces the government to be available to the parliament and also compels the governments' responsiveness to parliamentary questions, its participation in debate, and its public defense of its positions. This system is tremendously advantageous compared to that of those active and vulnerable legislatures in which the executive, controlled by forces outside parliament, need not account directly to the legislature for its actions.

However, the presence of the government in this system is predicated upon its command of a loyal majority of the members of the parliament, which provides the government with the opportunity to restrict the effectiveness of various oversight activities. Thus in France question time is restricted to Friday afternoon (King, 1976:23) and the government controls the allocation of questions among the parties. Questions from the opposition are not suppressed, but they are not given priority either. Therefore the opposition is deprived of its ability to "decide for itself when to exploit a tactical opportunity to inflict the greatest possible embarrassment or damage on the government" (Williams, 1968:49). In Germany the Basic Law allows one-fourth of the House to create a special investigating committee to look into the administrative conduct of the government. However, the fact that the government dominates the membership of such committees has prevented the use of these committees as an effective means of overseeing the executive (Loewenberg, 1967:419; Edinger, 1968:306). In the Canadian Parliament the government has consistently opposed any increases in the specialization and the autonomy of its committees on the grounds that such steps would mean the "abdication of Parliament." Put differently, it would mean the weakening of government control of the legislative process (Mallory, 1971:258). British governments, no matter what their partisan complexion, have resisted the growth of select committees and supported the nonspecialized nature of the "standing" committees, again because of their desire to continue to control the parliamentary process. And Storing (1963:88) traces the decline of the Norwegian committee system to the emergence of strong Labour Party majorities in the Störting.

This is not to say that what happens in these legislatures is unimportant in regard to oversight. However, where oversight is to be performed effectively the problem of bureaucratic dominance of information and expertise must be surmounted. Legislatures are able to surmount this problem only through the development of arenas of specialized knowledge. Committees of experts are, in the final analysis, the only legislators capable of knowing enough about the administration to effectively oversee its activities. And that is exactly why the governments in reactive legislatures, with the exception of West Germany, have kept these committees from developing that degree of expertise and have maintained strong party control over the operation of these committees.

Chapter 6

POLICY MAKING IN MARGINAL LEGISLATURES: THE EXECUTIVE VS. THE PLENUM

Like reactive legislatures, marginal legislatures can impose certain constraints on executive-centered elites even though they are generally dominated by these elites. But the differences between marginal and reactive legislatures are more important than their similarities. First, political parties are generally weak or nonexistent in marginal systems. While a strong governing party may exist on paper, in reality it is likely to be nothing more than the personal clique of incumbent executive elites with no real capacity of its own to control the legislature. Thus, the order and predictability that the strong party systems bring to the policy-making process in reactive legislatures is missing in marginal legislatures. Also missing is elite support for the legislature. Unlike reactive legislatures, to which executive-centered elites are bound through the structure of the governing party, marginal legislatures are separated from executive elites and have very little support from them. Thus, the marginal legislature can impose constraints on executive-centered elites, but with some degree of risk involved, for it constantly faces the prospect of closure or other extraconstitutional reactions from the executive.

Data for this analysis comes from legislatures in Latin America (Argentina, Brazil, Guatemala, Venezuela, Ecuador, Colombia, Peru), Asia (Afghanistan, Iran, Jordan, Thailand, Malaysia, Lebanon, Pakistan), and Africa (Kenya, Uganda, Zambia, Ethiopia).

POLICY FORMULATION

Executive Domination. In most marginal legislatures the bulk of legislation originates with the executive branch of government. One exception is the Colombian Congress where, between 1958 and 1974, 77 percent of all legislation and 61.4 percent of the more important laws, were initiated in the Congress (Hoskin, 1976:38). The Brazilian Congress was moderately active in this regard; between 1964 and 1973 23 percent of the laws ultimately passed by the House of Deputies originated in the legislature (Astiz, 1974:7). However, the percentage of legislature-introduced bills passed was quite small compared to the success rate for bills sponsored by the executive branch. During its 1964–65 session, the Brazilian Congress passed just under 11 percent of the bills introduced by legislators, while passing *all* of the bills introduced by the executive (Astiz, 1973a:10).

Other legislatures in this category perform even less impressively than the Brazilian Congress in regard to formal policy initiation. Findings from six other marginal legislatures are summarized in Table 6.1.

Of course, most legislation is actually formulated in the bureaucracy rather than by the "political" executive. In Zambia "the per-

Table 6.1
Initiation of Legislation By Marginal Legislatures

Legislature	Time Period	Finding and Source
Guatemala	1966–67	Congress initiated 15% of the legislation that it ultimately passed (Verner, 1969:93).
Jordan	1964–74	Twenty-four proposals were submitted by members of the lower house (Jaber, 1975a:6).
Kenya	1963–69	One bill was introduced by a private member (Hakes, 1970:299).
Zambia	1959–69	One bill was introduced by a private member (Helgerson, 1970:215).
Afghanistan	1965–71	All bills are cabinet initiated (Weinbaum, 1972:65).
Ethiopia	1957–67	One law is known to have originated in Parliament (Markakis and Beyene, 1967:213).

manent secretaries in the various bureaucracies had long been the people actually responsible for the drafting of bills" (Helgerson, 1970:262), while in Iran "bills have most commonly originated in the ministries" (Schulz, 1969:44–45).

Consultation. Some members of some marginal legislatures appear to be involved in the initiation of legislation through informal consultation with members of the executive branch. About one-third of the Venezuelan senators, for example, report that they are consulted by the president or his ministers (Kelley, 1973:146). In Iran the government's supporters in the Majlis are asked to react to government bills before they are formally proposed and, on occasion, the government responds to criticisms by making amendments (Weinbaum, 1975:53).

In Kenya this type of consultation takes place within the structure of the Government party. Sometimes bills are discussed in the KANU caucus before they are proposed to the legislature; legislators are also permitted to suggest topics for future legislation, but there is little evidence that the government takes such suggestions seriously or otherwise attempts to allow legislators to be effective actors in policy formulation (Hakes, 1970:321; Stultz, 1969:114).

The absence of more general consultation through party channels is evidence of the weakness of political parties in marginal systems. Extraparliamentary party organizations are virtually nonexistent; in only one country in this category—Zambia—is there any evidence that nongovernmental party elites have an influence on the formulation of policy (Helgerson, 1970:268, Saidi, 1976).

Committees. Committees in marginal systems are weaker than those in reactive legislatures. The institutional instability and the fluidity of membership that characterize these legislatures deprive legislators and those committees that exist of any degree of expertise, and thus of any possible role in policy formulation. One partial exception to this generalization is the Venezuelan Senate where, according to Kelley (1973:168), "several low level pieces of what may be called 'project legislation' emerged from less important committees." The examples Kelley cites were legislation to establish a National Council of the Sciences and Technology and the initiative for the construction of a new congressional office building.

DELIBERATION

Marginal legislatures, like reactive legislatures, are much more capable of involving themselves in deliberating than in formulating public policy. They perform their deliberative activities under conditions of wide-scale favor giving by the executive and under the omnipresent threat of extraconstitutional actions directed against the legislature. Such conditions tend to reduce the freedom and the effectiveness of the deliberative instruments that these legislatures might use to constrain the executive.

Executive Cooptation. In the first instance executive-centered elites attempt to gain legislative support by encouraging the selection of their supporters to the legislature. The Shah of Iran, for example, carefully controls the nomination process for membership in the Majlis, ensuring that candidates that would be difficult to control are stricken from the nomination list (Bill, 1971:363–65). Once legislators are elected, a variety of positive inducements can be offered to encourage legislators to support the government. In Zambia and Kenya the government uses "the distribution of jobs, development funds, and political influence and prestige to elicit responsible behavior from appreciative MPs" (Helgerson, 1970:158; Hakes & Helgerson, 1973:351–53). The situation in Lebanon is similar: "The deputies find that the most effective way to share in the proceeds of the society is to be in favor with the strongest power, the president and his ministers, who are in direct control of the administration and resources of the government" (Crowe, 1970:298).

When such persuasive techniques are ineffective, executive elites resort to force and intimidation against marginal legislatures. Between 1947 and 1971 the Thai legislature was, on six occasions, abolished by military coup (Mezey, 1975:113–17). Legislatures have been suspended at least once during the last ten years in Afghanistan, Malaysia, Pakistan, Bangladesh, Ghana, Nigeria, Uganda, Peru, and Ecuador, as well as other countries in this category. Such constitutional confrontations are encouraged and exacerbated by the fact that most legislative policy making takes place in public rather than private arenas. Caucus and committee arenas which in reactive legislatures provide forums in which the government can compromise or retreat without confrontations or embarrassment are underutilized in marginal legislatures while plenary arenas tend to dominate.

Caucus. In some marginal legislatures caucuses occasionally exercise perceptible influence on public policy. In the Kenyan Parliament important matters are usually discussed in KANU caucuses before being brought to the floor, while less important bills have been returned to caucus for discussion after preliminary plenary debate revealed divisions within the party. Even so, backbenchers seem to think that caucuses aren't held frequently enough; in one survey of government MPs, only 41 percent indicated that they met regularly to discuss matters of public policy (Hakes, 1970:167–72; James, 1975:10).

In Zambia government backbenchers indicated that they regularly availed themselves of their right to speak out in the party caucus; on a few issues backbench opposition did cause the government to change its mind, one example being the government's decision to postpone the 1969 referendum on constitutional reform. Nonetheless, backbench dissent was constrained by the fact that MPs owed their seats in the legislature to the party (Helgerson, 1970:135–38).

A case study of the Ugandan Parliament's actions in regard to an important land reform act passed in 1969 showed a substantial influence of the government party caucus on at least this one occasion. The first time that the bill was submitted to the caucus it was rejected outright. After it was redrafted several additional amendments advocated in the caucus were accepted by the government before the bill was ultimately passed (Ocaya-Lakidi, 1975:32). Only in the case of the Venezuelan Senate is there a report that the caucus discusses all bills before they go to the floor. Although such discussions are dominated by the party leader who represents the views of the party's executive committee, 44 percent of the senators interviewed in one study suggested that the caucus meeting was a place where executive-introduced bills could be modified (Kelley, 1973: 114, 149).

In the rest of the marginal legislatures party policy-making arenas have no influence at all. In some countries, such as Afghanistan, no parties exist. In other countries, such as Lebanon, substantial numbers of legislators are not members of political parties; between 1951 and 1968 as few as 13 percent and as many as 37 percent of the deputies were political party members, or put differently, for all of this period, at least 60 percent of the members were independents (Baaklini, 1972:253). In Iran the government regularly held meetings of their parliamentary supporters, but altered legislation as a result of these meetings on only the rare occasion when a deputy detected an error or a significant omission (Schultz, 1969:120; Weinbaum, 1975:53). The situation has been similar in the case of the government's Alliance party in Malaysia:

Caucuses are infrequent and backbenchers are usually as ignorant of government intentions as the opposition. . . . From time to time caucuses are called to explain some aspects of government policy to the membership but for the most part, these sessions are simply announcements and exhortations from the leadership with no opportunity for the ordinary members to raise criticism or inquire into details (Grossholtz, 1970:105–6).

Similarly, in Thailand during the 1969–71 period, Government party members met regularly to hear cabinet announcements of proposed legislation. However, the efficacy of such meetings was reduced for legislators because they were usually convened only a few days before the proposed bill was to go to the floor, and the inclusion of government bureaucrats and appointed senators in whatever voting took place assured support for the government's position (Mezey, 1975:133–34).

Committees. Committees in marginal legislatures are somewhat more effective at deliberating than in formulating public policies, but that activity is also hindered by the lack of legislative expertise, the fluidity of committee membership, and the absence of competent professional staff. In all of these legislatures members are assigned to committees almost at random and frequently change their committee assignments. In Afghanistan, for example, "deputies have little inclination or opportunity to develop legislative expertise, for geographic rotation of committee assignments and annual elections leave few committee veterans" (Weinbaum, 1972:61). In Colombia most legislators serve no more than one term on a committee because of a high turnover among the congressional membership generally, and because of the practice of reelecting members to committees biennially (Kline, 1977). Generally, the personal backgrounds of legislators does not provide an alternative source of expertise. As the former speaker of the Zambian Parliament told an interviewer:

Most members are politicians rewarded for participation in the struggle, for organizing meetings, etc. They are not specialists—accountants, lawyers, businessmen, and so on—so the select committee system cannot work here (Helgerson, 1970:180).

One possible exception to this generalization is the Iranian Majlis where expertise has been a factor in committee assignments:

Most of the Chairmen of the Public Health Committee have been medical doctors. Many of the chairmen of the Military Affairs Committee have been military officers. . . . Also, chairmen of the Education Committee were commonly among the most educated deputies. (Schulz, 1969:208)

This degree of expertise seems to have made the Iranian committees slightly more influential than other committees in these legislatures. Floor debate on bills, for example, is monopolized by the committee chairmen and from time to time a chairman who is particularly close to the executive will influence the content of legislation (Schulz, 1969:207). This pattern of occasional influence characterizes the performance of most of these committee systems. Studies of the Congresses of Colombia and Peru indicate that the committee system is generally weak, but they also indicate that the Peruvian agrarian reform law of 1964 and the Colombian agrarian reform law of 1961 were significantly influenced by the deliberations of the committees to which these bills were assigned (McCoy, 1971:349; Duff, 1971: 394–96).

The Lebanese Chamber of Deputies and the Venezuelan Senate have committees that can modify a larger percentage of legislation than the committees already discussed. Lebanese committees amended 61 percent of the bills that they considered during the years 1950, 1955, 1960, and 1966 (Crowe, 1970:292) and a survey of Venezuelan senators conducted in 1965 found that 56 percent of the members assessed the possibility of modifying executive-introduced legislation in committees as "great," while 28 percent said the possibilities were "few" and 12 percent said that it "depends" (Kelley, 1973:145).

In three marginal systems there is evidence that the committees charged with considering the budget are somewhat more influential than other committees. The Budget and Finance Committee of the Lebanese Chamber works closely with ministry officials and while they are prohibited from increasing cabinet appropriation requests, they are permitted to lower these requests. However, the lack of committee expertise means that these deliberations tend to be dominated by the government (Crowe, 1970:296). In Afghanistan the

Budget and Finance Committee also cannot increase appropriations, but has "relentlessly sliced nondefense appropriations, reorganized government positions, and eliminated perquisites of government personnel (Weinbaum, 1972:68). In Thailand the national budget was considered by a Budget Commission composed of legislators and bureaucrats. While these meetings tended to be dominated by the expertise of the Budget Bureau representatives some changes in cabinet requests were made to accommodate the political concerns of the legislators on the committee. Frequently such concerns involved trade-offs between development funds and military expenditures, with legislators lobbying heavily for the former. Conflict over this matter was in no small part responsible for the 1971 military coup which suspended the legislature (Mezey, 1973:311–12).

Even those committees which exercise some degree of influence on the shape of legislation are not really autonomous. In Lebanon, for example, despite the fact that committees can amend legislation, the executive may certify a bill as "double urgent" and thereby avoid its consideration by a committee, or it may certify it simply as "urgent" and restrict committee deliberations to one week, or the Chamber may recall a bill from committee, assign it to another committee, or take it directly to the floor (Baaklini, 1972:265). In Peru all bills not reported out of committee within eight days automatically go to the full house (McCoy, 1971:329) and in Afghanistan "most committee recommendations are ignored in plenary sessions" (Weinbaum, 1972:61). In Venezuela, which appears to have the strongest committee system in this category of legislatures, the committees are still "unable to act autonomously in large measure owing to the constraints on their activity established by the functioning of the party system," which places the committee chairman and the committee majority under the control of the party leadership (Kelley, 1973:133, 228). Nonetheless the parties do find the committees to be useful arenas within which to reach compromises when that is necessary:

[Committees] provide the parties with a forum which is at once removed from public view and the dramaturgical press-oriented politics of the Senate and yet is sufficiently visible to add legitimacy to the interparty bargaining which may develop as a result of the parties' representatives in the Senate meeting face to face. (Kelley, 1971:501)

In sum, the deliberative activities that take place in the committee arenas of marginal legislatures can be characterized as generalized rather than specialized, occasionally rather than regularly significant and usually subordinate rather than autonomous.

Plenary Arenas. Plenary sessions of marginal legislatures are generally free to criticize and amend government proposals as long as they remain within parameters established by the executive-centered elites who run these political systems. The most important of these parameters is that the government not be defeated on legislation that is important to it; however, there is reason to believe that the government in certain instances may well back off even from important proposals if confronted by strong opposition from the legislature.

One way in which these systems protect themselves from legislative opposition is through constitutional and political provisions that restrict the scope of legislative activity. Perhaps the most extreme restrictions are those imposed on the Brazilian Congress by the Fifth Institutional Act of 1969. Under that act, the president can require any bill sent by him to the Congress to be considered within thirty days by each house, or at his discretion, within thirty days by a joint session of both houses. Any bill not considered and rejected within the period specified automatically becomes law. Bills creating or increasing public expenditures may be initiated by the president only, and the Congress may not amend these bills to increase expenditures (Packenham, 1971:268). Such restrictions on budgetary amendments also exist in Pakistan (Rashiduzzaman, 1969–70:485), Jordan (Jaber, 1975b:8–9), and Lebanon (Crowe, 1970:296). In Brazil these limitations, together with the power of the president to issue decree laws, clearly limit the deliberative activities of the Brazilian Congress (Astiz, 1974:8).

These restrictions on legislative activity make amendments of any kind difficult to secure in plenary sessions of marginal legislatures. Of these legislatures the Jordanian Parliament appears to amend legislation most frequently; during the 1964–74 period Parliament amended 35 percent of the bills that it considered, rejected 13 percent, and passed the remainder in the form that they were submitted (Jaber, 1975a:30). The Lebanese Chamber amends less than 19 percent of the legislation that it considers on the floor; however, more than 60 percent of the bills have been amended previously in committee (Crowe, 1970:292, 295). Similarly, in Venezuela the committees and the party caucuses seem to be more likely arenas in which to achieve amendments; a survey of Venezuelan senators indicated that 16 percent would direct their efforts at modifying executive-introduced legislation to the Senate floor, compared to 44 percent who would focus on the party caucus, and 28 percent who would try to act in the committees (Kelley, 1973:149).

Studies of other marginal legislatures indicate that amending legislation on the floor of the legislature is an occasional thing, frequently reserved for particularly controversial acts. For example, the Agrarian Reform Act of 1964 and the proposed Constitution of 1967 were significantly amended by the Brazilian Congress (Packenham, 1971:275). During the Ayub Khan period in Pakistan (1962–69) several major pieces of legislation were extensively amended by the National Assembly, including bills dealing with political parties, film censorship, wealth taxes, corruption, and national security (Rashiduzzaman, 1969–70:492).

When it comes to the possibility of defeating the government, these legislatures are much less efficacious. Aside from Jordan where, as we have seen, Parliament defeated 13 percent of the bills that it considered, the only other place where legislative defeat for the government has occurred with any frequency is Kenya. There the government was most vulnerable on the less essential matters embodied in private member motions which the government was not required to implement even if they were passed by the Parliament. Thus from 1963 to 1969 the National Assembly acted on 213 such motions and defeated the government on 44. However, the story on essential matters was quite different; on these issues the government's position was supported by backbenchers 99 percent of the time (Hakes, 1970:191, 196). Such strong support was often attributable to the personal intervention of the president on many matters (Stultz, 1969:114).

Aside from amending or seeking to defeat legislation, members of marginal legislatures can criticize government policies as long as they recognize the limits involved in such criticism and the risks assumed when those limits are ignored. In Malaysia, for example, MPs are prohibited from discussing sensitive racial and communal issues. However, the parliamentary debate that does take place is said to involve "considerable criticism" of government policies, criticism to which many of the MPs questioned in one study felt the government responded (Musolf and Springer, 1977:119; Musolf and Springer, 1975:24). Zambian MPs never defeated the government and seldom forced amendments on it; however, they were able to express their own views and exercise considerable independent judgment in debates on the budget and on motions (Helgerson, 1970:116). Similarly, in Iran, the small opposition party "has been conceded the privilege of verbal criticism without effective voting strength" (Schulz, 1969:119), while in Peru, cabinet instability has been due on several occasions to pressures both from the parliamentary opposition as well as from government supporters in the Assembly (McCoy, 1971:351).

These findings do not mean that criticism of the government or indeed verbal participation of any sort is widespread in plenary sessions of marginal legislatures. From 1965 to 1968 the number of speeches per bill in the Zambian Parliament declined from 4.2 to 3.5 while the number of speeches per MP declined from 3.3 to 1.8 (Helgerson, 1970:122). In Iran approximately 70 percent of the deputies do not participate in debates (Schulz, 1969:221), while in Afghanistan there is a great deal of difficulty even getting members to attend. Between November 1969 and May 1970 a quorum could be attained for only four of a scheduled thirty-two plenary sessions of the Wolesi Jirgah. The remaining twenty-eight sessions were cancelled (Weinbaum, 1972:63).

There is little evidence that debates in marginal legislatures take place at a very sophisticated level. One observer of the Kenyan Parliament says that "debates generally are remarkably uninformative and evidence a lack of expertise among nearly all persons who are not in the cabinet. Members of Parliament appear content to speak from their own direct, but limited personal experience and often, it seems, spontaneously, in reaction to initiatives of the government (Stultz, 1970:324)."

Serious deliberative activity in marginal legislatures tends to be episodic, usually focusing on a "big issue" which tests the limits of elite support for the legislature. Traditionally, a confrontation develops in which the government implies that the abolition of the legislature will be imminent unless the legislators back down and the legislators, perhaps sensing that the government is bluffing, hold firm. The result is either a constitutional crisis or a small-scale victory for the legislature. Examples of both outcomes are found in the recent constitutional history of Thailand.

One incident occurred in 1970 when the government proposed to raise import duties and excise taxes on more than two hundred commodities. Many MPs reacted negatively, feeling that additional revenues ought to be raised by creation and enforcement of an equitable income tax and by new taxes on land, property, and inheritance. Government party MPs voiced their dissent privately at party meetings and publicly in the press, and there were strong rumors in Bangkok of possible dissolution of the legislature. In the end the cabinet agreed to a compromise in which the two largest increases—on gasoline and cement—would be rescinded in return for support on the rest of the package. With the threat of a coup hanging over the legislature unless the compromise was approved, the package passed the House by a one-vote majority and the crisis was averted (Morell, 1975:18–21).

One year later the result was different. Again the government proposed tax increases, and again the government's supporters in the legislature dissented, fearing that a tax increase would endanger their chances of reelection. Also involved was a demand by the MPs for more funds for local development projects, something which they also felt was necessary for their reelection chances. This time the cabinet chose not to negotiate and on November 17, 1971, the military closed the legislature, banned political parties, and placed the nation under martial law (Morell, 1975:22–23; Mezey, 1973:313).

Similarly, in Brazil in 1967 the Congress rejected an important tax bill submitted by the Executive Branch; in 1968 it blocked an international trade bill, and in the same year it rejected an armed forces request to lift a congressman's immunity from prosecution. These actions were factors "which precipitated the issuance of Institutional Act No. 5, the temporary suspension of congressional activities, and further tightening of electoral and legislative procedures, as well as party discipline" (Astiz, 1973a:17).

What all of this indicates, of course, is lack of support, which, as noted at the outset, is one of the defining characteristics of marginal legislatures. Institutional elites only tentatively accept the legislature's policy-making role and implicitly retain the right to abridge their actions when they think such steps are necessary.

Party Discipline. There is as we have seen a great deal of variation in the strength of political parties in marginal legislative systems, and therefore the importance of party discipline varies as well. In countries such as Afghanistan, Ethiopia, Thailand, and Lebanon, where parties either do not exist, or where large numbers of legislators are independents, party discipline is a meaningless concept. The government is usually able to round up a majority to support its programs, but that does not happen through the machinery of a disciplined majority party as was the case with reactive legislatures; rather, as we have seen, the executive uses a variety of techniques to coopt, coerce, or otherwise convince legislators to go along with government proposals.

However, in some marginal legislatures party discipline is important, and sanctions do exist that have the effect of encouraging legislators to support leadership positions. In Venezuela, Zambia, and the Peruvian Aprista party, party policies emanate from extraparliamentary party committees and a variety of sanctions are employed to encourage legislators to go along. In Venezuela party dissenters may be subjected to verbal admonitions, fines, and expulsion from the party (Kelley, 1973:124). Aprista MPs in Peru sign undated letters of resignation which are deposited with the party and are to be filed with appropriate officials in the event that the member dissents from party policies (McCoy, 1971:239). In Colombia support for the party is encouraged by the use of the list electoral system. Duff (1971:381–83) suggests that party leaders punish recalcitrant members by either failing to renominate them or by placing them at such a low point on the party's list that their chances for reelection are minimized.

Discipline in these systems does not apply to all matters. In Zambia, for example, party members are strongly discouraged from verbally opposing the government on significant issues and never vote against the government position on legislation; but on motions which do not require the government to act but which nonetheless were often quite controversial, members were permitted to vote against the government. "In practice, this meant that cohesion eroded among UNIP spokesmen from what had been unity in the consideration of bills" (Helgerson, 1970:192). In Colombia party unity is required on issues that party leaders deem to be of "strategic" importance to the party group, but on "program issues" such as fiscal and monetary policy, or social and economic measures, party "directorates did not take positions and were not expected to take positions" (Payne, 1971:184).

The most disorganized one-party system in this category is in Kenya where members regularly vote against the party on big and little issues alike. In 1965, after the declaration of a one-party state in Kenya, the index of cohesion for MPs on formal divisions was 39.9. This figure, low as it is, probably overstates the degree of party consensus in the Parliament "for many backbenchers who accepted the government whip at formal divisions of the House felt free to speak against programs of the Government in House debates and, indeed, voted against the Government in unrecorded voice votes" (Stultz, 1970:314).

OVERSIGHT

The oversight activities of marginal legislatures, like their deliberative activities, tend to be performed in plenary arenas rather than in committee arenas. However, in at least four of these legislatures— Ecuador, Argentina, Brazil, and Afghanistan—it has been reported that committees have undertaken investigations and issued reports of their findings. Pyne (1973:14) says that committee investigations in Ecuador have on occasion been effective in altering the conduct of administrative elites. In Argentina there are records of committee investigations of such disparate and important matters as management of national pension funds, rural labor conditions, misconduct of the federal police, and the granting of export licenses: "Even when such investigations bring no substantive change in policy or procedure, they serve the function of bringing the alleged problems to the attention of the public" (Fennell, 1971:159).

In Brazil and Afghanistan committee investigations have also covered a wide range of activities, but it seems that they seldom provoke any changes in government policies. From 1963 to 1971 the committees of the Brazilian House of Deputies initiated 117 investigations; they completed 82 of these, had 75 reports approved by the House, 59 of which were forwarded to other branches of the government. However, only three reports provoked remedial action by another branch of the Brazilian government (Astiz, 1974:10). Similarly, in Afghanistan, committees have held hearings on topics such as hospital and prison conditions, administrative graft, and food costs. While these investigations often proved embarrassing to the government the legislature was never capable of following through with remedial action (Weinbaum, 1972:66).

The committee oversight role in most marginal legislatures is typified by the committees of the Lebanese Parliament which have the power to ask for any government documents, listen to witnesses, and ask for explanations from those involved. But, "in practice, this power has not been resorted to frequently, since its use is tantamount to a lack of confidence in the existing government. . . . Few government officials, elected or appointed, have been subjected to parliamentary investigation or legal prosecution as a result of malpractice or fraud" (Baaklini, 1972:272–73).

Unlike committee systems in reactive legislatures, there is no evidence that the committees charged with budgetary oversight exercise effective control in this area. One exception is the Public Accounts Committee of the Zambian Parliament which, according to Helgerson, played an active role in overseeing government expenditures, was chaired by a minority member, and frequently called ministers and secretaries to account for their budgetary actions: "Public Accounts committee reports were often stinging indictments against general malfeasance and incompetence, yet the government lived up to its official policy by approving the revelation of any misuses of public funds" (Helgerson, 1970:272ff).

More typical of marginal legislatures is the performance of the Public Accounts Committee of the Malaysian Parliament. Its reviews of administrative financial records usually lag three to four years behind; in addition, the committee is chaired by a government supporter rather than by an opposition member as the Westminster tradition dictates (Musolf and Springer, 1975:20).

Plenary Arenas. Question time or its equivalent is the customary vehicle for oversight in plenary arenas. Data on the use of questions in four marginal systems influenced by the Westminster model are summarized in Table 6:2. The heavy volume of questions in these systems can be assumed to be a product of three factors: the ineffectiveness of committee oversight activities, a parliamentary form of government which requires the presence of the government in Parliament, and the formal designation of a particular period as question time.

Like the questions asked in reactive legislatures, a large proportion of those asked in marginal legislatures involve domestic issues with direct constituency implications. In Malaysia, well over half of the questions asked involved service issues such as education, health, agriculture, construction, and housing, or social issues such as employment, social welfare, government welfare, information, and the law (Chu, 1974:194). In Pakistan the last part of the Ayub regime saw an increasingly large percentage of questions directed toward the issue of regional disparities (Rashiduzzaman, 1969–70:483).

In other marginal legislatures questioning is somewhat restricted by the presidential form of government in which ministers do not sit in the Parliament. Thus the Brazilian Congress can request ministers to appear before them and from 1968 to 1971, 39 such requests were made (Aztiz, 1974:15). However, when ministers made such appearances, they "spoke from a rostrum ten feet above the floor of the Congress and delivered long initial speeches, which could not be interrupted by congressional questions, and which were subject to only a limited number of scheduled questions after the formal address" (Packenham, 1971:279). At one time question period in Brazil was augmented by the right of legislators to request information from ministers. Between 1963 and 1968 there were as many as thirty-six hundred such requests a year, but between 1969 and 1971 there were a total of only thirty-two requests for information (Astiz, 1974:15).

The same "distance" between legislators and ministers apparent in Brazil is also apparent in Iran where in one session eighty-seven questions were put to the government but only forty-seven responses were made (Schulz, 1969:36). Ministers in Argentina are responsible only to the president who on occasion has ordered them to ignore congressional demands for testimony (Fennell, 1971:158). And in Afghanistan the government seldom knows in advance who will be asking questions during question time or even what topics will be covered. As a result "questions rarely elicit lengthy or detailed replies from the ministers. More typically, answers are evasive, incomplete, and argumentative" (Weinbaum, 1972:67).

TABLE 6.2
Questions in Four Marginal Legislatures

Legislature	Time Period	Finding
Pakistan	1962–69	15,420 starred questions received; 9,357 admitted; 9,086 answered (Rashiduzzaman, 1969–70:484).
Malaysia	1959–60 1963–64 1971–72	2,060 questions raised (Chu, 1974:155).
Kenya	1965–67	4,677 questions submitted; 4,408 answered (Hakes, 1970:129).
Zambia	1965–68	173 questions asked (Helgerson, 1970:104).

However, in other marginal systems, legislators do get the opportunity to question the government. The Ecuadorian Congress has frequently exercised its right to invite ministers to appear before it to discuss the department's policies and how they are being implemented (Pyne, 1973:15). Members of the Colombian cabinet regularly appear before Congress, and there is evidence that ministers are at least partially inhibited in their official actions by the fear they they will have to defend what they do before the legislature (Duff, 1971:370). And in Ethiopia officials can be compelled to testify before Parliament; according to two observers of that legislature, "members of Parliament are at their most aggressive when they have a Minister or high administrative official on the stand. Such sessions can be quite rough on officials" (Markakis and Beyene, 1967:214).

Adjournment debates have been used on occasion in both Zambia and Pakistan as a means of exercising further control over the bureaucracy. In Pakistan, 678 motions for adjournment debates were received between 1962 and 1969, but only 42 were actually admitted for discussion (Rashiduzzaman, 1969–70:485). In Zambia 107 adjournment motions were debated between 1963 and 1968 (Helgerson, 1970:124).

More formal methods of control such as censure motions and interpellations are used quite infrequently in marginal legislatures. In Peru Congress can censure individual ministers or the Council as a whole, in which case resignation is mandatory and must be accepted by the president. During the periods in which Peru's legislature has been active "many ministers and even entire cabinets resigned under threat of censure" (McCoy, 1971:334, 352). In Afghanistan the Wolesi Jirgah may withdraw confidence from the government, but only by a two-thirds vote, a constitutional provision which understandably has restricted the use of this legislative prerogative. Nonetheless pressures from the legislature were instrumental in causing the government's resignation in 1971 (Weinbaum, 1972:67–68).

Limitations. The limitations on the effectiveness of legislative oversight in marginal systems include all of those which we discussed for other types of legislatures, plus additional ones peculiar to this category. As usual, there is the almost complete absence of professional staff support. In Venezuela, for example, staff members were without any professional expertise and their activities, according to one observer, often resemble that of "servants more than secretaries," a situation exacerbated by rules which require that all administrative personnel be partisan appointees (Kelley, 1973:156). In most marginal legislatures parliamentary oversight is further hindered by short annual sessions. And in Venezuela there are long periods during which committees do not meet at all, and when they do meet absenteeism is very high, especially for meetings of the less important committees (Kelley, 1971:484).

As we observed earlier, another impediment to effective parliamentary oversight is the fact that ministers in most marginal systems are responsible to the executive rather than to the parliament and thus the legislature has few sanctions that it can exercise against ministers whose performance they find wanting. More importantly, legislators may be dependent on administrators for a variety of personal and political favors, and therefore may be reluctant to call them to account. Lebanese parliamentarians

in their day-to-day work, particularly in serving their constituencies . . . are more in need of the cooperation and favors of the bureaucracy than vice-versa. The members of the civil service, having strong career security and immunity granted to them by law, cannot be arbitrarily removed except after a hard and tedious procedure that involves a decision by the highest administrative court. (Baaklini, 1972:274)

Finally, in all marginal systems legislatures and their members are subjected to implicit and explicit intimidation by executive elites and this must obviously affect the zeal with which they conduct their oversight activities. In Zambia "most backbenchers are hesitant to criticize the government, for they remembered the sanctions invoked against those who had antagonized the party leadership" (Helgerson, 1970:94–95). According to one member of the Brazilian Congress the legislature could exercise control of the bureaucracy if it had the audacity to issue implementing legislation to put into practice the various constitutional provisions that deal with this function. But in 1967 when Congress tried to do this, the executive vetoed the legislation. Congress overrode the veto, but then the executive promulgated its Fifth Institutional Act under which it eliminated all devices for the control of the executive that the Congress had enacted (Astiz, 1974:11–12). And in Kenya in 1975 the Parliament voted 62 to 59 to reject a government motion to censure a committee that had accused the police and high officials of complicity in the murder of a prominent political leader. In the view of one observer of Kenyan politics, this incident, coupled with economic problems, "led to substantial tension in Kenya" and marked a "period of growing frustration and a resurgence of demands for loyalty to the government." Kenyan leaders banned certain speeches, fired cabinet members, and vociferously comdemned their critics (Hopkins, 1975b:25, 28).

What all of this means is the legislators operating under the constant threat of extraconstitutional actions directed against themselves or against the prerogatives and even the existence of the legislature will always find it difficult and uninviting to exercise any type of continuing and effective control of executive-centered elites.

Chapter 7

MINIMAL LEGISLATURES: PRIVATE POLICY MAKING

Minimal legislatures are dominated by executive-centered elites whose influence permeates the entire policy-making process. The base of this influence is a dominant political party whose control extends not simply to public policy making but throughout the entire society. In this context the minimal legislature can impose only the weakest constraints on these elites and situations seldom arise when executive-centered elites are compelled to deal with or to accept dissenting views articulated in legislative arenas. Contrary to the experience of marginal legislatures, when conflictual situations involving legislators and executive elites arise in minimal legislature systems, they are certain to occur in private committee arenas rather than in public plenary arenas.

Our data for the analysis in this chapter come from the minimal legislatures of the Soviet Union, Poland, Yugoslavia, Tanzania, Singapore, and Spain.

POLICY FORMULATION

Executive Domination. The decision to initiate legislation in minimal legislature systems is always taken in extraparliamentary arenas dominated by the ruling party. In the Soviet Union, for example, "it is clear that the decision to enact major legislation . . . has always emanated from the highest level of leadership in the regime, which was of course Stalin in his time and the Party apparatus since" (Vanneman, 1972:254).

In all of these systems the bureaucratic sector of the executive elite plays a dominant role in policy formulation just as it does in the other legislative categories. In Singapore it is argued that the People's Action party is completely bureaucratized and has therefore de-politicized public policy making; thus, "power and leadership are concentrated in a handful of men who see themselves as architects of a new society; in their view, the allocation of resources in the de-politicized political system is a matter to be programmed and scheduled with the assistance of competent and efficient civil ser-vants" (Chee, 1976:427). Initiatives by individual members of mini-mal legislators are almost unheard of. In Singapore, in August 1974, "a backbencher initiated the Roman Catholic Archbishop's Bill, the first [private member bill] since the Third Parliament began session in 1972 and according to one MP, the first in 'donkey's years'" (Chee, 1976:426). In Tanzania private member bills are seldom offered, but private member motions sometimes succeed in encouraging the gov-ernment to introduce its own legislation on a particular subject (Kjek-shus, 1974:22). Similar resolutions are occasionally offered by members of the Polish Seym; they usually request the government or an individual minister to adopt some particular policy. Only eighteen have been adopted between 1952 and 1969 (Modelski, 1973:80).

Legislative initiatives in minimal legislatures can come from those legislators who participate in leadership arenas. In Tanzania MPs who are members of the cabinet "are normally involved in the preparation of legislation" (Hopkins, 1970:764). In the Soviet Union a count of important governmental decisions between 1964 and 1972 indicated that while only 16 of these decisions were embodied in laws passed by the Supreme Soviet, 59 were decrees of the Presidium of the Supreme Soviet and 176 were decisions of its Council of Ministers (Hough, 1975:17–18).

Committees. In several minimal legislatures committees appear to be acquiring a perceptible role in initiating and drafting legislation. In the Soviet Union during the post-Stalin period the commissions and the subcommissions of the Supreme Soviet have become arenas for both drafting and deliberating legislation. The commissions meet in secret "and draw on expert advice from a variety of sources. From mere administrative conduits and final review boards, the commis-sions are being transformed into organizations for integrating propo-sals emanating from various funds of expertise into rough draft bills" (Vanneman, 1972:299).

A similar pattern has emerged in post-Stalin Poland as well. Seym committees have been structured to encourage specialization. One of the criteria for assignment to committees is the possession of expertise in the subject area under the committee's jurisdiction. As examples scientists, teachers, and journalists make up 68 percent of the membership of the Education and Science Committee, and physicians, social workers, and physical education teachers make up 59 percent of the membership of the Committee on Health and Physical Culture. Finally, each committee has at least one full-time deputy who, because he is able to spend more time, becomes an expert in that particular legislative area, and quite frequently serves as chairman of the committee (Modelski, 1973:64, 66, 70).

Seym committees also possess the power to adopt a *desideratum*, which, like a motion, is addressed to the government, the prime minister, or individual ministers, and urges them to adopt a particular course of action. Those to whom the desiderata are addressed are required to respond, although they usually take somewhat longer than the constitutionally mandated limit of thirty days (Modelski, 1973:81ff).

Lest the impression be left that committees in these systems have become truly autonomous centers of power, it should be said that the party apparatus in the Soviet Union maintains tight control over the commissions (Vanneman, 1972:275) while in Poland, the party apparatus seizes "the commanding heights of the Standing Committees, namely their chairmanships" (Modelski, 1973:75). In sum, minimal legislatures, particularly in the private committee arenas, are permitted some degree of influence on the formulation of public policy as long as the strict and narrow parameters for such influence, established by the governing party, are respected.

POLICY DELIBERATION

The deliberative capacities of minimal legislatures are not very great because they do not meet very often in plenary session. Between 1954 and 1966 the Supreme Soviet held twenty-three sessions, each one lasting about one week (Vanneman, 1972:163). Other minimal legislatures meet somewhat more frequently; the Polish Seym had 55 sittings between 1962 and 1969 (Modelski, 1973:57), the Yugoslavian Federal Assembly held 376 sessions between 1963 and 1968 (Cohen, 1977:128), and between 1965 and 1970 the Tanzanian Bunge convened each year for an average of 48 days (Kjekshus, 1974:21).

These relatively brief sessions mean increased deliberative activities within those legislative arenas that are able to meet more frequently, such as leadership groups and committees. In the Soviet Union the Presidium of the Supreme Soviet "is actually a working legislature, exercising the entire spectrum of state powers between Supreme Soviet sessions," a period that extends throughout most of the year. Thus, there are about 50 *ukaz* (edicts) of the Presidium for every *zakon* (law) of the Supreme Soviet (Vanneman, 1972:320, 322). In Yugoslavia the ratio is not quite as extreme. In fact, during the 1963–68 period there were 993 laws, decisions, and other acts adopted by the Federal Executive Council (Cohen, 1977:128).

Committees. As suggested before, a great deal of deliberative activity takes place in committee arenas of minimal legislatures. For one thing, committees meet more regularly than the legislature does. Modelski (1973:76) suggests that one reason why the bulk of the Polish Seym's work is carried on in committee meetings is because the committees, unlike the Seym, are constantly in session. When the Supreme Soviet set about studying the 1969 budget and the new five year plan, they "formed thirty-two sub-commissions composing over 200 deputies of the Supreme Soviet plus other persons who may be co-opted, all of which held 100 sessions. In addition, there were 27 plenary sessions of the Planning and Budget Commission of each chamber" (Vanneman, 1972:243). Similarly from February 12, 1974, to February 12, 1975, the sixteen committees of the Spanish Cortes held a total of 194 sessions (Linz, 1975:I–23).

According to various sources committee sessions do result in modifications of many pieces of legislation. The Soviet Pension Law of 1956 was passed by the Supreme Soviet in the form that it was proposed but "certain important inequities were removed in the Legislative Proposals Commissions before the session began" (Juviler, 1960:356). Vanneman (1972:263) cites a public health law in the 1960s that had forty-six of its fifty-five articles altered in the subcommissions. Minor budgetary adjustments are frequently made at the behest of the commissions: "The chairman of the education, science, and culture committee of the Council of the Union reported . . . that over a four-year period his committee (together with its counterpart in the Council of Nationalities) had been able to obtain 274 million rubles for his branch in addition to that included in the drafts which they had received" (Hough, 1975:25). Even in the 1950s the Budget Commissions of the Supreme Soviet were succeeding in making minor changes in the proposed budget "usually about one tenth of one per cent of the total" (Juviler, 1960:385).

Committees of the Polish Seym are perhaps the most aggressive and the most successful in this category in achieving changes in proposed legislation. From 1957 to 1969 the Seym passed 327 statutes of which only about sixty were approved without modification. Most changes were made in committees and approved in that form on the floor. Some amendments constituted only slight changes in the original proposal while others were so extensive as to be "almost a substitution of the original measure" (Modelski, 1973:91). Almost all committee amendments showed "a definite concern for the protection of the interests of citizens in the substance of the policy itself as well as in the procedures by which the policy was to be applied" (Modelski, 1973:96). Although committees have never rejected any government measure, there have been occasions on which the government has withdrawn legislation as a result of opposition from the committee involved. The committees, in turn, obey the rules of the game by not challenging the general political line that guides the government's proposals (Modelski, 1973:92, 96).

One reason for the relative success of committee arenas is that they are private, and can therefore affect policy without embarrassing the government. The subcommissions of the Supreme Soviet "can collate suggestions from experts and the public on the circulated draft, then deliberate upon the incorporation of these suggestions without revealing the dirty linen" (Vanneman, 1972:268). In Poland the closed committee sessions provide the party with the opportunity to "find out the truth about the merits and demerits of their proposals and correct the flaws in them" (Modelski, 1973:56).

In the Supreme Soviet subcommissions have the opportunity to hold public sessions in order to hear reports of spokesmen for government agencies, ministries, and heads of the departments; the commissions can also summon representatives of government agencies and scientific and public organizations (Juviler, 1960:384–85). According to Vanneman (1972:268), such open meetings provide embryonic public deliberations—something quite unique for the Soviet legislative process.

Plenary Arenas. Plenary arenas provide an opportunity for dissent in all categories of legislatures. In minimal legislatures some mild dissent is permitted, but it takes place within very strict limits. It must be prefaced and softened with praise and support for party and governmental leaders, and it must avoid matters of party principle and concentrate instead on the technicalities or practical considerations involved in the issue at hand. One source describes statements in the Supreme Soviet as composed initially of oratorical bunting extolling the party, the government, and the people of the Soviet Union, and giving glowing accounts of economic and cultural progress. Only after these rituals have been scrupulously observed do deputies add certain critical phrases calling attention either to shortcomings in the proposal before the legislature or to deficiencies in previous government performance in that policy area (Juviler, 1960:317–18). Thus in the summer of 1973 the Supreme Soviet gathered in joint session to discuss education and to deliberate on a bill defining the "Principles of Legislation about Education": "Thirty-nine deputies spoke on the reports, and at least in some portion of their speech, each called for some new governmental action or some changes in governmental policy" (Hough, 1975:29). In Poland even the most vehement criticisms "stop short of questioning the fundamental policies" of the party; the criticism is usually focused "on the more technical problems and issues of economy and administration" (Modelski, 1973:52).

In the non-Marxist countries in this category legislative debate is a bit less inhibited. In Spain during the last days of Franco, Linz (1975:III–3) reports that debates in the Cortes were "freer" and "livelier" than they had been in the past. In Tanzania legislators have been told that they may criticize or oppose government policy in party discussions or within the Assembly before the Assembly votes, as long as they confine their opinions to the "practical" aspects of the policy and avoid questioning the principles involved. However, they may not publicly oppose a policy decision of the party's National Executive Committee and once a policy is passed by the Assembly, they must support it among their constituents (Hopkins, 1970:768–69). But events in Tanzania have convinced MPs that even these limited rights to oppose government proposals in the Assembly are somewhat tenuous and should not be exercised very zealously. During the first two years after independence, more than 50 percent of the speeches of some MPs were critical of the government. This practice has ceased, presumably because the critics were either placed in detention or were forced to opt for an early retirement from political life (Hopkins, 1971b:147).

Similarly, in Singapore PAP backbenchers may oppose government proposals, but may not in this role criticize the principles of policies but only details involving implementation. As in the Soviet Union, "some MPs preface their remarks with lavish praise of the senior ministers before they launch their criticism" (Chee, 1976:426).

The effect of plenary debate is not very great. There is no evidence from any of these countries that legislative debate actually changes the substance of legislation. Such changes, if they are to be made, will be made in the committees of these legislatures or as a result of deliberations and consultation in leadership or extraparliamentary arenas.

Discipline is a given in minimal legislatures. In Marxist countries all votes are unanimous. In Tanzania the expulsion of legislators from the party and thus from Parliament has effectively stopped MPs from voting against government positions (Kjekshus, 1974:31), and PAP in Singapore maintains party discipline in the same manner (Shee, 1971:112).

OVERSIGHT

Committees. In the post-Stalin period marxist systems began vesting increased oversight responsibilities in the standing commissions of its legislatures. In the Soviet Union the process is called *Kontrol*, which refers to monitoring the "effective as well as the faithful execution of policy as embodied in legislation and involves the power to judge whether the laws, policies, and execution should be arrested, reversed, expanded, or modified" (Vanneman, 1972:192). Between 1966 and 1970 the standing commissions held 170 sessions, the bulk of which dealt with *Kontrol* (Vanneman, 1972:200). In Hungary the 1956 Standing Orders of the National Assembly "authorized committees to act on their own initiative in investigating all social and political problems" while the new Czechoslovakian Constitution of 1960 emphasizes the role of committees "in giving impetus to the activities of other state organs" (Modelski, 1973:58).

In pursuit of these oversight activities, these committees have exercised the right to investigate complaints and to issue recommendations addressed to responsible officials. In the Soviet Union the Constitution requires that all institutions and officials must submit whatever documents and materials these committees may request

(Juviler, 1960:417) while those who receive the *desiderata* of Seym committees must given an answer to the committee within thirty days (Modelski, 1973:83). In addition, the Seym committees receive written reports from the government departments on a regular basis and the reports are often supplemented by the personal appearance of ministers and undersecretaries before the standing committees. Finally, the Seym committees may hold "thematic" discussions focusing on a particular problem not necessarily related to specific legislation (Modelski, 1973:110, 113).

The major weakness in this entire process is that the committees have no sanctions at all at their disposal to enforce compliance with their requests or recommendations. In the Soviet Union, the most that can be said is that the current practice of requiring ministers to at least examine the recommendations of the commissions "is a significant step, since they were often ignored altogether previously" (Vanneman, 1972:304). In Poland, Modelski (1973:84–85) claims that the *desiderata* are effective even though they are not enforceable because there are normally good relations between the committees and the bureaucracy, and because the party organs expect the bureaucracy to be responsive to the requests of the committees.

There is no report of equivalent oversight activities by committees in other legislatures in this category. The Public Accounts Committee of the Tanzanian Bunge does submit reports in writing to the Bunge after examining the accounts of the various ministries, but there is no indication of how important or effective these reports are in controlling administrative actions. Other committees in Tanzania apparently have no oversight impact at all (Kjekshus, 1974:21).

Plenary Arenas. Oversight activity in plenary arenas of minimal legislatures is not very intensive. Question period does not exist in marxist countries except for Yugoslavia. There, questions increased from a total of 59 for the 1953–57 period, to 243 for the 1958–63 period, and 498 for the 1963–67 period (Cohen, 1977:128). In Spain, there also has been an increase in the frequency with which questions are asked, from a total of seven for the entire eighth legislature to 122 for 1968 and 1969 (Linz, 1975:I–225).

In Tanzania the trend has been in the opposite direction. During the 1966 session, 1,169 questions were asked, most having to do with local or constituency issues; they are described in these terms:

A typical question might be: "What are the government's plans to tarmac the road between Dodoma and Morogoro?" or "Will the government build an extension to the overcrowded dispensary in Tukuyu?" These questions and responses constitute a dialogue reflecting persistent and important, though not explosive, demands by constituency representatives attempting to bring the problems of their constituencies to the government's attention and to secure whatever relief or development funds may be available. (Hopkins, 1971b:144)

However, by the 1969 session, the volume of questions had dropped to 571, reflecting a government decision to impose a limit of four oral questions per member per meeting as well as a decrease in the government's enthusiasm for public criticism (Kjekshus, 1974:23).

In the Supreme Soviet attempts to exercise oversight during plenary sessions are rather stilted; time is set aside for "scheduled" criticism, which is usually "ex post facto criticism of faulty implementation of policy by ministries" (Vanneman, 1972:168–69). Again, as was the case with committee oversight activities, no specific sanctions attach to plenary oversight activities.

The most important limitation on the effectiveness of the oversight activities of minimal legislatures goes to the basic defining characteristic of such an institution. The minimal legislature exists by the grace of the executive-centered elites and only exercises the authority that these elites care to allow it. If effective oversight means that the legislature can make it necessary for the executive to do something that it doesn't care to do, then clearly minimal legislatures do not and cannot have such a capacity. It is reasonable to believe that should they try to establish such a capacity, they would quickly cease to function. The imprisonment of Tanzanian MPs has firmly established the limits of oversight and criticism in that country.

Even the oversight capacities that are allowed are restricted by the usual variables that we have encountered in other categories of legislatures. Time is very limited; Hough (1975:25) suggests that Soviet commissions must limit themselves in practice to a detailed examination of one policy question a year. The more active committees in the Polish Seym lack staff and must rely entirely on the bureaucracy for the information that they need to oversee its activities (Modelski, 1973:89–90). All of these problems are exacerbated by the fact that minimal legislatures often function in states with maximum governments—with active governments pursuing a vast array of policies and programs throughout the nation. The work load required to effectively oversee the activities of the Soviet bureaucracy would stagger the most well-staffed legislature in the world; a legislature that meets briefly, that is heavily populated by nonprofessionals, and must stay within quite clearly understood limits concerning what can be said, asked, and done, can do nothing significant in this area.

Part III

REPRESENTATION

Chapter 8

LEGISLATURES AND POLITICAL DEMANDS:
A THEORETICAL FRAMEWORK

The great variation in the extent to which legislatures and their members engage in policy-making activities stands in marked contrast to the data on legislative performance of representational activities. Legislators from all over the world and from all types of legislatures devote a substantial portion of their time and effort to dealing with the problems, requests, and needs of mass publics as these are expressed either by individuals or by interest groups. This relative uniformity in behavior is attributable in the first instance to a near unanimity of mass expectations concerning representation, the substance of which is that legislators, because of their elected status, are obligated to be responsive to the needs and demands of those who elect them. These expectations, along with other factors, also encourage legislators to perceive their role as that of trustee and defender of the interests of the people, either narrowly conceived as the constituency that elects them, or more broadly conceived as the entire citizenry of the nation.

In the chapters that follow I will be concerned with describing the representational activities of legislators, with identifying and assessing the variables that influence the way in which legislators perform representational activities, and with suggesting the consequences of effective and ineffective legislative performance for both the legislature and the nation.

POLITICAL DEMANDS

The term "political demand" can be used to refer to all requests for assistance, support, or some other service or action directed to a political institution or actor. These demands can be divided into four categories depending on their *source* and on the *scope* of the response that they require.

First, demands can be labeled as *organized* if they emanate from groups, such as a labor union, or a farm cooperative, or a corporation, or demands can be classified as *individual* if they come from a worker, a farmer, or a business executive.

Second, demands can be either *generalized* or *particularized* (Almond and Powell, 1966:87). Generalized demands are those that require government actions that can affect the nation as a whole. Particularized demands are couched in narrow terms relevant to a small group of people and therefore require government actions of a more specific nature. Responses to both types of demands can take the form of a law or an individual action by a legislator or another government official. The distinction is not between statutory and nonstatutory responses, but between laws or other government actions with a predominant effect on the individual or group initiating the demand and laws or other actions that have a generalized effect throughout the country.

These two dimensions—source and scope of demand—can be combined to yield a four-fold classification of political demands:

Particularized-Individual Demands. An army veteran asks his representative to contact the bureaucrat who is responsible for holding up his disability check, an unemployed laborer asks a party leader to get him a job on the government payroll, or a street vendor asks a customer who is an army officer to help her obtain the appropriate license. These demands emanate from individuals; they do not seek the passage of legislation, but rather a discrete action by an officeholder on behalf of a citizen confronted by a specific problem.

Particularized-Organized Demands. A farmers' cooperative petitions a legislator to see to it that funds for a dam in their province are included in the next budget, a trade association asks a bureaucrat to work for a high tariff to protect the industry, or a town council asks a national party leader for help in securing funds for a new hospital in the area. All of these demands come from organized groups; all call for a particularized response from those who are recipients of the demand.

General-Individual Demands. A university student writes a letter to his representative asking that a land-reform bill be introduced, a newspaper editor demands that the Foreign Ministry sever ties with another nation whose internal policies he does not like, or an economist calls on the government to raise taxes in order to avoid inflation. All of these are demands by individuals that the government take action that would affect all of its citizens.

General-Organized Demands. A labor union adopts a plank at its convention calling for higher tariff rates on foreign products that in its view compete unfairly with domestic products, or a minority party asks the government to draw up legislation that would raise the income of poor people. These demands come from organized groups and call for the government to take action that will affect the entire nation.

These four categories of demands taken together constitute the political system's total demand flow with which legislators and other political actors must contend. In the remainder of this chapter I will identify the variables that account for the volume of demands that legislators receive and the way in which legislators perform in response to these demands. The consequences of successful and unsuccessful legislative performance also will be assessed. As a guide to this discussion, the schema depicted in Figure 8.1 identifies the variables with which we will be concerned and indicates the way in which they will be shown to be related to one another.

DEMAND VOLUME

Only a portion of the demands generated within a political system find their way to the legislature and its members. Demands also can be dealt with outside of legislative arenas by structures such as the bureaucracy, interest groups, political parties, local government institutions, and local elites, to name some obvious examples. The volume of demands that the legislature receives is determined by several variables: the accessibility and capability of the legislature, the performance of other political institutions that deal with demands, the expectations that members of the political system hold concerning the legislature, and the role perceptions of legislators.

Accessibility and Capability.[1] Accessibility refers to the ease with which an institution or person can be approached by those with demands to make. Certain structures are open in the sense that they have regular mechanisms and procedures linking them with the individuals and groups from whom demands emanate. Other structures are closed; those who populate them insulate themselves from all but extraordinary demands coming from highly select publics. For example, civil servants are usually more accessible than army colonels but less accessible than political party or interest-group personnel.

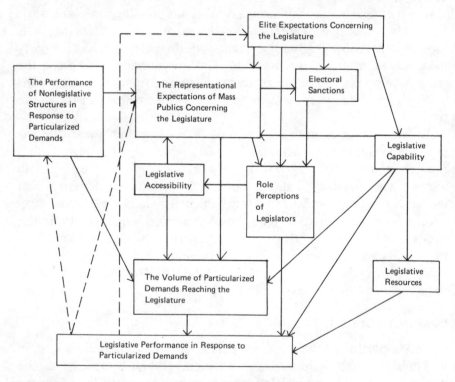

FIGURE 8.1   Legislatures and Political Demands: A Model

Certain participants in the political process are more capable of responding to political demands than others. The more dominant elements of the political system can get things done where others may fail. The American Congress has a greater capacity to respond to demands than American political parties, while the PRI—the governing party of Mexico—is more likely to respond successfully to demands than the Congress of that country.

These two dimensions can be combined to produce the four categories shown in Figure 8.2. Institutions and actors located in the highly accessible–highly capable quadrant—for example, the United States Congress—will be primary targets of demands. Those located in the low-accessibility–low-capability cell—for example, the military in Japan—will receive no demands whatsoever. Those in the highly accessible–low capability cell—for example, the Thai National Assembly—will receive a high volume of demands, many coming from those who cannot gain access to those structures in the low-accessibility–high-capability cell—for example, the Thai bureaucracy.

As a rule, the more structures in a system that are accessible to demand makers and capable of responding to demands, the lower the demand volume will be for any one structure or group of actors (Easton, 1965: part two). From a legislative perspective, this means that the existence of alternative structures with such demand-handling potential *reduces* the volume of demands that reach the legislature.[2]

		LOW	HIGH
CAPABILITY	HIGH	Thai Bureaucracy	United States Congress
	LOW	Japanese Military	Thai National Assembly
		LOW	HIGH
		ACCESSIBILITY	

FIGURE 8.2   Factors Affecting Demands on Political Institutions

The reasoning behind this assertion is quite simple. Assuming that there is a certain volume of demands in every political system, the greater the number of potential targets for demands, the fewer the number of demands that will reach any one target. For example, if the bureaucracy is accessible as well as capable, citizens with complaints will go directly there to seek redress rather than going to their legislator as they would if the bureaucracy was inaccessible. If power in a political system is decentralized—if local units of government with capacities of their own exist—fewer demands will reach the national level than if the political system was highly centralized. Similarly, the existence of accessible local party organizations that are also capable of responding to demands will reduce the volume of demands that impinge upon the legislature and its members.

On the other hand, the volume of legislative demands can be increased if these nonlegislative structures are inaccessible, or if they are not capable of responding effectively. Also, the way in which these institutions perform their activities may generate more political demands than they resolve. Arbitrary or corrupt bureaucrats will cause citizens to complain; ineffective local government units will fail to resolve problems or even exacerbate them, thereby increasing the number of demands reaching national government institutions. Aggressive parties and interest groups—highly accessible but lacking in capability—may politicize a dormant or traditional society and thereby cause a flood of demands to be directed at national political institutions.

Expectations about the Legislature. The volume of demands that the legislature receives is also affected by the expectations that people have concerning the legislature. As noted in Chapter 1, mass and elite publics hold various expectations about what the legislature should and should not do. The performance of representational activities bulks particularly large in the expectations of mass publics. No matter how other institutions perform, representation will be one of the main expectations people have of their legislators, and there always will be a certain volume of demands directed at the legislature because of these expectations. The more accessible and the more capable the legislature is, the more intense these expectations will be and the heavier its demand volume will be.

The performance of nonlegislative institutions, in addition to having a direct effect on legislative demand volume, also affects demand volume indirectly through this intervening variable of mass expectations. For example, if political parties are active and efficacious demand handlers in the manner of the Communist party of the Soviet Union or the PRI of Mexico, they will be the objects of representational expectations and will be subject to a steady demand flow. This, in turn, should reduce the intensity of the representational expectations directed at the legislature. Alternatively, political parties such as the American Democratic and Republican parties, or the Kenyan African National Union may be inactive and inefficacious as demand handlers, in which case few will expect representation from them and few demands will flow to them. This should increase the intensity of the representational expectations directed at the legislature.

Elite expectations about the legislature may be either supportive or hostile to the representational expectations of mass publics. If elites hold different expectations—for example, expectations heavily oriented toward the system-maintenance activities of legislatures— the representational expectations of mass publics may be less intense. Alternatively, if elite and mass expectations are congruent—if both focus heavily on representational activities, for example—then representational expectations of mass publics will be reinforced.

In sum, the accessibility, capability, and performance of nonlegislative structures combined with the expectations of elite publics about the legislature affect the intensity with which mass publics will expect representational activities from their legislators, and thereby affect the volume of demands that the legislature receives.

Role Perceptions of Legislators. The role perceptions of legislators are influenced by any number of variables. Studies have sought and discovered correlations between representational role perceptions and various personal background characteristics of legislators such as faith in people, political socialization experiences, level of education, and party and campaign experiences (Jewell, 1970:474–75). However, the expectations of those with whom a role occupant such as a legislator must interact will have a particularly strong effect on the incumbent's role perceptions (Hopkins, 1971b:48–57). Thus, if mass and elite publics expect the legislature to be actively involved in policy making, legislators will construct their role perceptions accordingly. Alternatively, if executive-centered elites forcefully articulate a set of expectations that emphasize the legislature's system-maintenance activities, this too will have an effect on the role perceptions of legislators. Ideally, legislative role perceptions should be congruent with expectations but this may be difficult, especially in systems where elite and mass expectations conflict.

In most political systems, the effect of mass and elite expectations on the role perceptions of legislators is reinforced by electoral sanctions. As I will demonstrate in chapter 11, legislative membership is generally attractive and valuable in all political systems and thus it is likely that legislators will be responsive to those who are responsible for their continuance in office. By threatening a legislator's tenure in office, mass and elite publics may encourage the legislator to perceive his role in a manner that is congruent with their expectations.

In some political systems this reciprocal relationship between legislators and their constituents is almost a cultural imperative. Patron-client relationships in many countries link leaders and their supporters in a set of diffuse, informal mutual obligations. Clients (constituents) provide services (votes) to their patrons (legislators) and the legislator is expected to provide services in return. When legislative-constituency relations are of this nature, the representational expectations directed at the legislator are intensified and have an even more substantial impact on the manner in which legislators perceive their roles.

Certainly electoral sanctions are not the only ones available. The penalty for violating the expectations of some elites may be a good deal more severe than simply being retired from office as our discussion of political risk in chapter 11 will show. But in terms of the representational expectations of mass publics, the electoral sanction appears to be particularly potent.

Role perceptions have an indirect effect on demand volume through the accessibility variable. Legislators who perceive their role as one of being responsive to demands will act to increase their accessibility to those who have demands to make, and by so doing they are likely to increase the volume of legislative demands. Legislators who do not perceive their role in these terms will take no action to increase their accessibility and may even take steps in the opposite direction, thereby reducing legislative demand volume.

To this point we have been concerned with explicating the variables that affect the volume of demands that reach the legislature and its members. The expectations of mass and elite publics, the accessibility and capability of the legislature and of other political institutions, and the role perceptions of legislators have been identified as the key variables affecting demand volume. In a political system where no political actors other than legislators are concerned with demands, legislators will have a very heavy demand load; representational expectations will be focused exclusively on them and they are quite likely to define their roles accordingly, assuming that there are no strong countervailing elite expectations. In contrast, in those political systems where other institutions and actors are involved with handling political demands, legislators will have a more manageable demand load. Although the legislators will continue to perceive satisfying these demands as a part of their role, other actors in the political system will also perceive it as part of their role, and thus the burden for the legislator will be less.

PERFORMANCE

Once demands are received by the legislator they must be dealt with in some manner. In this analysis the way in which legislators deal with demands will be called "performance." Legislators have several options available to them. First, demands can be ignored. If the volume of demands the legislator receives is particularly high, it may be impossible to acknowledge or deal with each one. Also, a legislator may ignore demands for which he has no sympathy, or a demand emanating from a group or individual toward whom the legislator feels no óbligation.

Second, a legislator may try to bring the demand to the attention of those with the capacity to resolve it. For example, he may act inside the legislature by asking a question of the minister whose responsibility includes the substantive area of the demand, or he may act outside the legislature by writing a letter or telephoning to the appropriate administrative official.

Third, a legislator may act within the legislature to secure general relief for the needs expressed in a demand. If a legislator receives requests from several young constituents to act on their behalf against the arbitrary rulings of local draft boards, the legislator may respond by introducing legislation calling for the elimination of conscription. As we saw in the preceding chapters, legislators in many countries use their prerogative of introducing private member bills as a means to respond to both particularized and generalized demands. Part of this response may be purely symbolic; the private member bill may have little chance of enactment, but the fact that the legislator has introduced a bill may be sufficient to satisfy the representational expectations of those who initiated the demand.

Finally, a legislator may react to a demand by resolving it. A legislator asked to find a job for a deserving constituent may hire the person as a part of his congressional staff. A constituent's problem in securing a payment from a federal agency may be solved by the personal intervention of the legislator with the agency involved. A project for the legislator's constituency may be secured by a deal between the legislator and the president.

How legislators respond to demands and how successfully is determined by four variables: the volume of demands with which legislators must deal, the capabilities of the legislature and its members, the role perceptions of legislators, and the resources that legislators have at their disposal.

Volume. The relevance of volume to performance is simply this: if legislators have fewer demands to deal with they are more likely to be successful than they would be if they were overloaded with demands. For example, if people with individual demands carry them to interest groups first, and these groups aggregate these demands into one organized general demand that is then conveyed to the legislator, the legislator's job is easier. Instead of dealing with several discrete demands, he deals with only one organized demand. Similarly, if local political institutions have a degree of autonomy and capability to go with their accessibility, they will deal with many demands which will therefore never reach the national level, let alone the national legislator. If demand volume is reduced in this way, the legislator will be more effective in dealing with those demands that he ultimately receives. Legislators who are overloaded with requests simply will not be able to deal effectively with more than a few.

Role Perceptions. The performance of the legislator in dealing with political demands is affected to some extent by the way in which legislators perceive their roles. For example, legislators may see their role as being exclusively that of a constituency agent and they may gear their behavior in the legislature entirely to the performance of those activities. If they also see themselves as policy makers, they may channel their efforts towards seeking legislative solutions for the different kinds of political demands directed at them. Alternatively, they may see themselves primarily as intermediaries between demand makers and those executive-centered elites with the real capacity to do something about the demands. If so, they will deal with demands by using methods both inside and outside the legislature to

influence the behavior of executive-centered elites. Those who perceive themselves as strong partisans may work through party organizations; those who see themselves as overseers of the administration
may use such instruments as parliamentary questions or committee
investigations. And, of course, those who do not perceive their job as
including an obligation to respond to these demands (as unlikely as
that might be) will not perform at all as demand handlers.

Legislative Capability. As we have seen in the last four chapters,
legislative policy-making capabilities vary substantially both across
and within the five legislative categories, and this capability is important in determining what legislators can do to respond to demands. In
reactive, marginal, and minimal legislatures, legislators have only a
peripheral policy-making role and it is therefore unlikely that they can
respond to many demands by initiating policy proposals that will
ultimately become law. In comparison, members of active and vulnerable legislatures are somewhat more likely to be able to pursue this
course. However, members of all except minimal legislatures may be
able to respond to demands by seeking amendments or modifications
in proposals submitted to the legislature by executive-centered elites.
Thus, projects of constituency interest can be inserted into a budget
authorization bill, or a change in tariff regulations sought by an
industry interest group may be incorporated into a general tariff
revision.

In all save minimal legislatures all types of political demands can be
brought to the attention of those with the power to resolve them by
raising them during plenary session debates. The deliberative activities of legislatures provides legislators with the opportunity not
only to address the issue at hand but also to discuss other related
problems.

If a legislature is able to effectively oversee the administrative
branch of government, these capabilities can be usefully employed in
performing demand-related activities. A legislator may respond to an
interest group's problem by raising a question on the floor of the
Parliament, thereby forcing the issue to the minister's attention. A
powerful member of a legislative committee may evoke a favorable
response to a constituency problem from an agency over which the
committee is charged with oversight responsibilities.

The relative capability of different legislative arenas will also be a

factor in determining to whom demands are directed. Interest groups
will be particularly sensitive to this variable. Thus, in active and
vulnerable legislatures, where committees are significantly involved
in the policy-making process, interest groups will attempt to seek
access to committee arenas to press their demands. In reactive systems where parties are dominant, interest groups will seek access to
caucus or leadership arenas in order to secure a hearing for their
problems.

Resources of Legislators. The resources of legislators, quite apart
from the capabilities of their institution, affect their performance of
representational activities. If, within the legislature, members have
qualified staff at their disposal to assist them in dealing with the
various demands that are directed at them, they will be able to deal
with their demand load more effectively. Secretaries can help to
answer letters from constituents. Aides can make telephone calls or
write letters to relevant administrators on behalf of aggrieved constituents. Legislative assistants can help the legislator to understand
the policy proposals before the legislature so that he may be better
able to make those policies responsive to those who are making
demands on him.

In addition, the personal resources of a legislator are relevant. As
we shall see, in many countries legislators must deal with personal
problems of constituents that do not require government action but
may require small amounts of cash. If legislators are personally
affluent, they can deal with these demands on their own. If legislators
aren't well off, they will have to find ways to get the funds from
government sources if they hope to respond to these types of demands successfully.

The possession of sufficient resources is also related to legislative
capability. Members of highly capable legislatures will see to it that
they are supplied at public expense with a staff of sufficient size and
competence to enable them to deal effectively with their demand load.
They also will see to it that they themselves receive a salary that is
high enough to enable them to bear whatever expenses might be
involved in successfully performing demand-related activities.

THE CONSEQUENCES OF LEGISLATIVE PERFORMANCE

To this point we have been primarily concerned with legislative
performance as a dependent variable. However, as Figure 8.1 indi-

cates, there are several feedback loops from the legislative performance variable.

First, successful legislative performance in response to demands can affect the performance of nonlegislative structures. For instance, bureaucrats can be made more accessible and more responsive as a result of legislative intervention. Second, legislative performance affects the extent to which people direct representational expectations toward the legislature. If legislators have a record of successfully responding to demands, more people will more intensely expect such services from legislators, thereby further increasing legislative demand volume. If legislators consistently fail to respond to demands, then representational expectations will become less intense and demand volume will decline. Legislative performance affects elite expectations and elite performance. If elites perceive the legislature as too effective in dealing with demands contrary to their expectations, elites may take action to reduce legislative capabilities and thereby reduce their rate of success in dealing with demands. Alternatively, the record of legislative performance may alter elite expectations concerning the legislature or reinforce existing expectations. Finally, as suggested in Chapter 2, the fit between performance and expectations has consequences for the level of support accruing to the legislature and its members.

Intuitively there should be a connection between the legislature's demand-handling performance and support for the institution and its members. Successful demand performance will be congruent with representational expectations and will increase the level of support for the legislature among those who hold these expectations. But, as we have suggested, elite and mass publics might not have the same expectations and therefore successful performance in the view of mass publics may not be evaluated in the same way by elite publics.

This conflict between mass and elite expectations stems from the different values of each group. Mass publics tend to look at public policy particularistically; they are concerned with benefits and response that are immediately relevant to them and to their problems. Elites profess a greater concern with the total effect and long-range implications of policy. Because they are of higher status, their needs and demands are less immediate than those of mass publics, and they also tend to benefit from what they conceive of as rational public policy. In their view, public policy designed to incorporate the particularistic demands of interest groups and mass publics is often inefficient and irrational. Thus, as legislators strive to respond to the particularized demands they receive, they may satisfy interest groups and constituents and thereby increase their support from those precincts, while simultaneously irritating elite publics and decreasing their support from those sectors.

The situation with the more generalized demands articulated by highly organized interests may be a bit different. In most countries, executive-centered elites will establish linkages of their own with these groups and seek in one way or another to incorporate them into their own policy-making processes. Groups will view legislative representation as supplementary to their more efficacious ties with executive-centered elites. Thus, in representing organized interests legislators may not run quite as great a risk of affronting the expectations of elites.

In the next chapter we will be concerned with particularistic demands that come to the legislator from individuals or groups in his constituency—from those whom the legislator is "supposed" to represent. The generalized demands made by interest groups will be dealt with in Chapter 10. I will not deal explicitly with either generalized demands made by individual citizens or with particularistic demands that come to the legislator from individuals outside his constituency.

NOTES

1. See Mezey (1976) for an earlier formulation of these concepts.

2. Clearly the presence of alternative demand handling structures may also serve as a stimulus to demands. That is, because there are accessible and capable structures in existence, people may be encouraged to make demands that they otherwise might withhold. The validity of this point does not invalidate the argument presented in the text, if the following mathematical conditions prevail:

If x = the flow of demands toward one structure, and

If y = the increase in demands stimulated by the presence of an additional structure, and

$$\frac{(x + y)}{2} < x$$

then the addition of another structure reduces the demand flow per structure. However, if $(x + y)/2 > x$, then the argument presented in the text does become vulnerable.

Chapter 9

LEGISLATURES AND PARTICULARIZED DEMANDS

If you were asked to name the one activity that legislators are most likely to perform regardless of the country in which they serve, your best response would describe the job of receiving and dealing with particularized demands coming from constituency-based individuals and groups. Members of every type of legislature say that they are subjected to an incessant flow of such demands, and they indicate that coping with them requires a substantial portion of their time and resources. In this chapter we will be concerned with the volume and substantive content of these demands, the expectations that evoke them and cause them to be sent to legislators, the way in which legislators respond to them, and the role perceptions that legislators adopt in regard to this aspect of their work.

CONTENT

We have already divided particularized demands into two broad categories defined by whether the demands were initiated by a group or by an individual. These demands can be described further in terms of their substance, or more specifically, what the legislator is being asked to do. Some demands involve the constituency as a whole; others involve the political needs of an individual or a family; still others deal with problems that are not ordinarily considered to be political.

Protection of Constituency Interests. One category of demands asks the legislator to see to it that the actions of the central government have the effect of protecting and promoting constituency interests. Public works projects are an important part of these concerns. Every nation expends a sizable portion of its national budget on roads, airports, dams, hospitals, schools, and other projects which, in addition to improving the quality of public services, also provide employment and generally bolster the economy of the area in which the funds are spent. Legislators in both developed and less developed nations are asked to ensure that their constituencies get their share of these projects. In sub-Sahara Africa, for example, these undertakings

run the gamut from schools, health centers, cattle dips, and irrigation works to feeder roads, crop and settlement schemes, and various forms of cottage industries. Despite their limited size, projects of this type have a tangible effect on the lives of the rural population, are highly visible, and constitute the substance of most demands made by the people for government assistance to their development efforts. (Barkan, 1975:10)

And one American congressman told a researcher that "you've got to take care of the folks back home. . . . They've got to see something; it's the bread and butter issues that count—the dams, the post offices and the other public buildings, the highways. They want to know what you've been doing" (Murphy, 1968:10).

Usually, legislators are pressed for these constituency allocations by local officials, or by groups of local citizens rather than by private citizens acting individually. In the Philippines, for example, "most of the demands for local legislation come from local politicians who are under their own constituents' pressure to make a change, but do not have the power" (Franzich, 1971:144).

Even if legislators cannot deliver all the projects that their constituents would like to have, they are still asked to bring constituency problems and needs to the attention of policy makers at the national level. Colombian legislators said that this was the second most important constituency service task that they performed (Hoskin, 1971:424), and in 1970 the Yugoslavian Chamber of Nationalities was reported to have become bogged down in a "continuous deadlock concerning the criteria by which funds for economic development would be collected and dispersed. Rather than attempt to reach a mutually acceptable solution, the federal deputies positively articulated the various demands and objections of their respective regional constituencies in an unyielding manner" (Cohen, 1977:145–46).

Members of active and vulnerable legislatures are asked to do much more than simply articulate constituency needs. They are asked to use their power to help pass laws that will directly benefit the constituency. In the Philippines the load of such "local" bills was so heavy that Fridays were usually set aside exclusively for their consideration (Franzich, 1971:144), and in Chile

Congressmen could support their clients either by obtaining specific legislation or more often by amending a law, such as the budget law, to earmark resources for a particular end. Private laws providing pensions and other dispensations for individuals have always been important in the Chilean Congress. . . . At the same time, through legislation Congressmen often obtained special consideration for local governments in their *zonas*. (Valenzuela and Wilde, 1975:18)

Problems of Individual Constituents. A more substantial portion of a typical legislator's demand load consists of the problems of individuals rather than the needs of their constituency as a collectivity. Indian MPs, for example, say that about 75 percent of the problems brought to them are individual in nature compared to about 25 percent which are relevant to the entire constituency (Maheshewari, 1976: 337). Ninety-three percent of a sample of Philippine congressmen reported that individuals seeking help with personal problems came to them "very often" while only 26 percent said that groups seeking help with group problems came to them that frequently (Styskal, 1967:59). And one audit of an American congressman's casework for a year found that 86 percent of the requests involved individual cases, with group cases constituting the remaining 14 percent (Olson, 1967:341).

Expedition. A large number of the requests from individuals ask the legislator to act as an intermediary between the citizen and the government bureaucracy so that a service may be expedited, an adverse decision reversed or a positive decision evoked. Examples of this type of demand come from all types of legislatures. Canadian MPs report that the bulk of their mail was from constituents who wanted their assistance on matters such as pensions, income tax, veterans' payments, unemployment insurance payments, and passports and visas. Other correspondence asked for information such as the identity of the appropriate officials to whom complaints and questions could be addressed (Kornberg and Mishler, 1976:191).

Responding to these types of demands was mentioned as their most important service activity by 55 percent of the members of the Colombian Congress (Hoskin, 1971:424), accounted for 68 percent of the individual case load of one American congressman (Olson, 1967:341), and was an activity in which *all* Bangladeshi MPs were involved (Jahan, 1976:366). The reason why these demands are directed at legislators is suggested by these comments about deputies in Romania: "Simply put, to get any service done, and done right, one needs to 'know someone'—to 'have an in.' A deputy is for many citizens a means of avoiding bureaucratic tangles, and he (the deputy) therefore becomes a dispenser of favors, and an interlocutor" (Nelson, 1975:29).

Pensions and social security matters account for a large portion of this demand category. Austrian provincial legislators said that it was the issue that they dealt with most frequently (Crane, 1961–62:169), and British MPs say that it is the second most frequently raised issue in their meetings with constituents, or "surgeries" (Dowse, 1972:53). The situation in Chile is perhaps typical of many other countries. There, the most important type of particularistic demand "related to the complex and overburdened Chilean social security system. There simply [were] not enough resources to cover all the potential claims on the system. As a result the system would not settle a claim unless specifically forced to do so. . . . Several congressmen had a full-time secretary working only on matters related to social security" (Valenzuela and Wilde, 1975:17).

Bureaucratic Corruption. Complaints of citizens often involve corrupt bureaucrats. Members of the South Vietnamese Parliament, besieged by complaints about corrupt provincial chiefs who were appointed to their position by the executive branch, launched campaigns for the removal of the worst offenders (Goodman, 1975:185), while in India, one MP suggested that he got involved only when bribery failed to bring action: "Corruption is now regarded as but a part of life. If by greasing an official's palms the work gets done, it is no longer a grievance as such. But if even after bribing, nothing gets done, it becomes a grievance" (Maheshewari, 1976:339).

Intervention in the Judicial Process. In some countries legislators are asked to intervene with the police or the courts on behalf of constituents. In South Vietnam "groups of deputies applied varying degrees of pressure, much of it successful, to government agencies to have students, peasants, and religious leaders released from detention" (Goodman, 1975:185). Thai MPs said that their constituents asked them to help them in court cases or bail relatives out of jail (Mezey, 1972:697), and members of the Afghani Wolesi Jirgah (Weinbaum, 1977:112) and the Supreme Soviet (Juviler, 1960:149) have been reported as performing similar services. One Malaysian MP told his colleagues that he "had the unfortunate experience of having parents and relatives coming to me at all hours of the day and night and saying 'My son has been arrested, my daughter has been detained yesterday. The police say I cannot see them'" (Chu, 1974:225).

Civil Service Cases. In many countries civil servants ask legislators to intervene on their behalf in regard to promotions and transfers. One Indian MP described these demands in these terms: "The largest number of cases are for postings in or nearer the home town. Some people get superseded when promotions are made and they come to me for redressal of grievances" (Maheshewari, 1976:340). It has been reported that similar demands are made upon MLAs in the Indian states of Orissa (Mohapatra, 1971:122–23), Uttar Pradesh (Brown, 1971:254), and Himachal Pradesh (Bhatnagar and Dogra, 1973:139). These cases are not peculiar to India. Afghani legislators report similar demands (Weinbaum, 1977:112), and for at least one American congressman, one-third of his constituency case load consisted of military and civilian personnel matters (Olson, 1967:341).

Patronage. In developing countries where good-paying jobs are often very difficult to come by, legislators report that a large quantity of the demands that they receive involve requests for assistance in finding employment. In India it is the most frequently raised individual problem (Maheshewari, 1976:338), and in the Philippines, one study found that 17 percent of an adult sample had at one time or another personally asked their representative for help in getting a job. One congressman stated that his main job was "as an employment agency for the people of his district" (Franzich, 1971:148). In Costa Rica, at the time of year when the Ministry of Education assigns teachers to temporary positions that will be open for the next school year, the activity of the deputies at the ministry reaches a feverish pitch as they try to procure these positions for their constituents (Baker, 1973:235–36). In the United States congressmen still influence hirings in parts of the federal bureaucracy as well as in the Congress itself (Tacheron and Udall, 1966:87–89).

Schools and Hospitals. In some countries admission to schools and hospitals can be influenced by political pressures. Legislators in Japan (Morey, 1971:16), Thailand (Mezey, 1972:696), and Chile (Valenzuela and Wilde, 1975:17) have reported that they are asked by parents to help their children gain admission to certain schools, while legislators in Costa Rica (Baker, 1973:235) and the Philippines (Franzich, 1971:143) have been asked to help constituents get into state-run hospitals.

Private Services. Sometimes the demands that some legislators receive extend far beyond what westerners usually think of as political matters. Legislators in the Soviet Union (Juviler, 1960:138) and Singapore (Chee, 1976:436) have been asked to help find run-away husbands or wives, and Japanese legislators say that they are asked to act as go-betweens in arranging marriages (Morey, 1971:16). Indian (Maheshewari, 1976:338) and Thai (Mezey, 1972:697) legislators are regularly asked to lend or give money to constituents in need. Bangladeshi MPs distribute relief funds and are also asked to mediate private disputes among their constituents (Jahan, 1976:366–67), and in Lebanon the presence of a legislator at a funeral, wedding, or baptism in his constituency is essential for political survival (Baaklini, 1972:225).

EXPECTATIONS

In the preceding chapter I have suggested that the expectations of mass and elite publics play an important role in evoking this broad range of particularized demands that has just been described. Systematic comparative data on expectations about the legislature or indeed about political institutions generally have not been available until recently and even now this information has been generated for only a relatively small number of countries. From what has been done, however, we are able to piece together a partial picture.

Mass Expectations. Mass surveys administered in Kenya, Korea, and Turkey by the Comparative Legislative Research Center at the University of Iowa asked citizens to assess the importance of various activities performed by members of these three legislatures (Jewell and Kim, 1976a:13). The results are shown in Table 9.1, and provide an indication of the expectations that Kenyan, Turkish, and Korean citizens hold about their legislatures.

Tribune of the People. The expectation that legislators will tell the government what the people in the district think received the most "very important" designations in all three countries. This expectation also has been found to dominate the views that American voters have about their legislators. The tribune role for the legislator—defined as "discovering popular feelings and desires, defending popular interests, or advocating popular demands" (Jewell and Patterson, 1973:409)—was the legislative expectation articulated by 41 percent of a sample of 2,500 American respondents. The author of that study summarized his data in the following terms: "The tribune role is so commonly expressed that it must be interpreted as a cultural norm for legislative performance, a collective specification as to what individuals think is proper" (Davidson, 1970b:654-55).

One study of the perceptions of Tanzanian citizens concerning the role of their MPs also found evidence of the tribune expectation. When asked what their MP should do in a situation where the central government had a different view of an issue than the people in the respondent's constituency, 79 percent indicated that the MP should try to explain the requests of the people in his constituency to the government, while only 17 percent indicated that he should agree with the government (Barkan, 1975:23).

Thus, evidence has been found of tribune role expectations among the citizenries of two countries with marginal legislatures, one coun-

TABLE 9.1
Comparative Expectations: Kenya, Korea, and Turkey

	Percent saying activity is "very important"		
Legislators should	Korea	Kenya	Turkey
Explain government policies	35	68	18
Tell government what people in the district think	52	84	46
Obtain projects and benefits for the district	41	79	46
Help constituents who have personal problems with the government	40	68	21
Help solve conflicts in the community	25	55	21
N=	(2,274)	(4,128)	(2,007)

try with an active legislature, one with a reactive legislature, and one country with a minimal legislature.

Pork Barrel Projects. The Korean-Kenyan-Turkish data also indicate the strength of the expectation that legislators will work to obtain projects and benefits for the district, an expectation that is second in salience only to the aforementioned tribune expectation. Studies that asked citizens of two constituencies in the Philippines to identify the criteria they used in deciding who to vote for in congressional elections provide an indication of mass expectations in that country; not surprisingly, the procurement of pork-barrel projects was the most frequently mentioned criterion in one constituency and the second most frequently mentioned in the other (Franzich, 1971:157).

Intervention. Although articulating popular wishes and bringing home the pork are accorded the highest priority by the Korean, Turkish, and Kenyan respondents, a substantial percentage also expect their legislators to intervene on their behalf with government agencies and to help solve community problems. Indirect evidence of this mass expectation among French voters is provided by a recent survey of French MPs, 66 percent of whom perceived a difference between the way they viewed their jobs and the way in which the voters saw the legislative task. Of those deputies who mentioned this perceptual difference, 64 percent went on to say that the problem was that the voters were primarily concerned with local problems and the deputy's role as an intermediary. Members used such terms as "social worker," "solicitor," "servant," and "valet," to describe the role in which they were cast by their constituents (Cayrol et al., 1976:74–76). While the cultural as well as the geographical distance between France and Afghanistan may be sizable, differences in mass expectations concerning the legislator seem minor. There, individuals who want to approach agents of the central government are expected to seek the intercession of powerful people. Thus, legislators in Afghanistan "are accustomed to requests to intercede where constituents have run afoul of the law or to help settle family quarrels." The legislator is also "expected to treat petitioners cordially and, where called for, to extend his hospitality by offering food and temporary lodgings. Legislators are prepared to find constituents camped in their courtyard or their business establishment, and to be accosted in any public place" (Weinbaum, 1977:111).

A Delegate. Another expectation looked at in Korea and in Tanzania, as well, concerned mass views of the importance to be accorded constituents' opinions when a legislator has a decision to make. In all three countries citizens articulated delegate expectations, indicating that the views of the constituency should be more important than any other factor. It was assessed as "very important" by 59 percent of the Korean respondents (Kim and Loewenberg, 1976:380) and by 83 percent of the Kenyan respondents (Barkan, 1975:23); 88 percent of the respondents in a Tanzanian survey said that if an MP's ideas differed from the ideas of his constituents, he should vote according to the views of the people in his constituency (Barkan, 1975:23).

The Mail. Another rough indicator of mass expectations is the volume and content of mail that legislators receive. In Canada 80 percent of a sample of MPs interviewed said they received a large volume of mail each week from their constituents. In addition, 84 percent reported receiving telephone calls and 53 percent said they were visited in their parliamentary offices or when they returned to their districts. Most of the mail requested services that involved the MP as an intermediary between the citizen and the bureaucracy (Kornberg and Mishler, 1976:191). Half of a sample of British MPs reported receiving more than fifty letters a week from their constituents, with about 9 percent reporting one hundred letters or more a week (Barker and Rush, 1970:174). Mail to American congressmen is subject to great variation, but one congressman from a geographically large area reported receiving an average of two hundred letters a day (Tacheron and Udall, 1966:61), and in 1963 one United States senator from a moderately large state reported receiving between eight hundred and a thousand letters a day (Jewell and Patterson, 1973:361). Finally, about one-third of a small sample of Indian legislators reported receiving more than five hundred letters a month (Maheshewari, 1976:344).

Expectations of Institutional Elites. As suggested in the last chapter, the expectations of executive-centered elites may have a greater impact on the legislature than the expectations of mass publics. In minimal legislatures particularly the representational activities of legislators may be viewed as exclusively the product of these elite expectations.

In the Soviet Union, for example, dealing with citizen grievances "is increasingly a major task of the individual Supreme Soviet deputy" (Vanneman, 1972:247). As early as 1938 statements made in the Supreme Soviet officially urged the deputy "to adopt measures through local and central state and public organs designed to clear up matters raised by his constituents" (Juviler, 1960:136). According to one source by the late 1950s there had been enough reported examples of this type of deputy activity "to make people who read the central press expect help from their Supreme Soviet deputy" (Juviler, 1960:157). By 1967 the deputies had been given statutory authority to conduct on-the-spot studies on their own initiative and a 1968 decree by the Presidium of the Supreme Soviet required that ministries "reply to a deputy's inquiry within one month and inform the deputy in person as to what action had been taken to remedy the alleged grievance" (Vanneman, 1972:247). However, legislators were still required to accept the premise that the interests of their constituency in terms of public works projects must defer "to projects with a higher priority which are centrally determined" (Juviler, 1960:139).

In Yugoslavia representational activities are both encouraged and tempered by the Federal Assembly's Rules of Procedures, which "require that the federal deputy follow events in his district, inform his constituents, and carry requests from the local level to the assembly, but that in doing so he can also present his own opinions and take a stand on these matters accordingly" (Cohen, 1977:139). Similarly, in Singapore and in Mexico legislators are encouraged to maintain contact with their constituents both to assist the government and to represent constituency grievances. In Singapore the Peoples Action party requires legislators to attend weekly "Meet-the-People" sessions and reprimands those legislators whose attendance is irregular (Chee, 1976:436), while in Mexico, some legislators claim that those deputies who do not attend to the requests of their constituents are not advanced by the party hierarchy as quickly as those who do (de la Garza, 1972:97).

In countries with supported legislatures elites appear to accept the legitimacy of legislative representational activities. Kornberg and Mishler (1976:201) report that Canadian bureaucrats do what they can to facilitate MP efforts to assist constituents with their problems. Agencies of the American bureaucracy have entire offices with large staffs devoted exclusively to the task of dealing with citizen complaints brought to them by legislators (Fiorina, 1977:67–70). For nonsupported legislatures the situation is different; bureaucrats are not as accommodating, as indicated by this blunt statement of an Italian bureaucrat about his interaction with deputies who are not members of the Christian Democratic party: "We find little need to pay attention to the demands or the threats of the other political parties, or their representatives, or their deputies, or their senators" (LaPalombara, 1964:319).

Comparative data on bureaucratic attitudes provide further evidence that in those countries with less-supported legislatures bureaucrats are less tolerant of the representational activities of the parliament than are bureaucrats in countries with more-supported legislatures. One study reported on the attitudes of bureaucrats in Britain, Germany, and Italy. Responses to four questions as summarized in Table 9.2 show that compared with bureaucrats in Britain and Germany, Italian bureaucrats are less tolerant of intervention by politicians in their affairs, more concerned about technical than politi-

TABLE 9.2

Comparative Political Values of Bureaucrats:
Britain, Germany and Italy

	Percent agreeing, or agreeing with reservations		
Question	British (N=129)	German (N=134)	Italian (N=102)
The interference of politicians in affairs which are properly the business of civil servants is a disturbing feature of contemporary public life.	9	43	83
In contemporary social and economic affairs it is essential that technical considerations be given more weight than political factors.	22	49	77
Although parties play an important role in a democracy, often they uselessly exacerbate political conflicts.	53	30	85
In a world as complicated as the modern one it doesn't make sense to speak of increased control by ordinary citizens over governmental affairs.	44	38	63

cal factors, more willing to see political parties as a source of useless political conflicts, and less tolerant of citizen control over governmental affairs (Putnam, 1972:15, 21). Data such as these demonstrate the comparatively low level of support that the vulnerable Italian legislature has from the Italian bureaucratic elite and suggest the reasons why many deputies are less than successful in their dealings with the bureaucracy.

Members of marginal legislatures are frequently caught between the representational expectations of their constituents and the system maintenance expectations of elites. Kenyan and Korean legislators have been urged by their leaders to explain the government's positions to their constituents and generate support for government programs, but as the data in Table 9.1 indicate, these expectations have a very low priority for mass publics. In South America it has been suggested that the representational activities of Brazilian (Astiz, 1973a) and Chilean (Valenzuela and Wilde, 1975) legislators run counter to the development views and thus the legislative expectations of the technocratic elites who now dominate these countries. And in Iran the deputy's "relationships with the Shah and with the elite are the ones which are most significant" (Schulz, 1969:48).

ROLE PERCEPTIONS

The expectations of mass and elite publics should have a marked effect on the role perceptions of legislators—their ideas of what they should be doing. Before looking more closely at the role perceptions relevant to representational activities, a few preliminary words are in order about role analysis.

During the last twenty years students of legislative behavior have devoted considerable energy to the analysis of legislative role perceptions. One major problem with this work is that research designs for role studies have been heavily influenced by the role orientation categories originally developed by Wahlke et al. (1962). These categories were quite useful for Wahlke and his colleagues but have proved to be less relevant to some kinds of legislative behavior than to others, and less relevant to some types of legislatures than to others. Some researchers, appreciating that fact, have developed different categories that were more appropriate for their research, but they paid a price for such innovations in terms of lack of comparability between their findings and other work using other categories. All of this has led to serious questions about the utility of role analysis for cross-national research. That is unfortunate because the essence of the concept—that how political actors perceive their jobs is important data for understanding behavior—is as accurate today as it was when role analysis was first used in legislative research.

The problem is most apparent in the case of representational role perceptions. When they introduced this concept, Wahlke and his associates were interested in the extent to which legislators felt bound by the views of their constituents when they were deciding upon public policies. They suggested that a "delegate" would attempt to reflect faithfully the views of his constituency, that a "trustee" would adopt the Burkean view and follow his conscience alone, and that a "politico" would attempt to combine both orientations. Researchers have searched for these role perceptions in several legislative settings; some of their findings are summarized in Table 9.3.

What are we to make of these data? Are we to assume that because trustees outnumber delegates in all of these legislatures except the Japanese Prefectual Assemblies, the Canadian House of Commons, and the Korean *Kukhoe*, that legislators are flouting the mass expectation that they represent and defend the interests of their constituents? Not at all, because we must recall that the classification scheme is based upon responses to questions asking how important constituency views were in helping legislators to decide about policy, and not on questions about whether or not legislators felt an obligation to represent their constituencies by securing public works projects or by articulating constituency needs, or by assisting constituents who need help with the government.

Orientations such as these are found by asking legislators what they do with their time, and not how they make up their minds. When these purposive questions are asked, role orientations emerge that are quite congruent with the representational expectations of mass publics. Thus, sample surveys of members of the United States Congress, the Kenyan Parliament, the Thai National Assembly, and the Colombian Congress found substantial numbers of legislators who perceived their role as defending or articulating the interests of the people. These findings concerning the tribune role are summarized in Table 9.4. Generally, the tribune role orientation is the most frequently mentioned after the obvious ritualist orientation. Thus it appears that

TABLE 9.3
Comparative Representative Role Perceptions

Country (Source)	Type of Legislature	N	Trustee (%)	Politico (%)	Delegate (%)
United States House of Representatives (Davidson, 1969:117)	Active	87	28	46	23
American state legislatures (Wahlke et al. 1962:291)	Active	283	63	23	14
Philippine House of Representatives (Franzich, 1971:266)	Vulnerable	40	20[a]	0	12
Japanese House of Representatives (Morey, 1971:4–5)	Reactive	40	80	7	13
Japanese Provincial Assemblies (Kim, 1973:403)	Reactive	193	38	26	57
Canadian House of Commons (Kornberg, 1967:108)	Reactive	165	15	36	49
Indian Uttar Pradesh Legislative Assembly (Brown, 1971:656)	Reactive	162	46	30	24
Belgium (Loewenberg and Kim, 1976:8)	Reactive	125	60	0[b]	40
Switzerland (Loewenberg and Kim, 1976:8)	Reactive	191	75	0[b]	25
Turkey (Loewenberg and Kim, 1976:8)	Reactive	101	52	0[b]	48
Colombian House of Representatives (Hoskin, 1971:428)	Marginal	219	28	52	20
Korean National Assembly (Kim and Woo, 1975:264)	Marginal	112	22	0[b]	78
Kenya (James, 1972:25)	Marginal	46	54	0[b]	32

a. Franzich (1971:267) believes that his large "no response" category should be included in the trustee column.
b. The politico role orientation was not used in these studies.

even though trustees and politicos far outnumber delegates in these countries, legislators nonetheless consider the representation of constituency interests an important part of their job.

Other studies have also uncovered an explicit orientation toward constituency service functions in a number of legislatures and these are summarized in Table 9.5. In addition, some legislators have indicated that they perceive their role primarily in terms of getting public works projects and other improvements for their constituencies. In Kenya 44 percent of a sample of MPs said that they found the greatest job satisfaction in promoting the economic development of their constituencies (James, 1972:21) and 16 percent of a sample of Tanzanian MPs indicated that promoting the constituency was the most important aspect of their role (Hopkins, 1971b:167).

Even in those legislatures where systematic surveys of role perceptions have not been done, there is evidence of the constituency service orientation among legislators. The French deputy during the Fifth Republic has been described as "a lawyer with a monthly salary, an interpreter, an indefatigable broker . . . and also an extremely busy and often the most efficient social worker in his department" (Ehrmann, 1971:292). A survey of British MPs found that 39 percent derived "a great deal of personal satisfaction" out of their constituency work and found it the most valuable part of what they did; 60 percent welcomed, or accepted, or expected the role of welfare officer, while only 12 percent said that the role had been taken too far (Barker and Rush, 1970:192).

Another indicator of this role perception is the amount of time that members devote to this type of activity. This measure has to be treated carefully, however, because it discriminates against members of active and vulnerable legislatures who necessarily spend a great deal of their time on legislative matters and in favor of members of legislatures in which policy making is not as salient and who consequently have more time available to devote to constituency service. Thus, members of the United States Congress report spending about 28 percent of their average work week on constituency service compared to 65 percent on legislative work; however, their staff members spend 65 percent of *their* time on constituency related services and only 14 percent of their time on supporting the representative's legislative activities (Saloma, 1969:184–85). Similarly, only three of twenty-four Costa Rican deputies responding to a questionnaire indicated that they spent more time on constituency work than on legislative tasks even though most viewed the service function as their primary role (Baker, 1973:236).

TABLE 9.4
Tribune Role Orientations: Selected Legislatures

Legislature (Source)	Type	Percent Mentioning Tribune Orientation	Salience of Tribune Orientation
United States House (Davidson, 1969:80)	Active	40	First
Colombian Congress (Hoskin, 1971:418)	Marginal	27	Second to "ritualist"
Thailand National Assembly (Mezey, 1972:695)	Marginal	37	Third to ritualist and overseer
Kenya (James, 1972:24)	Marginal	75	First

TABLE 9.5
Service Role Orientations: Selected Legislatures

Legislature (Source)	Type	Orientation and Percent Mentioning It
Philippines (Franzich, 1971:256)	Vulnerable	*Service*, mentioned by 62% of sample
Orissa State Legislature (India) (Mohapatra, 1971)	Reactive	*Intervener*, mentioned by 82% of sample
Uttar Pradesh State Legislature (India) (Brown, 1971:692)	Reactive	*Servitor*, mentioned by 65% of sample
Himchal Pradesh State Legislature (India) (Bhatnagar and Dogra, 1973)	Reactive	82% of sample support the view that members should help their constituency
Mexico (de la Garza, 1972:89)	Reactive	14 of 23 PRI deputies defined their role primarily or secondarily as petitioners for constituents
Thailand (Mezey, 1972:695)	Marginal	43% of sample say they should oversee the government
South Vietnam (Goodman, 1975:172)	Marginal	31% of a sample classified as service oriented

Estimates of time spent on constituency work tend to be higher among members of reactive legislatures. Thus, a survey of a sample of British MPs revealed that 26 percent of the respondents spent more than two hours a day on constituency service activities, with an additional 37 percent spending between one and a half and two hours a day (Barker and Rush, 1970:190). Of a sample of members of Canadian provincial legislatures, 41 percent reported spending 26 to 50 percent of their time on constituency problems, and 31 percent reported spending 51 to 75 percent of their time on these matters (Clarke, Price, and Krause, 1975:530). And 16 percent of a sample of Austrian Provincial legislators indicated that constituency service work was "practically all I do" while an additional 68 percent said that such tasks took up "much" of their time (Crane, 1961–62:168).

In contrast, in those countries where elite expectations are not supportive of legislative representational activities, legislators spend very little time on these activities. In Korea 69 percent of a sample of legislators report spending little of their time interceding with the government on behalf of their constituents, while 72 percent say that they make no more than one visit to their district each month (Kim and Pai, 1976:18). In Zambia the government has coopted its MPs and thus has reduced their ability and their willingness to deal with constituency demands. The bureaucracy is a good deal more immediate to the people in the constituency than the legislator who is obliged to visit his district only four times a year. Not surprisingly demand volume is quite low and "very few MPs claim to receive more than a handful of requests for favors from constituents each year" (Hakes and Helgerson, 1973:342–47). Similarly, in Iran, the deputy's relationship with the Shah and his associates is crucial and provides a "disincentive to the deputy who might attempt to communicate with his constituents." (Schulz, 1969:48). And in Tanzania the inclination of legislators to view their job as representing their constituency is significantly tempered by the stronger elite expectations that the legislator will not publicly disagree with the party (Kjekshus, 1974:32).

REINFORCEMENT OF EXPECTATIONS

The impact of expectations on role perceptions is reinforced by sanctions, or, to speak more positively, inducements that favor congruence between expectations and the perceptions of those who are the objects of those expectations. In the case of legislators the most effective inducement has to do with continued tenure in office, which means quite simply that unless legislators do what is expected of them, they will be voted out at the next election.

There is evidence that legislators from all of our five types of legislatures know or think that their continuance in office is contingent on their satisfactory performance of representational activities. One member of the Public Works Committee of the United States House of Representatives put it this way: "If you're going to stay around here, you've got to take care of the folks back home—and, if you're not, you don't belong here—you're supposed to be representing them and if you don't somebody else will" (Murphy, 1968:10). One student of the Congress has argued that all American legislators feel the need to do things for their constituents in order to aid their reelection campaigns and that it doesn't even make much difference if a congressman is from a safe or a competitive district; the only thing that a safe district implies is that constituency efforts are very likely to be rewarded by reelection (Mayhew, 1974:37). Some congressmen keep a running list of people to whom they have rendered assistance so that they can call upon them for help during the campaign. An aide to one senator reports that these people are much more likely to volunteer campaign assistance than the average citizen (Olson, 1967:327). In Costa Rica, where there is another active legislature, the parties expect their deputies to maintain their popularity among their constituents and, in the view of one student of that legislature, a deputy "courts disaster" when he loses contact with his constituency (Baker, 1973:240–41).

In the Philippines legislators perceive their reelection opportunities as closely related to their representational activities. Part of this is rooted in the patron-client system which characterizes Philippine political and social relations and which suggests that votes are given in direct exchange for favors (Franzich, 1971:125; Grossholtz, 1964:97). In this cultural context it is not surprising that when a sample of congressmen were asked what a potential candidate should do to line up the political support necessary for election, the most frequently mentioned responses after the obvious "get oneself well known" were "be of service to the constituency" and "do personal favors." When asked to indicate the reason why they themselves won their last election, the first reason given by 57 percent of the respondents was their demonstrated ability or their future promises to bring public works and other benefits to the district; the next most favored response, mentioned first by 23 percent of the respondents, was past personal favors for constituents (Franzich, 1971:153, 155).

The accuracy of these perceptions was demonstrated in an analysis that divided thirty-three legislators into a group with a high success rate in passing local bills and a group with a low success rate; 58 percent of those with a high success rate but only 29 percent of those with a low success rate were reelected. When the same sample was divided into a group whose constituencies had received a relatively high public works allocation and a group whose constituencies had received a low allocation, the more successful group had 67 percent of its members reelected, while the less successful group had a reelection percentage of 44 percent (Franzich, 1971:377, 379).

In the Philippines and in the United States as well the effect of pork barrel success on reelection chances is so clear to legislators that they make certain that they can claim credit for any and all local improvements (Mayhew, 1974:52; Franzich, 1971:146). In reactive legislatures such as the British Parliament, where the legislator's reelection chances are tied quite closely to the fortunes of his party, constituency service should not have such a pronounced effect on reelection chances. Thus, most MPs in one sample indicated that they didn't think the surgeries that they held in their constituencies won them votes (Dowse, 1972:51). However, another study of instances in which MPs were not renominated by their constituency organizations attributed the second largest number of such cases to the MP's neglect of constituency duties (Dickson, 1975).

The situation in marginal legislatures is similar to that in active and vulnerable legislatures. Again, the legislator is very much on his own in election campaigns and his constituency record is likely to influence the outcome. In one analysis of the attitudes of South Vietnamese deputies, many of the legislators thought that their constituency activities would hinder their reelection chances because the people would expect more of them than they could be reasonably expected to deliver. But these opinions were inaccurate. The same study indicated that deputies who were service oriented were reelected at the rate of 41 percent whereas only 23 percent of their nonservice-oriented colleagues were reelected (Goodman, 1975:194).

In Kenya, another marginal legislature, the defeat in the 1969 election of 60 percent of the incumbents who ran for reelection has been attributed to their poor performance in securing government services for the constituency: "Here, the past record of incumbents tended to tell against them because they had not been able to secure enough benefits either from lack of influence or because they had not tried hard enough" (Hyden and Leys, 1972:401). In Kenya, as in the Philippines, there is a strong strain of clientelism which encourages legislators to seek votes through promises of postelection favors (Hopkins, 1975a:212). Some legislators have adopted an entrepreneurial role, "mobilizing the resources of the constituency for community development projects on the one hand, and extracting resources from the central government for these projects on the other" (Barkan, 1975:10). The legislator who performs this task successfully can establish his own personal political machine as he builds up a contingent of clients for whom he has performed favors either collectively through public works projects or individually through personal services. One analysis of the 1969–71 Thai legislative experience suggests that legislators there made a similar attempt to build their own local political bases by manipulating development funds, an activity that was ended by military coup (Morell, 1975:37).

The electoral system might have an intervening effect on the capacity to apply electoral sanctions to legislators. Hoskin (1970:414) suggests that the demand load of Colombian legislators, although accelerated by a patron-client system, is to some extent mitigated by a proportional representation system which insulates legislators from some constituency pressures. But in Lebanon the proportional system appears not to have had this effect. There, the "successful candidate remains the one who has maintained close relationships with his constituency and has delivered enough personal services to the influential members of the various villages" (Baaklini, 1972: 222–23).

Finally, there is evidence from two minimal legislatures that despite the overwhelming effect of elite expectations, constituency performance constitutes a significant variable in determining whether or not a legislator will continue in office. In the Soviet Union the party determines who will be allowed to seek reelection to the Supreme Soviet, but there is an indication that at least some popularity among one's constituents is considered desirable by the party leaders who make these decisions (Juviler, 1960:157–58). In Yugoslavia electoral sanctions held by constituencies reportedly do put deputies under some pressures:

As delegated representatives of their republics and provinces whose future political careers increasingly hinged on the goodwill of local and regional elites, the deputies in the Chamber of Nationalities were under considerable pressure to follow the direction of their regional constituencies in formulating federal legislation. Any deputy who failed to comply with such instructions faced personal ostracism in his native region and possible recall from office (Cohen, 1977:142).

However, in minimal legislature systems and in some marginal systems, the satisfaction of elite expectations is more important for continued tenure in office than the satisfaction of mass expectations. In Iran, for example, "loyalty to the Shah is the first [criterion] for nomination, rather than loyalty to constituents. Furthermore, the rapidity with which the Shah breaks down the independent power bases of other politicians offers a disincentive to the deputy who might attempt to communicate with his constituents—be they interest groups or electoral constituents" (Schulz, 1969:48). Similarly, in Tanzania opposition to decisions of the National Executive Committee of TANU is grounds for expulsion from the party and thus from the Parliament, so there are strong "electoral" inducements to sacrifice the interests of constituents to those of the party (Hopkins, 1975b; Kjekshus, 1974:32).

ACCESSIBILITY

One indication that a legislator is responding to the representational expectation of mass publics is when he takes steps to increase his accessibility beyond what would normally be expected of him. One technique is to hold regular office hours in the constituency so that citizens can have the opportunity to speak privately with their representative about their problems. Approximately 90 percent of the British MPs hold these "surgeries," most at least once a month and many as frequently as once every two weeks (Barker and Rush, 1970:182–83). In West Germany such sessions are more likely to be held by rural than by urban members (Loewenberg, 1967:427) while only 19 percent of a sample of Canadian MPs reported holding such meetings (Kornberg and Mishler, 1976:192).

In at least two minimal legislature systems—the Soviet Union and Singapore—the governing party mandates regularized contacts between legislators and their constituents. The People's Action party requires its legislators to attend the weekly "meet the people" sessions, (Chee, 1976:436) while Soviet MPs are encouraged to meet their constituents at their places of work (Juviler, 1960:136).

In contrast, research on Kenya has suggested that many legislators try to avoid seeing their constituents despite the invocations of party leaders. By reducing accessibility they hope to reduce demand volume. As one observer put it: "The assumption that a problem can be solved if only it can be presented to the MP is not challengeable if it cannot be tested. Hence, limiting accessibility has become important, and this has reinforced the distance between the political elite and the average Kenyan" (Hopkins, 1975a:216). This assertion appears to be supported by the data. Interviews with more than eight hundred citizens living in four constituencies revealed that 56 percent had not seen their MP within the last six months, while another 15 percent had seen him once. Local elites fared somewhat better; 47 percent reported seeing their MP "many times" during the six-month period (Barkan and Okumu, 1974:18). A parallel survey of MPs showed that many legislators did little to increase their visibility. Only about half attended public meetings once or twice a month, and 8 percent reported maintaining an office in their constituency. However, most reported that they were available to see constituents at their homes (Barkan and Okumu, 1974:20).

The effect of any action directed toward increasing accessibility is felt most heavily by those in society who are least likely to initiate contacts with their MPs. A study of British MPs concludes that "writing to one's MP is primarily a middle-class custom and that working class people write only under grave provocation, preferring if possible to visit the Member's surgery" (Barker and Rush, 1970:176). Of the Conservative MPs questioned about their surgeries, 48 percent were of the opinion that they were attended primarily by working class people, a view shared by 89 percent of the Labour MPs (Dowse, 1972:54).

Thus, when legislators take steps to increase their accessibility, they are making themselves more available to mass demands; demands of middle and upper-class people and of governmental elites will reach them regardless of what they do.

ALTERNATIVE STRUCTURES

In addition to the representational expectations of mass and elite publics, the role perceptions of legislators, and the accessibility of the legislature, legislative demand volume can be affected by the performance of nonlegislative structures. For example, an inefficient, corrupt, or nonresponsive bureaucracy can cause citizens to develop grievances against bureaucrats that they then bring to their legislators. Alternatively, accessible and capable local government institutions can reduce the demand volume of legislators by dealing with demands before they reach the national level.

In two countries with vulnerable legislatures—the Philippines and Italy—and in two countries with marginal legislatures—Kenya and Thailand—and in the case of the reactive Fifth Republic Parliament, there is evidence that these two factors combine to further increase rather than to reduce a heavy load of particularized demands.

The failures of the bureaucracy are suggested by public opinion analyses that show that only 42 percent of the Philippine respondents and 53 percent of the Italian respondents expected equal treatment from their government, compared with figures of 65 percent for Germany and 83 percent for the United States and the United Kingdom (Franzich, 1971:117–18; Almond and Verba, 1963:70). In France the bureaucracy has been described as "closed" and "isolated" and as characterized by an "intense dislike for all outsiders of whatever social origin" (Ehrmann, 1971:151). All three countries are also highly centralized. In the Philippines the most minor decisions such as changing a village boundary or renaming a school had to go through the Congress (Franzich, 1971:144) and in Italy 51 percent of a sample of 400 legislative proposals were classified as "microsectional" by a panel of judges (DiPalma, 1977:84). In France local government institutions are quite weak and final authority in just about all matters rests with the local prefect and his superiors in Paris (Ehrmann, 1971:84).

Similarly in Kenya and Thailand, legislators have attested to an overwhelming volume of particularized demands and have complained that their constituents expect more from their MP than he is able to deliver (Barkan and Okumu, 1974:12; Mezey, 1972:696). In Kenya bureaucrats are usually strangers in the province and legislators "are likely to be accorded a higher tenet of trust by the residents of the rural areas than that accorded civil servants and others trying to penetrate these areas from the outside" (Barkan, 1975:9). In Thailand a large proportion of particularized demands are a product of a notoriously nonresponsive and corrupt bureaucracy. In fact, the existence of the legislature give citizens "a chance to safely persist in pressing their complaint [and] the temerity to pursue their grievances through the traditional channels of Government" (Morell, 1972:641).

In contrast to these five countries, the West German legislator receives a comparatively low volume of constituency requests, partly because the German citizen seems to feel relatively efficacious in dealing with administrative organs (Almond and Verba, 1963:218, 225–27) and partly because he "is inclined to look to local government officials rather than to his Member of Parliament for a redress of grievances" (Loewenberg, 1967:427).

In India decentralization appears to reduce but certainly does not eliminate the flow of particularistic demands to national legislators. Much of the authority over local development projects in India is in the hands of the state governments and this, combined with the local visibility of the legislative assembly members and the general nonresponsiveness of the bureaucracy (Mohapatra, 1971:129–30) makes for such a heavy demand load that the conscientious MLA must devote nearly all of his time to dealing with these demands (Sisson and Shrader, 1976:25). Still, members of the national Lok Sabha "are approached by villagers for tube wells, road, irrigation projects and other local needs, even though these things can be obtained only through the state government" (Weiner, 1962:16). One researcher asked a sample of Indian MPs to list the types of demands that were put to them by constituents in order of frequency. Eleven members received "communal" demands most frequently, 149 members said subjects of state and local concern, and only 24 reported receiving national demands most frequently (Hart, 1971:136). In addition, Question Period in the Lok Sabha is heavily dominated by issues of constituency concern (Berry, 1971:100). Nonetheless the MLA is more involved with his constituency as this statement by an MP who previously served as an MLA suggests:

I was much more effective—and happy—when I was an MLA. The ordinary citizen has his problems which demand state action, not central action. As an MP, I can't give as much time to my constituency as I did when I was a state legislator. The population of my constituency is nearly 10 lakhs and it is a sprawling one. The central government is a remote entity so far as the problems of the ordinary citizens are concerned (Maheshewari, 1976: 336–37).

PERFORMANCE

Although the relationship is far from perfect and hard comparable data are simply unavailable for most political systems, there does appear to be a tendency for the heaviest volume of demands to be associated with the least supported legislatures. Thus vulnerable legislatures such as those in the Philippines and Italy, and marginal legislatures such as the Kenyan and Thai parliaments are characterized by an extremely heavy demand load. However, demand volume is also high for the active American Congress, for the reactive legislatures in Mexico (de la Garza, 1972:88), India, and France, and for the minimal legislature in the Soviet Union. The difference appears to be that members of the more supported legislatures seem to manage their demand load effectively while the burden of dealing with demands appears to be more onerous and less manageable in the less supported systems. This raises the final question with which we will be concerned in this chapter: how our different legislatures perform in response to particularistic demands.

Legislative Capability and Performance. Legislative performance in response to constituency demands can involve activities that are performed within the legislature as well as activities that take place outside of parliamentary arenas. The techniques that are used and the way in which they are used are heavily influenced by the policy-making capabilities of the legislature. Because their legislatures have a significant policy-making role, members of active and vulnerable legislatures have been able to protect and advance the interests of their constituents by incorporating their needs into legislation. They can also use less formal processes involving personal interaction with bureaucrats and constituents outside the parliamentary arenas. Members of reactive, marginal, and minimal legislatures must rely almost exclusively on these less formal and more personalized techniques as they seek to deal with particularized demands because their institutions are not capable of having a continuous and significant impact on the shape of public policy.

In the United States Congress much of the legislation passed is relevant to the particularistic demands of a variety of legislative constituencies. Public works bills, for example, provide funding for construction projects all over the country, and legislators contest and bargain in order to ensure that their districts get their fair share (Ferejohn, 1974). Farm bills group subsidies for many different crops into one omnibus bill so that a majority coalition is created out of the individual crop interests of different states and districts. Appropriations to the Department of Interior provide funding for reclamation projects to be carried out throughout the country, and the military appropriations bill provides funding for military construction and weapons purchases which affect the economy of every state and almost every congressional district in the country. In addition, Congress, as a matter of courtesy, passes thousands of individual relief bills a year granting citizenship or providing relief from other laws or regulations for individual citizens. Tax legislation frequently includes sections so artfully written that they apply to only one individual or company that the legislature wishes to relieve of a tax obligation. The list of examples is limitless; the point is that a legislature like the United States Congress, which writes its own legislation in its own committees and can amend all legislation on the floor at will, can protect and advance constituency interests by seeing to it that those interests are incorporated in general legislation.

The same can be said for vulnerable legislatures. In Chile private laws providing pensions and other dispensations for individuals accounted for more than 55 percent of the total of all laws passed between 1959 and 1968 (Hughes, 1971:66). Legislative amendments to the budget law could not provide for increases in expenditures beyond what had been requested by the president, but legislators saw to it "that money allotted for a particular line item in the budget would be destined to their own particular projects," and bureaucrats could be pressured into responding to the needs of a legislator's constituency by threats to reduce the appropriations for the agency involved (Valenzuela and Wilde, 1975:27). In the Philippines the budgetary allocations for public works were separated from the rest of the appropriations. Since the practice began in 1922, separate lists were kept for the House and Senate "with the party caucuses dividing the total amount available for individuals, each majority party member receiving a larger figure than his minority party counterpart, and with some variation within each group. Individuals in leadership positions in each chamber received appropriations significantly larger than rank-and-file members" (Stauffer, 1975:15). Also, like the American and Chilean Congresses, the Philippine Congress passed numerous local bills relevant to particularized problems in individual constituencies. In the House 63 percent of all bills introduced in 1970 were particularistic while in the Senate, elected at large, the figure was 20 percent (Stauffer, 1975:13).

Members of these legislatures may also use informal negotiations with executive elites to resolve constituency demands. Members of the United States Congress and their aides write or telephone responsible bureaucrats seeking solutions to the problems of individual constituents as well as benefits for the entire constituency. Administrators are obviously influenced by the fact that the legislator, as a member of the branch of government with control over the agency's budget, has the power to back his requests with political muscle. Similarly, legislative contacts with agencies on behalf of individual citizens with grievances are likely to be successful because the agencies are aware of the legislator's capacities to make things difficult for the agency involved.

In Chile legislators seeking assistance from bureaucrats were often quick to remind them that legislative support could help advance a civil servant's career (Valenzuela and Wilde, 1975:30). Because the bureaucracy and ultimately the president in Chile, the Philippines, and the United States has something to say about whether or not funds will be spent, legislators have devoted a great deal of time to bargaining with the executive so that pork barrel funds will be dispensed to their districts (Stauffer, 1975:15–16; Valenzuela and Wilde, 1975:22–28).

In reactive legislatures the resolution of constituency demands is less likely to involve the formal legislative process and more likely to be characterized by public or private negotiations or interactions between legislators and executive-centered elites. Legislators write letters to bureaucrats, call them on the telephone, see them in their office, and otherwise attempt to place constituency problems before them. In the case of the Austrian state legislators interviewed by Crane (1961–62:169) 80 percent said that these efforts were usually successful. Kornberg and Mishler (1976:189) report that 21 percent of the Canadian MPs that they interviewed had not been successful in their contacts with cabinet ministers, while 27 percent had failed in their contacts with deputy-ministers or parliamentary secretaries. The remainder called the results of their work successful.

As indicated in Chapter 5, in Britain and West Germany question period is frequently used to raise issues of special concern to the constituency of the legislator initiating the question. Matters of collective concern to the constituency such as roads, hospitals, and schools are brought up (Rose, 1972:106–7; Loewenberg, 1967:412) rather than issues of immediate concern to individual constituents. When a sample of British MPs was asked how frequently an individual problem raised with them during their surgeries led to a question on the floor of the House, 30 percent replied "never" and 49 percent said rarely, which meant less than ten times during the previous two years (Dowse, 1972:56). MPs apparently deal with most of their constituency casework by using a fairly standardized form to correspond with the appropriate ministry. Ministers can be expected to reply, often in detail, and then the MP simply forwards the reply on to the constituent, saying in effect, "I have taken up your complaint with the minister and this is his reply." One former minister insisted in an interview that "for the great majority of cases, the Minister is forced by modern conventions to appear to help the Member to go through the motions of taking up a case with the Government and thus impressing his constituents" (Barker and Rush, 1970:203). On the other hand, there are certainly instances in which the intervention of an MP is much more than a formality and results in genuine alterations in bureaucratic behavior leading to a redress of a constituent's grievance (Leonard and Herman, 1972:61–73).

In India a sizable percentage of MPs prefer writing to the relevant minister on behalf of their constituents, feeling that the minister is more likely to take a written communication seriously (Maheshewari, 1976:347). At the state level members prefer private contacts with responsible administrators to questions as a means of resolving constituency problems. Only one of forty-five MLAs interviewed in Himachal Pradesh indicated that they would deal with a constituent's request by raising the issue on the floor of the House (Bhatnagar and Dogra, 1973:141). In Rajasthan Congress party MLAs were less likely than Opposition members to raise constituency grievances in the House, presumably because they felt that they could gain private access to responsible officials (Narain and Puri, 1976:328). In Uttar Pradesh members seemed to use question time as a means to dispose of constituency problems that they were not able to resolve in private. By asking the question in the House the member simultaneously publicized his effort to do something while at the same time absolving himself of responsibility for the absence of remedial action (Brown, 1971:537).

The apparent distaste for legislative arenas as a means for dealing with constituency demands in the case of reactive legislatures may be attributable to the greater support and hence the greater responsiveness of bureaucrats to legislative demands in these systems. In contrast, members of many marginal legislatures use legislative arenas to a somewhat greater extent because their support from and access to bureaucratic elites is not as dependable as that of their counterparts in reactive legislatures.

Thus in Kenya (Stultz, 1970:315), Thailand (Morell, 1975:15), and South Vietnam (Goodman, 1975:185) legislators used the plenary and committee arenas of the legislature to attack government programs, articulate rural grievances to the central bureaucracy, and publicize instances of bureaucratic corruption. While such activities did not always remedy the situation, they did provide mass publics with the sense that their representational expectations were being fulfilled.

However, members of marginal legislatures do interact with executives when they can. For example, members of the Wolesi Jirgah of Afghanistan spend most of their time calling on ministers and very little time in the parliament building itself. They enjoy easy access to the highest levels of officialdom and are usually treated cordially and responsively (Weinbaum, 1976:113). Similarly, Colombian legislators are judged to be much more effective as brokers with the executive branch than as agents in the legislative process, so their interactions with the bureaucracy often bring results for constituents while their policy-making activities are less likely to bear fruit (Hoskin, 1971: 453).

In Kenya some legislators are now beginning to work in their constituencies, spurred on in large measure by President Kenyatta's endorsement of MP involvement in establishing local development projects. Many MPs are involved with organizing self-help programs among their constituents and attempting to get funding and other resources for these projects from the central bureaucracy (Barkan and Okumu, 1974:11–12). While there are still apparently a sizable number of MPs who do not engage in these activities or engage in them with little success (Stultz, 1970:322; Hopkins, 1975a:216), the increasingly strong expectation on the part of both elite and mass publics that legislators will adopt this entrepreneurial role is likely to result in the removal from office of those who lack either the will or the skill to do it effectively (Barkan and Okumu, 1974:21). Similarly, Government party MPs in Malaysia have been publicly exhorted by the prime minister to increase the level of their entrepreneurial ac-tivities in the constituencies. "Enforcement of these norms is said to be backed up with signed resignations in the hands of the leadership for use if necessary" (Musolf and Springer, 1975:30).

In Thailand, the involvement of legislators in local development programs is not well received by the executive elites of that country, but during the 1969–71 constitutional period, legislators were very active in this respect. By lobbying the bureaucracy both in Bangkok and at its district office, MPs succeeded in changing the locales of certain projects—presumably in response to constituency demands or needs—and in shifting part of the development emphasis away from large projects to smaller infrastructure projects with a more immediate impact on local residents (Morell, 1975:26–33). Again, the "success" of these legislative efforts has to be judged in the context of the closure of the legislature by a military coup in 1971.

Finally, in at least one marginal legislature there seems little evidence of legislative activity of any sort in response to constituency demands. Only 2.5 percent of a sample of Korean legislators reported that they had acted on behalf of constituent interests during the previous two years (Kim and Woo, 1975:267).

In minimal legislature systems any sort of legislative performance is tied quite directly to the expectations of executive-centered elites. Activities within these legislatures have involved such concerns as articulating regional demands in the case of Yugoslavia (Cohen, 1977:147) or raising local issues during question period in the case of Tanzania during the 1960s (Hopkins, 1971b:143–144). Outside the legislature the legislator finds it difficult to act as an autonomous agent on behalf of his constituency. Thus Tanzanian MPs are much less involved in local development projects than their counterparts in Kenya (Hopkins, 1975b:16), and in Tanzania, the Soviet Union, and other minimal legislature systems there is a strong expectation that the legislator will be the government's agent in the constituency rather than an active representative of the constituency (Kjekshus, 1974:32; Juviler, 1960:139–43).

The Effect of Party. The situation in the minimal legislature raises the question of the effect that political parties have on the MP's performance of constituency-related activities. In the strong-party minimal legislature situations, it is clear that the party seeks to make the legislator its agent rather than allowing the legislator to become the agent of his constituency.

In the weak-party marginal and vulnerable legislatures parties render no assistance to the MP but they also do not hinder him in carrying out constituency-related functions. Thus, Barkan (1975:11–16) attributes much of the Kenyan MP's ability to perform the entrepreneurial role to the absence of a strong party which not only allows the MP to run his own constituency operation but makes it a virtual necessity if the legislator hopes to be reelected. Because KANU cannot assure the MP's reelection, he must build his own constituency machine through effective entrepreneurship. Clearly, Thai legislators were aware that their position was similar and therefore attempted the same type of entrepreneurial strategy.

In Chile and in the Philippines there is no evidence that local party organizations helped the legislator deal with constituency demands. If anything, the legislator was the object of pressures from local party elites to produce for the constituency or else face the loss of his seat. In this context party was important only in regard to whether the legislator was affiliated with the president's party or with the opposition. Affiliation with the president's party meant greater access to pork-barrel projects and therefore more success in delivering the goods to his people (Valenzuela and Wilde, 1975:28; Stauffer, 1975:15).

Most American legislators also receive no assistance from local party organizations in dealing with constituency problems and only a little bit of assistance from the president if they are members of his party. The key factor in successful legislative performance of representational activities in the American Congress is the degree to which the legislator succeeds in establishing his own power in the Congress. Once he succeeds in doing that, influence with the bureaucracy follows quite naturally; for the run-of-the-mill constituency inquiry there is no evidence that legislators are treated any differently by the bureaucracy because of their party affiliation.

In stronger party systems such as those in reactive legislatures the party can be of some assistance to the legislator. The control of the ministry by MPs in leadership positions of the majority party ensures that the bureaucracy will be responsive to legislative interventions on behalf of their constituents. However, strong local parties can also generate demands. In India local party leaders frequently accompany constituents who come to see their MP, and the presence of the party leader makes it difficult for the MP to ignore the complaint (Maheshewari, 1976:343). However, local MLAs in Uttar Pradesh (Brown, 1971:256) and Orrissa (Bailey, 1960:137–38) report that local party organizations assist them in dealing with constituency demands. One Uttar Pradesh MLA described his setup in these terms: "In each area of my constituency, I have party workers to whom people may go for their requests. Smaller requests which can be taken care of at the local level are done so without my having to be involved. The more complicated or high level problems are sent or brought to me" (Brown, 1971:255).

Staff. Legislators can deal with constituency demands more effectively if they have the assistance of qualified staff members. The reason why American legislators are so successful with their constituency work is because in addition to the political power that comes with their membership in a powerful legislative body they have also provided themselves with large personal staffs, most of whom are assigned to constituency casework. The smallest staff in the United States Senate consists of eight people while the largest may go as high as thirty (Olson, 1967:334), and in 1973 the average number of staffers per member of the House of Representatives was 12.6 (Hammond, 1974:120). Members of American state legislatures have a lower case load than national legislators, but it appears to place a heavier burden on them because they "lack the large staffs that congressmen assign to this work" (Crane and Watts, 1968:90). Philippine legislators also provided themselves with large staffs, again almost exclusively assigned to constituency service work (Stauffer, 1975:13).

In comparison with the United States and the Philippines the absence of staff in most other legislatures around the world is striking. In Canada it has been suggested that the lack of staff accounts for many of the situations in which legislators have been unsuccessful in dealing with constituency problems (Kornberg, 1970:96). In Great Britain legislators have no publicly provided staff and no private offices (Crick, 1968:57–62). In one poll 23 percent of the members reported that they had one or more secretaries and/or assistants working for them; not surprisingly, 30 percent of the Conservative MPs had such assistance compared to 15 percent of the Labour MPs. Most MPs (54 percent) either shared a secretary with one or more colleagues or had no regular secretarial help at all (Barker and Rush, 1970:191).

In marginal legislatures such as Lebanon and Iran members have no personal staff at all and sometimes press their families into service to help them meet their obligations to their constituents (Crowe, 1970:286; Baaklini, 1972:224–25; Schulz, 1969:47). Recent attempts to increase staff support in these legislatures have been aimed more at the legislator's policy-making activities than at his constituency service activities (Baaklini and Heaphey, 1976).

PERFORMANCE AND SUPPORT

As suggested in Chapter 8, there should be a connection between the legislature's performance of representational activities and the degree to which it is supported, and this connection should depend on whether or not legislative activities are satisfying the expectations of both mass and elite publics. In the absence of data we only can assume that the high level of support accruing to active and reactive legislatures means that both sets of publics are satisfied with legislative performance or at least not so dissatisfied as to significantly affect their support for the institution. In the case of the minimal legislatures the representational activities of those institutions take place within the expectational framework of executive-centered elites and their support is essential to the existence of the legislature. Thus, our attention should be directed at vulnerable and marginal legislatures in order to determine whether or not there is any connection between the low level of support for these legislatures and the way in which they deal with the particularistic demands made upon them.

First, it should be noted that the representational activities of some of these legislatures are not directed at mass publics. One student of Latin American legislatures attributes the relatively low level of support for these institutions to the fact that most legislators represent middle and upper class elements in society and do not respond to mass needs (Astiz, 1973b:118). In the case of Colombia Hoskin (1971:453) points out that the responsiveness of legislators is largely to their clientele groups and not to their constituency as a whole.

Second, for many marginal and vulnerable legislatures their representational activities come into conflict with the expectations of executive-centered elites. The latter argue, for example, that if the political system is forced by legislative pressures to respond to particularistic demands, the resources of the nation may be so badly depleted as to court economic disaster (Barkan, 1975:19). Planning officials, in particular, are consistent in their distaste for intervention by politicians on the grounds that such activities threaten what they believe to be the inherent rationality of their development plans (Valenzuela and Wilde, 1975:24). This point of view is neatly summarized in these comments about the Brazilian Congress:

those running for legislative seats in the process of making themselves attractive to the electorate escalated the level of expectations of the electorate. Furthermore, in order to attract support from a given region's voters, they sometimes locked themselves into fixed positions which made negotiations, compromises, and the enactment of nation-wide legislation extremely difficult. Thus, the laws that "ought to be passed" are not approved, bills of limited applicability are enacted through vote trade-offs, and the level of disappointment among the constituents rises. When added to the general lack of resources to satisfy constituents' demands and a general lack of understanding regarding the functioning of the political system, it is no wonder that this picture leads people to conclude that the legislature is not working as "it ought to be" (Astiz, 1973a:5).

Similarly, in the Philippines "the politics of particularism was bitterly attacked by the urban-based media" who viewed the process as time-consuming, inefficient, and corrupt (Stauffer, 1975:16–17). In Chile the technocrats became so dissatisfied with the incessant particularistic demands that legislators directed at them and which, in their view, played havoc with their economic development proposals, that a "principal thrust of the Frei Administration was to do away with particularistic considerations in order to rationalize national planning." While there is no clearly demonstrable relationship between these tactics and the breakdown of Chilean democratic institutions,

the effort to cut back on the role of Congress as the key arena for compromise on issues of national importance as well as on the myriad of critical, but small, issues vital for electoral politics, led to a reduction of communication among political elites of divergent factions and made more difficult the center consensus necessary for preserving the regime (Valenzuela and Wilde, 1975:34, 41).

In Thailand, legislative involvement with the implementation of development projects had long been irritating to the executive-centered elites who dominate that country. The military was particularly disturbed by the possibility that military appropriations might be eroded to satisfy the demands of MPs for increased allocations of development funds. They argued that the particularistic activities of the legislators were ruining the country's economy, contributing to corruption, and constituted an inefficient and wasteful expenditure of resources. In November 1971 they cited exactly these reasons when they abolished the legislature for the sixth time in twenty-five years (Morell, 1975:10, 33; Mezey, 1973).

The question still remains as to whether or not this flouting of elite expectations is worth the price for the legislature: does the representation of particularistic demands increase support? Hard and definitive data are difficult to come by, but there are some preliminary reports that seem to suggest that the answer to that question is, tentatively, yes.

An analysis of survey data collected in Korea demonstrated that perceptions of legislative performance was a crucial variable in influencing the level of individual citizens' support for the legislature. However, it was found that modern, well-informed, and active citizens concentrated on how the legislature as a whole was doing while inefficacious, inactive, and ill-informed citizens were much more concerned with how individual legislators were doing. Put differently, the more modern sectors were concerned with the types of policies being produced, but the more traditional—and more numerous—sectors tied their support to the types of things that the legislator was doing in the constituency (Jewell and Kim, 1976b:481–83). However, a study using small samples of presumably "modern" Asian university students indicated that their support for the legislature was also contingent upon favorable evaluations of the activities of individual legislators (Mezey, 1976). Finally, a study conducted in Kenya indicated that the presence and performance of the legislator in the constituency was strongly related to favorable evaluations of him by his constituents (Barkan and Okumu, 1974).

For marginal and vulnerable legislatures the question then is how do legislators satisfy the representational expectations of mass publics, reinforced by electoral sanctions and possibly mass support, while maintaining or even increasing their level of support from elites who possess the ultimate sanction of being able to dismantle the legislature. One possibility, of course, is for elites to come to the belief that effective constituency activity by legislators is functional for them as well as for the legislature. Schulz (1969:48) suggests that the constituency activities of Iranian deputies reduces the demand load of the bureaucracy and consequently "makes the dissolution of the Majles less likely." Whether or not this appraisal is accurate is open to debate, but the general point seems relevant enough: legislators if they perform representational activities effectively can increase regime support as well as their own institutional support. However, this is a long-run strategy, and the evidence is that elites in marginal and vulnerable systems are more concerned with the short-run problems that stem from what they view as nefarious legislative meddling in what they think of as their own proper domain.

Chapter 10

GENERALIZED DEMANDS: LEGISLATURES AND INTEREST GROUPS

While all legislators appear to be the recipients of a constant and heavy volume of particularized demands from individuals and groups in their constituency, the extent to which they are the objects of organized demands of a general nature either from within or without their constituency is subject to a great deal of variation from one legislature to another. Much of this variation can be explained by the concepts that were introduced in Chapter 8 and used to analyze particularized demands in Chapter 9. However, part of the difference between particularized and general-organized demand loads is attributable to systemic factors relating to the existence and autonomy of interest groups.

INTEREST GROUPS: SOME PRELIMINARY CONSIDERATIONS

Whether or not interest groups are important structures in a political system depends upon the degree to which the system in question is "developed" and the extent to which dominant elites permit such groups to function.

In "less developed" political systems, "there are relatively few explicitly organized interest groups with functionally specific roles" and therefore the majority of demands that are made reflect individual or primary group interests rather than "common interests" of larger, more organized groups of people (Pye, 1958:480–81). As societies become more developed, secondary groups assume a more active role in the political process. What this means then is that within each legislative category there will be some countries in which there will be few general organized demands because there will be few groups capable of making such demands.

A second variable is the attitude of ruling elites toward interest groups. In countries with minimal legislatures, and in some countries with reactive or marginal legislatures, ruling elites do not permit autonomous interest groups to exist. An "autonomous interest group" is one that operates independently of other structures in the political system, and in countries such as the Soviet Union, Singapore, and Tanzania the party elites that prevent the legislature from exercising any autonomous influence on the policy-making process also prevent the emergence of autonomous interest groups by incorporating these interests into the structure of the ruling party. To a lesser extent, this appears to be the case in Mexico and Zambia as well.

Therefore, in less developed countries and in countries with hegemonic ruling elites legislators will be subject to few interest-group demands because groups either do not or cannot function. This analysis therefore must be restricted to those countries in which interest groups do function.

Where they do function, interest groups can affect the demand flow of a political system in several different ways. First, groups can reduce the volume of particularized demands either by aggregating many such demands into a smaller number of more generalized demands or by resolving particularized demands through its organization. The aggregative potential of interest groups is obvious; the demands of many companies for tariff protection may be aggregated by a trade association into one general demand for a new tariff law, or the individual appeals of farmers for protection against the vagaries of the rainfall may be aggregated by a farm organization into a generalized demand for more irrigation projects.

Modern interest groups also provide their members with a wide range of social, economic, and professional services which can satisfy a variety of needs. Were these services absent, many of these needs undoubtedly would be translated into particularized demands directed at legislators or other political actors. Thus, a union retirement fund means that a worker is not entirely dependent on government pension programs; an agricultural cooperative may provide a small farmer with facilities that he otherwise would have to seek from government agencies.

From another perspective, groups may increase the volume of demands in a political system. The availability of an interest group organization may raise the sense of political efficacy of group members and embolden them to make demands that they would not have voiced in the absence of the interest group. Thus, groups may be demand stimulators as well as demand reducers. On balance, groups will probably reduce the volume of particularized demands with which legislators must deal and increase the number of more general demands that they receive.

CAPABILITY AND THE VOLUME OF GENERAL DEMANDS

The general demands that interest groups make call for responses that require that the entire policy-making process be engaged to produce laws or decisions applicable to the entire nation. Making general policy normally requires a greater degree of capability than responding to particularized demands, and so interest groups must seek access to those few actors and structures with the greatest policy-making capacity. In contrast, individuals and groups with particularized demands may find the capacity to resolve those demands in a variety of actors and structures that would be incapable of producing general policy solutions—for example, local political elites and individual legislators. Thus, interest groups making general demands must be more sensitive to the comparative capabilities of institutions and actors than those who make particularized demands.

Interest Groups and the Bureaucracy. Considerations such as those suggested above have led interest groups in just about every country in which they function to seek and achieve access to the executive-centered elites who dominate so much of the policy process in the modern state. In all countries, there are reports of continuous and close relationships between interest groups and the bureaucrats who have jurisdiction over the policy areas relevant to the group.

The best term for this type of relationship between bureaucrats and interest groups is *clientela*. Coined by Joseph LaPalombara (1964: 262) in his classic study of interest group politics in Italy, the *clientela* relationship exists "when an interest group, for whatever reasons, succeeds in becoming in the eyes of a given administrative agency, the natural expression and representative of a given social sector which, in turn, constitutes the natural target or reference point for the activity of the administrative agency." Among his many illustrations of the phenomenon in Italian politics is the Ministry of Commerce, which, according to one bureaucrat in that agency "views industrialists and associations that represent them as its most significant clientele" (LaPalombara, 1964:264).

The relationship between administrators and bureaucrats in Fourth Republic France was similar: "The views of a branch of the administration tended to reflect those of its regular clients, shorn of their least reasonable demands" (Williams, 1964:378). According to Ehrmann (1971:178–79) the situation did not change very much as the vulnerable Fourth Republic Parliament yielded to the reactive Fifth Republic. In Great Britain a leading student of interest group politics in that country observes "the most close, continuous, and intimate relationship between the interest groups and Whitehall" (Finer, 1960:131), while the situation in Canada has been described in these terms:

the interaction between interest group leaders . . . bureaucrats, and politicians is permeated by the ethos of mutual accommodation. . . . The accommodation depends upon all parties receiving enough satisfaction that continued interaction is deemed worthwhile. Nowhere is the phenomenon of mutual accommodation more apparent than in clientele relations established between interest groups and government departments (Jackson and Atkinson, 1974:33).

In many of these countries the relationship between bureaucrats and interest-group leaders is institutionalized in the form of consultative committees that meet regularly, often have legal status, and play an important role in drawing up legislation and approving administrative decisions relevant to particular policy areas. In Chile business organizations served on advisory and policy-making government boards, a link which allowed for the "development of deep and pervasive relations between the interest groups and the executive," a relationship which often manifested itself in invitations from the president to these groups or to the government boards to draft legislation (Hughes, 1971:51). Such committees have also existed in one form or another in the French Fourth Republic, in West Germany, and in Great Britain.

Why do such strong ties emerge between the bureaucracy and its clients? The answer is that there are benefits for all who are involved.

Francis Rourke (1969:14–15) neatly summarizes the situation in the United States, but his terms are applicable to most other nations and therefore worth quoting at length:

. . . it is essential to every agency's power position to have the support of attentive groups whose attachment is grounded on an enduring tie of tangible interest. The groups an agency directly serves provide the most natural basis of such political support, and it is with these interest groups that agencies ordinarily establish the firmest alliances. Such groups have often been responsible for the establishment of the agency in the first place. Thereafter, the agency and the group are bound together by deeply rooted ties that may be economic, political, or social in character. From an economic perspective the agency usually carries on activities that advance the material welfare of members of the group. The group in turn may supply private employment opportunities for employees of the agency. Also, in return for the political representation with which the agency provides the group in the executive apparatus, the group ordinarily supports the agency in a variety of undertakings, including its request for financial support, its attempts to secure the passage of legislation expanding its powers, or its efforts to defend itself against legislative proposals which threaten its administrative status.

An additional benefit of such liaison is the interest group's utility to the agency as a source of information. In Colombia, for example,

the government has found it desirable, even necessary, to link more closely to it many of the *gremios* (economic interest groups) which often outdistance the relevant agencies of government in technical expertise and administrative capacity. Some interest associations have by law been granted official consultative status with particular ministries or government agencies and some of the professional associations have acted as regulatory instruments for their professions. (Dix, 1967:326)

The involvement of groups in bureaucratic policy making also has been justified on the grounds that if policy is to be successfully implemented, the support of those groups that are most affected by the policy is essential, and the way in which such support is guaranteed is by involving the group in every stage of the process out of which the policy emerges. Thus, the situation in the French Fifth Republic has been summarized in these terms: "From the perspective of the bureaucracy, interest groups are audiences, advisors, and clients, foremost participants in the process of bargaining over governmental policy, and instrumentalities for the enforcement of its rulings" (Ehrmann, 1971:179).

Interest Groups, the Bureaucracy, and the Governing Party. In most political systems the bureaucracy is not autonomous and operates at least ostensibly under the control of a political executive. Therefore groups, in addition to seeking direct access to the bureaucracy, will also attempt to gain access to the bureaucracy through good relations with the governing party.

In Italy LaPalombara (1964:306–48) has suggested that groups which have a close *parentela* relationship with the governing Christian Democrats have enjoyed better access to the bureaucracy than groups which are affiliated with opposition parties. In the case of Japan Kuroda (1975:10–13) has noted such a close relationship among bureaucrats, business groups, and leaders of the Liberal Democratic party that he has stated that the country is governed by this triumvirate. More generally, when a party controls the government, bureaucratic agencies will not be able to guarantee policies to its client groups if these policies are not in favor with the ministers of the governing party. No matter how intimate the relationship between the British Ministry of Employment and leaders of the Trades Union Congress, ministry policies under a Conservative government will not be as palatable to the unions as they would be if Labour were in power. Similarly, the relationship between the United States Department of Labor and the AFL-CIO changes when a Republican replaces a Democrat in the White House.

Legislative Capability. The vigor with which interest groups pursue access to executive-centered elites in the bureaucracy and the governing party suggests a judgment on the part of these groups that these structures are capable of affecting general public policy, and perhaps more capable of doing so than the legislature.

Such a judgment should not be at all surprising to us given our earlier discussions about the policy-making roles of legislatures. Even active and vulnerable legislatures—the legislatures with the greatest degree of involvement in policy making—are at best coequal with executive-centered elites at the policy formulation stage, and are at a distinct disadvantage in overseeing the way in which bureaucracies administer policy. Reactive and marginal legislatures are less capable than executive-centered elites at every phase of the policy-making process, while minimal legislatures have no autonomous capacity of their own to affect public policy. What this means is that active and vulnerable legislatures can expect a substantial load of interest-group demands, reactive and marginal legislatures somewhat less, and minimal legislatures none at all.

The data seem to support this generalization. American legislators are besieged by interest-group representatives; by one estimate Washington lobbyists outnumber legislators by almost ten to one (Schwarz and Shaw, 1976:330). Under a very vague lobbying law that invites circumvention, 269 groups filed reports on their 1969 lobbying expenditures with the Clerk of the United States House of Representatives, and in some state legislatures more than four hundred groups have registered with the appropriate legislative authorities. The groups that registered with the Clerk of the House reported spending $5.1 million in 1969 to influence legislation (Jewell and Patterson, 1973:334–35).

In the Philippines, 54 percent of a sample of legislators reported that they were either "very often" or "somewhat often" contacted by groups seeking help with their problems (Styskal, 1967:59). In Fourth Republic France groups maintained primary liaison with the bureaucracy because the constant fall of governments and the resulting parliamentary immobilism meant that the bureaucracy was the most stable policy-making organ in the state (Ehrmann, 1961). However, if a group found itself confronted by a hostile minister and therefore an unreceptive bureaucracy, it was more than willing to concentrate its energies on its parliamentary connections, often with the goal of bringing down the government and thereby creating a more congenial bureaucratic atmosphere. Thus, in 1956 the French Farmers Federation (FNSEA) failed to sway the finance minister to its way of thinking on the issue of farm prices; in 1957 deputies sympathetic to FNSEA were instrumental in turning out the government and securing a cabinet with a more friendly finance minister (Williams, 1964:380).

In reactive legislatures such as the British Parliament a similar pattern develops in which demands on legislatures by interest groups are a supplement, or fall-back position "if a pressure group finds its demands rejected in Whitehall, or if Whitehall ignores its claim to deserve consultation" (Rose, 1974:273). As France moved from the Fourth to the Fifth Republic, interest groups began to focus their primary efforts on impressing the appropriate administrative agencies while at the same time maintaining their influence in Parliament in the event that it was needed (Brown, 1963:524–25).

Clearly, interactions between legislators and interest-group representatives are less frequent in reactive than in active legislatures.

One study of four American state legislatures reported averages of 7.8, 8.5, 34, and 16 contacts per legislator per week with lobbyists (Zeigler, 1971:70). In contrast, a similar study of ten German state parliaments found a mean of 2.1 contacts per week across all of the legislatures with only one legislature exceeding 2.4 (Von Nordheim and Taylor, 1976:516). And one study of 139 Canadian MPs found 70 percent reporting no more than twice weekly contacts with interest-group representatives (Presthus, 1971:447).

In marginal legislatures groups are less concerned with their legislative liaisons than they are in reactive legislatures. In Iran deputies report very little contact with interest groups; instead, group representatives are invited to the ministries to give their views during the bill drafting stage, and the fact that decisions taken in these arenas are usually final makes interest-group involvement with the legislature a waste of time (Schulz, 1969:44). In Colombia, however, groups do expend some effort on congressional lobbying, even though they reserve most of their energies for the president, his advisors, and the bureaucracy (Dix, 1967:325–26).

In one study a sample of interest associations in Brazil was asked to indicate the frequency with which they contacted various authority groups and institutions. The results are summarized in Table 10.1.

TABLE 10.1[a]

Frequency of Interaction of Interest Associations with Authority Groups and Institutions in Brazil (Percentages)

Authority Group or Institution	Frequently	Occasionally
Legislative Groups		
Chamber of Deputies	20.7	46.5
Senate	17.2	43.1
Individual congressmen	24.1	41.4
Parliamentary commissions	12.1	29.3
State legislature	17.2	29.3
Executive-Centered Elites		
President of the Republic	13.8	32.8
Ministries	46.5	39.7
Semipublic agencies	36.2	29.3
Other fed. admin. organs	32.8	17.2
State Administration	20.7	29.3

a. Schmitter, 1971:258.

Clearly contact between interest associations and legislative arenas is "occasional" while contact with executive-centered elites is "frequent." When group leaders were asked simply, "Do you have more contacts with legislative, executive-administrative, or judicial organs?" 73 percent said "executive-administrative" while only 8 percent said the legislature. Nonetheless, 42 percent of the respondents said that it was necessary to maintain legislative contacts, while 16 percent said it was desirable, and 27 percent said it was not necessary, thus indicating once again that parliamentary contacts constituted a fall-back position in the event that the more important interaction with executive-centered elites failed. However, when pressed to name their major campaigns for governmental decisions favorable to their group, 54 percent could not mention a single campaign that involved an appeal to the legislature (Schmitter, 1971:257–62).

REPRESENTATIVE EXPECTATIONS AND THE LEGISLATURE

From what has been said to this point, we can assume that if a group finds the bureaucracy to be accessible and responsive to its needs, and if the legislature in question is not very effective, the group will direct only minimal representational expectations toward the legislature. However, if the bureaucracy is not accessible or not responsive and if the legislature possesses any capacities at all to alter this behavior, then groups will direct representational expectations toward the legislature. Because the response of the bureaucracy never can be guaranteed, and because all but minimal legislatures are capable of exercising at least some influence on the policy-making process, interest groups will always attempt to maintain some access to the legislature so that it may reasonably expect representation from these quarters if it is required.

Whether or not interest groups will receive such representation from the legislature depends upon the role perceptions of legislators, which are in turn conditioned by the electoral sanctions that groups can impose on them and by the general expectations about the legislature that are held by elite and mass publics. If legislative role perceptions are receptive to interest-group pressures, legislators are likely to make themselves accessible to the demands of group leaders.

Role Perceptions. Legislative attitudes toward interest groups have not been researched as intensely as attitudes toward constituents.

The research that has been done has been influenced by the Wahlke-Eulau study of American state legislators. Wahlke, Eulau, and their colleagues (1962) developed a typology of role orientations toward interest groups, classifying legislators as facilitators if they were knowledgeable about group activity and friendly toward it, resisters if they knew about group activity and were hostile toward it, and neutrals if they knew little about group activity or had no strong attitudes toward it. As was the case with representational orientations, these categories have been replicated in other studies. Table 10.2 summarizes data on the distribution of these role orientations in five American state legislatures, the United States Congress, the Colombian Congress, and five Japanese provincial assemblies.

Some of these data are difficult to interpret. The large number of neutrals in the United States Congress is puzzling given the ample evidence that most legislators have at least cordial relations with the interest groups represented in Washington and particularly with those groups who have members in their constituency. In Colombia, even though resisters outnumber facilitators, a survey of legislators indicated that members had substantial contact with interest groups: "Seventy-one percent reported contacts with spokesmen representing community-action groups, 61 percent with municipal governments, 60 percent with *campesinos*, 52 percent with clergy, 51 percent with labor unions, 50 percent with departmental governments, 46 percent with teachers, 41 percent with economic associations, and 30 percent with other groups" (Hoskin, 1971:425).

In marginal legislatures contact between legislators and interest groups appears to be almost entirely absent. In Iran (Schulz, 1969:44) and Zambia (Hakes and Helgerson, 1973:343), legislators report no contacts at all with representatives of interest groups. In Thailand 49 percent of a sample of legislators perceived that there were groups outside the government who were attempting to exert influence on the legislature; of these, only 14 percent indicated that they had ever sought the advice of these groups (Mezey, 1972:696). And in Brazil congressmen were aware of representative associations, received their publications, and knew of their policy pronouncements but "almost all felt that they were not very important in parliamentary life. No one perceived them as being regularly and systematically engaged in influencing individual deputies or the Congress as a whole; most felt that they were sporadically active and not particularly

TABLE 10.2

Interest-Group Role Orientations: Selected Legislatures

Country or State	Legislative Type	Percent Faciliators	Percent Resisters	Percent Neutrals	(N)
California[a]	Active	38	20	42	(97)
New Jersey[a]	Active	41	27	32	(78)
Ohio[a]	Active	43	22	35	(157)
Tennessee[a]	Active	23	40	37	(116)
Iowa[b]	Active	29	12	59	(85)
U.S. House of Representatives[c]	Active	29	21	49	(218)
Colombian Congress[d]	Marginal	44	56		(46)
Kyoto Pref. Assembly[e]	Reactive	65	33	2	(49)
Ibaraki Pref. Assembly	Reactive	57	41	2	(49)
Gunma Pref. Assembly	Reactive	56	33	10	(31)
Osaka Pref. Assembly	Reactive	55	45		(18)
Kumamoto Pref. Assembly	Reactive	67	22	11	

a. Wahlke, et al., 1962:327
b. Jewell and Patterson, 1973:413

c. Davidson, 1969:166
d. Hoskin, 1971:435

e. Kim, 1973:403

effective on specific issues" (Schmitter, 1971:263). However, some Brazilian legislators were more aware of and more receptive to the appeals and suggestions of associations; they were most likely to be the conscientious legislators, or legislators that represented more developed states where groups were more visible and more highly organized (Schmitter, 1971:264–66).

Expectations. The fact that American legislators are so reluctant to classify themselves as facilitators despite the substantial evidence of their close involvement with interest groups suggests that such an involvement may be contrary to the expectations of mass publics. The term "pressure group" or "special interest group" has always had a nefarious ring to it in American political culture and, one would expect, in other political systems as well because it connotes an interest different from and perhaps contrary to the general public interest. For instance, in a recent study a sample of American citizens was asked to indicate whether various political institutions could be trusted "to do what is good for the people" and also whether business and industry and labor unions could be trusted. While all of the political institutions were trusted by more than 50 percent of the sample and none were distrusted by more than 33 percent, only 26 percent agreed that business and industry could be trusted while 56 percent said they could not; similarly, 27 percent agreed that labor unions could be trusted, while 53 percent disagreed (Lehnen, 1976:71–72).

Elite expectations toward the legislator–interest-group relationship are likely to be a bit more complex. Obviously, if elites expect legislative support for their policy initiatives, close contacts between legislators and interest groups could reduce this level of support if executive policies run contrary to group interests. Thus, the Nixon Administration's proposal in 1970 to prevent an extension of the 1965 Voting Rights Act was blocked by the strong lobbying of civil rights groups in the Congress (Orfield, 1975:94–103). On the other hand, if elites are intimately connected with interest groups and if these groups are also connected with legislators, bargains between elites and groups will not be disavowed in the legislature. Thus, the close connection between American defense contractors and the Department of Defense is reinforced by an equally close relationship between the contractors and the members of Congress who must pass on Defense authorization bills (Katznelson and Kesselman, 1975: 184–88).

In reactive legislatures executive-centered elites want to ensure that they are the ones who do the bargiaining with interest groups with only a minimal amount of pressure from the government's legislative contingent. In these countries the firm expectation of partisan elites is that for the individual legislator, party should take precedence over the demands of interest groups. Thus, in the United Kingdom and West Germany, there have been several instances in which legislators who were demonstrably sympathetic toward an interest group's demand opposed the group's positions because of the contrary decisions of their party leaders (Schwarz and Shaw, 1976:338–39). In Italy leaders of interest groups have been elected to Parliament on the Christian Democratic ticket but once in Parliament some have been coopted by party leaders and have articulated the views of their interest groups with a good deal less vigor than they displayed prior to their election (Zariski, 1972:202–3). One reason why party expectations outweigh the demands of interest groups is that the party is the guarantor of the legislator's tenure in office. Put more generally, we may expect that in systems where executive-centered elites are responsible for electing their followers to the legislature, legislators will be relatively insulated from group demands that are contrary to the positions of those elites. In systems where legislators are elected largely by their own efforts, they will be vulnerable and receptive to the demands of groups that can assist their election or cause their defeat.

THE ELECTORAL CONNECTION

Electoral Techniques. Interest groups can use three strategies in seeking a legislature composed of members who are favorably disposed toward their concerns. First, in systems where the role perceptions of individual legislators are not entirely structured by elite expectations, a group may assist in the election of legislators who are friendly to the goals of the group in the hope that the legislator will act autonomously in behalf of the group. In systems where partisan elites dominate legislators, groups, in return for policy promises, may seek to assist the election efforts of an entire party rather than a specific legislator. Alternatively, groups may seek to help friendly members or particular factions of a party by making their support for the party contingent upon the party's nomination of candidates who will represent the interests of the group.

A group's success in pursuing any of these strategies depends upon the resources at its disposal. The most important resources of the group are money to finance campaigns, workers to help in the campaigns, and the capacity to deliver a substantial number of votes to the party or candidate of the group's choice.

In the case of active legislatures in the United States groups with sufficient resources follow the option of direct assistance to candidates. American elections are very expensive and legislative candidates receive little or no financial support from party organizations. Therefore, legislators are heavily dependent upon campaign contributions from interest groups (Green, 1975:1–27). Whether or not such assistance guarantees a candidate's election and whether or not it guarantees that the legislator will vote according to the wishes of the group are open questions.

The first question probably cannot be answered in a definitive manner, but certainly we can assume that candidates without any substantial financial backing will have a difficult time getting elected. For candidates endorsed by mass membership organizations such as labor unions, just as important as the financial support is the help of union volunteers in canvassing legislative districts on behalf of the endorsed candidate. One observer of the Congress suggests that the ability of labor unions "to deliver both money and campaign workers causes it to be both feared and respected as a force in elections" (Clapp, 1964:417).

Such campaign assistance from interest groups is obviously appreciated, but legislators steadfastly maintain that it does not necessarily guarantee a favorable response to the group's demands. When a sample of congressmen were asked to assess the effectiveness of campaign contributions as an instrument for getting favorable congressional action for the group making the contribution, 6 percent said they were very effective, 30 percent said they were either moderately effective or that they could be, and 46 percent said they were ineffective (Scott and Hunt, 1966:82). In other studies members of the Congress and members of four state legislatures were asked to rank the effectiveness of various interest-group techniques. In all five samples campaign contributions were ranked lower than the mean effectiveness rank for all techniques (Jewell and Patterson, 1973:344).

One of the best pieces of research on this subject suggests that a group's position on an issue will be important to a legislator's voting decision only if the issue is of high visibility in the legislator's constituency (Kingdon, 1973:140, 145). Clearly, interest groups will seek out legislators in whose districts their concerns are important and their members reside and make these legislators the primary targets of their demands. Legislators will be most likely to respond to the demands of a group if they see this direct connection between the group and their constituents and their election to the legislature. On the other hand, even a group outside the constituency should have some influence on a legislator if it can supply sizable infusions of campaign funds.

Group techniques in vulnerable legislatures depend upon the strength of the party system in the country. In the Philippines, where the parties play virtually no electoral role, 72 percent of a sample of legislators said that groups had supported them in their electoral campaigns (Styskal, 1975:240). "Business interests tend to support candidates through campaign contributions and by dealing with the congressman's law firm or family business," and some groups try to elect their own members to office (Franzich, 1971:191). In other vulnerable systems, such as Uruguay, the French Fourth Republic, Chile, and Italy, parties have been stronger and have therefore served as an intermediary between the groups and the legislators.

During the Fourth Republic groups contributed to the parties as well as to individual candidates but the postelection support of the recipients of these funds was never guaranteed (Williams, 1964:371–72). In Italy and in Chile groups also contributed to the parties, but in addition sought to have their own members nominated for seats in Parliament. From 1921 to 1965 the National Society of Agriculture in Chile and the National Society of Mining each had a yearly average of fourteen executive board members in Congress (Hughes, 1971:51–52).

In several countries the attempts of groups to gain nominations for their supporters is facilitated by the use of a list system of proportional representation. With several nominations to be made in each legislative district, the party is able to satisfy the demands of different groups among its supporters. In contrast, group-oriented candidate selection is unlikely to occur in single-member plurality systems "because the adoption of a group candidate implies the exclusion of all other groups from legislative representation" (Czudnowski, 1970:240).

The Italian Christian Democrats have a *parentela* relationship with several groups, such as Catholic Action, the *Coltivatori Diretti*, and the Italian Confederation of Workers Unions. These groups see the election as not only an opportunity for them to gain influence in the Parliament, but also as a chance to gain influence within the party by achieving more nominations and more parliamentary seats for politicians affiliated with the group. Thus the groups demand that their representatives be included on the Christian Democratic election slates and, having achieved this goal, they devote their campaign workers and their financial resources to the quest for preference votes for their nominees on the party's list. Sometimes the more interesting result is not which party wins the most seats in the Parliament but which Christian Democratic faction elects more of its members (Zariski, 1972:205).

There are some parallels between the Italian situation and the situation in certain reactive legislatures. In Japan the tie between the ruling Liberal Democratic party and established business groups is very strong and is reinforced by campaign contributions which in the 1972 election totaled about $30 million. The groups attempt to maximize their power by contributing to factions within the party that most closely represent their interests. Business-party ties are even further strengthened by the fact that at any one time about one-third of the Liberal Democratic members of the Diet are former businessmen (Kuroda, 1975:10–13).

In West Germany interest groups are actively involved in the process of nominating CDU/CSU candidates for seats in the Bundestag. Business organizations and industrial firms use their financial resources to convince the party to nominate candidates that they favor (Schwarz and Shaw, 1976:351). The CDU is particularly vulnerable to these pressures because it is a party of few dues-paying members and therefore completely dependent on outside financial contributions (Hirsch-Weber, 1960:108). Of course, the SPD also has its group obligations, as indicated by the substantial portion of its members who are associated with labor unions (Hirsch-Weber, 1960:110). Loewenberg (1967:122) estimates that 30 percent of the members of the 1957–61 Bundestag were interest-group representatives, in the sense that they were members or employees of interest groups. In addition, another 32 percent of the membership held part-time employment in the private sector, so it is reasonable to conclude that in a way they too were group representatives.

Again, it is important to balance this picture so as not to leave the impression that the German parties are subordinated to interest groups. Once in the Bundestag, legislators acquire allegiant attitudes toward their party which often counterbalance their connections with outside groups. In addition, there is evidence that the parties are more responsive to the demands of groups that can claim substantial voting strength in a constituency than they are to the demands of organizations that have financial resources only (Schwartz and Shaw, 1976:353).

In Sweden and Finland public financing of election campaigns means that the parties will distribute places on their lists to representatives of groups capable of delivering substantial numbers of votes to the party (Hecksher, 1960:164–65; Ahrenberg, 1960:44).

In the Fifth Republic and in Great Britain a single-member district system of electing members to Parliament plus a relatively strong party system compels a mixed bag of tactics for interest groups. There is no list, so places cannot be allocated to satisfy group demands. Therefore, groups contribute to the general party effort and also work for the election of particular legislators who will be articulate spokesmen within the party for the interests of the group, even if they do not have the freedom to vote for group positions that may be contrary to the views of the party. In France

groups still appeal to the candidates, and the candidates show deference or independence according to their temperament and lights. Although party discipline in the Gaullist party is strict, its candidates are nonetheless encouraged by the party leadership to seek communication with and support from organized interests as a means of sinking stronger roots in their constituencies (Ehrmann, 1971:175).

In Britain today campaign contributions do not seem to be very important in determining the outcome of parliamentary elections. Trade unions and the Cooperative party sponsor the candidacies of some Labour party nominees with a limited cash subsidy, but the party allegiances of British voters are quite firm and no pressure group can swing a sizable percentage of the vote. Thus, groups will seek out sympathetic MPs in the hope that they will act as representatives for the group, but they are in no position to back up their demands with electoral sanctions (Rose, 1974:266–67). Perhaps the more effective means for groups to gain supporters in Parliament is by encouraging their own members to go into politics. Certainly the social backgrounds of Conservative MPs have shown a marked bias in favor of business occupations, whereas many Labour MPs hold membership and even leadership positions in trade unions. While such affiliations do not always make these people advocates of these interests, there must certainly be a tendency in that direction (Rose, 1974:211–12).

In Canada groups that are concentrated in a legislator's constituency can have an impact on election outcomes (Jackson and Atkinson, 1974:37), and in India some MPs suggest that their affiliation with interest groups provide them with an independent base that helps them to win reelection and also increases their "clout" within the party organization (Maheshewari, 1976:349).

Because political parties are weak in marginal legislative systems, interest group ties tend to be directly with individual legislators. These ties take the form of direct group affiliations and campaign support. The Latin American systems which we have classified as marginal tend to be dominated by politicians from the wealthier sectors of society (Needler, 1968:130) whose activities generally reflect the economic interests of these groups. Senators in Venezuela are likely to be independently wealthy individuals (Kelley, 1971:486), and in Peru upper-class politicians meet with businessmen with whom they have family and financial ties in the confines of private clubs where political arrangements are made (Astiz, 1969:193–204). In Brazil many legislators have connections with an individual firm or economic group through family ties, direct professional interest, or indirect financial support, and "the major employers' associations have usually managed to have at least one of their leaders or employees in the Chamber." Groups will give financial support to individual candidates, but avoid any connections with political parties, partly because it is of questionable legality but also because most think that it is not a particularly effective tactic. As was the case in some of the reactive systems, these ties with interest groups in Brazil do not necessarily mean that the legislator will be an outspoken supporter of the group's positions because legislators must make other deals with local political machines in order to get elected and these may well supersede connections with interest groups (Schmitter, 1971:267–74).

In minimal legislatures efforts are made to represent groups that are part of the governing party in the membership of the legislature. Because much of the value of these legislatures to elites is symbolic, it is important to them that the membership of the legislature faithfully reflect all of the relevant interests in society. Yugoslavia has gone further than most of these countries in making this type of representation something more than symbolic. There, representatives of various economic sectors are elected to membership in several "second" houses of the Parliament: the Economic Chamber, the Educational-Cultural Chamber, and the Socio-Health Chamber. The passage of legislation through the Yugoslav Parliament requires the agreement of both the Federal Chamber and the specialized chamber in whose jurisdiction the legislative proposal falls (Djordjevic, 1960:214).

Nonelectoral Techniques. Interest groups have means apart from the electoral process to influence legislators. This is not the place to go into all of the techniques that groups can use to defend and advance their political interests, but some are worthy of note because of their connection with the legislative process. For example, American legislators report that they rely heavily upon the information that interest groups provide, and in one survey they ranked the presentation of research results as the second most effective technique that a group could employ to persuade a legislator to its point of view (Milbrath, 1963:392–93). Interest groups may establish private economic ties with legislators; it is not uncommon in the United States and the Philippines for the firms of lawyer-legislators to receive large retainers from groups in need of political as well as legal representation. In Great Britain the process is more open; MPs are put on retainer by an interest group, the connection is publicly acknowledged, and the interest group has purchased a voice (if not a vote) in the Commons (Rose, 1974:267). In Great Britain, and in other reactive legislatures where salaries are relatively low, legislators may find part-time work with interest groups that may provide them with an income supplement and also with a place to go in the event that their political career is terminated.

Interest groups also may help the legislator to accomplish his own policy goals. Group resources can be used to publicize particular programs and to create a climate of public opinion that favors or opposes them. British industry has spent a massive amount of money on public education programs aimed against nationalization, while the money spent by the American Medical Association to head off "socialized medicine" is legend. In these instances groups are, of course, helping themselves, but they are also being useful allies to the politicians who share their views. In the same way a labor union out on strike or the withdrawal of an important interest group from government consultations can embarrass the government to the benefit of the members of the Opposition.

PERFORMANCE

To this point I have outlined the factors that cause interest-group demands to be brought to the legislature. My next concern is with the types of activities legislators engage in on behalf of interest groups. Essentially groups want their views incorporated into general public policy. Exactly what the individual legislator can do in this respect depends a great deal on the policy-making capabilities of the legislative institution.

Members of active and vulnerable legislatures can be asked to act both as public advocates of interest-group positions and as intermediaries between the interest group and executive-centered elites. Also, because these legislators can participate in all phases of the policy-making process, they can protect group interests as they formulate, deliberate, and oversee the implementation of policy.

Members of reactive and marginal legislatures also will be asked to act as public spokesmen and intermediaries with executive-centered elites. In the case of reactive legislatures the legislator will be asked to intervene on behalf of interest groups with his parliamentary party or with the government should his party be in the majority. Because most of the members of these legislatures have only a peripheral involvement in the policy-making process. they are not approached as policy makers per se, but as people with the potential to influence those who hold more central policy-making roles. In marginal legislatures, the importance of executive contacts is so great that the only reason to go to the Parliament is "for initiating minor measures, or for making minor modifications in officially sponsored bills" (Schmitter, 1971:272).

Members of minimal legislatures are unlikely to be approached at all because of the absence of autonomous interest groups in these political systems. In the event that they are approached the most they can be asked to do is to advocate group positions to those who actually can make policy. Legislators can represent group interests in partisan, committee, or plenary arenas within the legislature.

Committee Arenas. In legislatures where they function committees provide the most effective legislative arenas for the defense of group interests. There are several reasons for this. First, committee systems usually divide labor by subject areas and groups therefore can easily identify and establish ties with those committees that have jurisdiction over the areas of their concern. Second, committee structures often parallel bureaucratic structures so committees will be convenient intermediaries between interest groups and the bureaucracies with which they must deal. Third, committees, as suggested earlier, are relatively private arenas and to the extent that the advocacy of organized group interests is viewed by mass publics as illegitimate such activities are more conveniently carried on in private rather than in more public arenas.

In countries such as the United States, Italy, and Germany, and in France during the Fourth Republic, committees have been the focus of the policy-making process and thus the focus of interest-group activity. In the United States the term "subgovernment" has been used to describe the relationship among committee members and bureaucratic and interest-group personnel who share an interest in a policy area:

A typical subgovernment is composed of members of the House and/or Senate, members of congressional staffs, a few bureaucrats, and representatives of private groups interested in the policy area. Usually the members of Congress and staff members are from the committees or subcommittees that have principal or perhaps exclusive jurisdiction over the policy area dominated by the subgovernment (Ripley and Franklin, 1976:6).

To reinforce this arrangement, groups seek to have legislators sympathetic toward them sit on the committees that are relevant to their interests, which yields "a decision-making system heavily predisposed toward the very interests under their purview" (Davidson, 1976:5). For some time the AFL-CIO was involved in clearing Democratic appointments to the Education and Labor Committees (Fenno, 1969:290). Legislators from farm states, elected with the assistance of farm groups and often themselves members of these groups, dominate the Agriculture Committees in both houses (Jones, 1969:155–74; Lowi, 1969:102–15) while people involved with banking interests have had a tendency to gravitate to the Banking and Currency Committees (Katznelson and Kesselman, 1975:301).

Not surprisingly, the effectiveness of committee representation is attested to by congressmen and lobbyists alike. Only 3 percent of a sample of congressmen felt that group contact through committee hearings was ineffective while more than half felt that testimony given by interest groups during committee hearings was a "very effective" method for gaining favorable action (Scott and Hunt, 1966:78). Lobbyists ranked presentation of research results (which often takes place in the context of committee hearings) and testifying at hearings as the second and third most effective techniques they used to influence legislation (Milbrath, 1963:392–93).

The relationship among interest groups, committees, and the bureaucracy in the United States is multifaceted, and the benefits are shared. Interest groups can use committee personnel to lobby the bureaucracy for certain policy decisions, as the House Judiciary Committee has frequently lobbied the Justice Department on behalf of civil rights legislation for black people. Or groups can help committees to defend their prerogatives, as several groups did when proposed changes in committee jurisdiction were being considered by the House of Representatives in 1973 (Davidson, 1976:19). Or the bureaucracy can use interest groups to lobby committee personnel for legislation that the bureaucracy wants to see passed: " . . . groups can often do for a department things that it cannot very easily do for itself. Interest groups can take a position on policy questions that department officials secretly hold but cannot publicly advocate because it may put them in disfavor with the President" (Rourke, 1969:18).

In Italy groups seek access to committees for two important reasons. First, the power of committees to enact legislation on their own without sending it to the full Parliament gives them tremendous authority over policy areas of importance to interest groups. The power is most frequently used for highly technical bills which few people understand but which may be of great moment to large economic interests; "export-import regulations, rules and procedures concerning state-owned industries, and matters affecting the tariff" are some of the issues dealt with *in sede deliberante* (LaPalombara, 1964:221). Secondly, committees provide a private arena within which interest groups may more easily achieve their goals. One leader of the Italian Banking Association put it this way:

Committees do not operate in the limelight and therefore do not become the subject matter for sensational treatment by the press. As a result of the committee's relative removal from public view, even those committee members who may be opposed to the ends or goals of the association do not very often make sensational or demagogic statements to the press concerning the discussion or debate that takes place within the committee (LaPalombara, 1964:221).

The relationship between committee personnel acting on behalf of interest groups and relevant administrative agencies is conditioned by the party variable. One official in the Ministry of Foreign Affairs said that his ministry tended to ignore interventions of single deputies or senators on behalf of interest groups but "an MP who represents the party in power is always accorded more respectful attention than any other. If the MP is also chairman of a parliamentary committee, he will receive more attention. If the lawmaker is on the Cabinet or close to the Cabinet, or if he is viewed as a potential Cabinet member, even greater attention will be accorded his requests" (LaPalombara, 1964:318).

During the Fourth Republic in France, committees were, in the words of one observer, "institutional facades for the operation of pressure groups" (Williams, 1964:247). The close relationship between committees and groups was essential to the groups because of the great policy-making power that these committees held, and it was facilitated by "their great number, their specialized character, and the great permanence of their staffs, which are small enough to make individual contact with each one of them possible" (Lavau, 1960:86). Pressure groups penetrated the committees by making certain that their own representatives, or those legislators who were sympathetic to them were members:

In 1952 MRP's trade unionists went to the labour or industry committee, but its extreme Indo-China diehards preferred to sit on Defense together with three Gaullist generals and one admiral. . . . The education committee, with its majority of teachers, included the most laic Gaullists, the anticlerical zealots of SFIO, and both the priests in the Assembly. The medical professions provided half the health committee. Agriculture drew all but six of its 44 members from the land, and no urban deputy ever stayed on it. . . . In 1956, two-thirds of the labour committee came from industrial areas, Merchant Marine attracted only seaboard members; of 18 representative of the Midi winegrowers, 13 were on Beverages (Williams, 1964:247–8).

This type of relationship between interest groups and committees also characterizes the West German Bundestag. In that Parliament the representation of interest groups varies with the committees, "from those in which the Members of at least some parties are outright interest representatives, notably the committees concerned with economic and social policy, to those like the Foreign Affairs Committee, where interest representation is remote" (Loewenberg, 1967:326). Thus, interest representatives constituted about 32 percent of the membership of all Bundestag committees during the 1956–61 period, but 66 percent of the membership of the Social Policy Committee, 59 percent of Food, Agriculture, and Forestry, 52 percent of Labor, and 45 percent of Foreign Trade. Furthermore, for these committees and others that directly affect organized interests, the chairmanship "has regularly gone to representatives of the interests within the committee's jurisdiction" (Loewenberg, 1967:197–98).

While there are no direct reports of the subgovernment relationship that characterizes interest-group–committee–bureaucracy relations in the United States, it certainly seems reasonable to conclude that such a relationship functions in Germany. In fact, if the same group that controls committee memberships also is on intimate terms with the bureaucracy, it is reasonable to conclude that the group serves as the mediator if not the arbitrator of policy in that particular area. Obviously, this great attention to committee membership is a function of the strength of the committee system in the Bundestag.

In other reactive legislatures with weaker committee systems there is somewhat less evidence of interest-group penetration. In Canada groups see committees as highly accessible but not very potent arenas to press their claims (Jackson and Atkinson, 1974:37), while in Great Britain groups have found the committee stage useful for clarifying or amending details of complex legislation of importance to the group, but not for shaping the basics of public policy (Rose, 1974:273). In France the change from the Fourth to the Fifth Republic saw a dramatic diminishing of committee strength through a reduction in the number of committees and an increase in the size of those remaining. All of this was designed to reduce the close contact between interest groups and specialized legislators presiding over key committee positions (Ehrmann, 1971:280–81). While interest groups continue to have some liaison with parliamentary committees, this activity is now distinctly secondary to the efforts they direct toward the executive branch.

In the marginal Iranian legislature, however, groups do not maintain any contact at all with legislative committees because these committees have so little influence in determining policy outcomes

(Schulz, 1969:45). But in Poland, where committees are the most efficacious arenas in that minimal legislature, representatives of groups testify at committee hearings, and because ministers and bureaucrats frequently attend committee meetings, the committee provides an arena to facilitate contacts between the groups and the bureaucracy (Modelski, 1973:97).

Partisan Arenas. In those reactive legislatures where parties have formed their own internal committee systems to deal with policies, groups have been quick to grasp the importance of these structures and have succeeded in gaining access to them. In Great Britain the National Farmers Union has abandoned its practice of sponsoring candidates in favor of "working closely with the agricultural committees in the Labour and Conservative parliamentary parties" (Schwarz and Shaw, 1976:332–33). In the German CDU party committees are often dominated by party members who are identified with the interests most relevant to the committee's concern (Hirsch-Weber, 1960:107), and interest groups, as a regular part of their procedure, maintain close contact with the policy committees of both parties (Schwarz and Shaw, 1976:333).

Aside from party committees, groups encourage legislators to speak out on their behalf in party meetings or in discussions with cabinet leaders. As one interest-group leader in Italy put it:

if the pressure group leaders can reach the party leadership so much the better. But this does not mean that the groups ignore the individual deputy. In fact, pressure groups often send whole delegations to talk with various members of Parliament for purposes not necessarily of influencing a single vote but of encouraging the single deputy to represent the position of the pressure group in the meetings of the parliamentary group (LaPalombara, 1964:214).

In reactive legislatures interest groups seek spokesmen in all the major parties but especially in those parties that form the government coalition. In doing this, of course, they are motivated by the belief that constant group pressure on the backbench may force a change in the cabinet's position on an issue critical to the group. While this strategy is obviously less desirable than one involving direct access to the cabinet, it may be the only course open, and sometimes it is effective. As we have seen in Chapter 5, backbench revolts in the British House of Commons have been the cause of changes in government policy, as they have been in Germany and in France as well, and it is reasonable to expect that groups will seek to foment such revolts as a last ditch effort to prevent government action that they deem harmful to their interests.

Plenary Arenas. As our earlier discussions have suggested, plenary arenas are probably the least efficacious places for affecting the shape of public policy and, not surprisingly, groups do not place a very high priority on achieving influence there. The only exceptions are those active and vulnerable legislatures in which party discipline in voting is weak enough to permit a bloc of group advocates to swing a vote one way or another. Thus, in the United States bipartisan groups of legislators representing oil interests or labor interests or commodity interests or the National Rifle Association are sometimes able to influence the outcome of votes. Similarly, during the Fourth Republic budget debates, "some groups with a wide base of parliamentary support could make trouble for the strongest government, and every year there was difficulty over the post office, education, and above all war pensions estimates" (Williams, 1964:375).

In reactive legislatures where party discipline prevents such revolts on the floor the most that a group spokesman can provide in a plenary arena is a voice in favor of the group's demands. Floor speeches may bring a group's interests to the public's attention, or may encourage those with more policy-making power to make proposals relevant to the group's needs. Such may be the function of sponsored candidates in the House of Commons, for example.

For the legislature and its members, the difference between particularized and generalized demands should be clear. The former are always there for just about every member of just about every legislature. The major questions to be dealt with were how heavy the volume of such demands were and how well the legislature performed in response to them. Generalized demands articulated by organized interests are another matter. In some political systems organized demands of this sort are not made at all. In many other countries these demands seldom reach legislators. Whether or not they do reach the legislature, and what the legislator is expected to do in response to them is a function of the policy-making capabilities of both the institution and its various policy-making arenas.

In sum, the individual citizens who articulate particularized demands usually have no one other than their legislator to go to in order to have these demands resolved. Organized interests, in contrast, are highly sensitive to the relative policy-making capabilities of political institutions and actors and will unerringly direct their expectations and demands toward those whom they perceive to be most efficacious. In political systems with reactive, marginal, and minimal legislatures, this means that the legislature will be a secondary or fall-back target in the event that other structures are inaccessible or nonresponsive. Only in the active and vulnerable categories will organized interests view the legislature and its members as primary demand targets.

Part IV

SYSTEM MAINTENANCE

Chapter 11

THE LEGISLATURE AND SYSTEM MAINTENANCE: POLITICAL RECRUITMENT

Those things that the legislature does that contribute to the stability of the political system and enhance its capacity to survive fall under the broad heading of system-maintenance activities. More specifically, system-maintenance activities are those that (1) recruit new members into the political elite, (2) increase the degree to which the system is integrated, (3) increase the level of support for the policies of the regime, and (4) legitimize the existence of the regime. In this chapter I will focus on the first of these activities, political recruitment; the remaining three system-maintenance activities will be considered in the next chapter.

PRELIMINARY CONSIDERATIONS

The political recruitment process touches the legislature in two different ways. First, the legislature can be the goal—the elite position to which people are recruited. Alternatively, a seat in the legislature may be a transitional position, either between nonelite and elite status or between one elite position and another. This is the case when new occupants of nonlegislative elite positions are recruited from the legislature. Thus, we can speak of both recruitment *to* the legislature and recruitment *from* the legislature.

Two methods can be used to analyze these two aspects of recruitment. The traditional method is to assemble and present background data on politicians who have entered into or passed through the legislature. Such analyses typically yield tabulations reporting how many politicians with certain sets of characteristics have come to and through the legislature (See Dogan, 1961; Frey, 1965; Verner, 1971). This method is characterized by its limited capacity to generate explanations. Questions such as why people pursue legislative membership, or why people of certain backgrounds are represented in or promoted from the legislature while others are not, generally go unanswered in simple career-line analyses.

A second approach begins from the perspective of the individual politician's perceptions of the recruitment process. The underlying assumption is that aspiring politicians make certain rational calculations when considering career decisions. The governing force in making these calculations is the ambition of the politician—his plans for his political future and his assessment of the opportunity structure that he faces (Schlesinger, 1966). When deciding whether or not to seek the legislature or to permit himself to be coopted into the legislature, he assesses the subjective value of a legislative seat to him against the costs and risks associated with seeking and holding such a seat.

These assessments are conditioned by the type of legislature in question as well as by the pattern of elite and mass expectations that surround that legislature. Thus the value of a particular legislative seat may be reckoned in one way rather than another because of the things that elites expect of the legislature and its members. Similarly, elites may raise or lower the cost of seeking a legislative seat and they may determine the degree of risk that will be associated with that undertaking. In this way the parameters that guide the career decision of politicians aspiring to legislative seats will vary from one legislature to the next; although some variation within types will exist, a general pattern can be generated for each legislative category.

THE VALUE OF A LEGISLATIVE SEAT

If a politician seeks membership in the legislature, he does so because he thinks that such a position will be of value to him. Membership may have immediate political value, long-range career value, and financial value, as well as value calculated in less tangible ideological and psychological terms.

A seat in a legislature may have immediate political value because it provides its occupant with opportunities to influence the policy-making process. A legislative position is more likely to be valued in this way if the legislature has a significant policy-making role.

If certain legislators have a great deal of influence while others have very little, and if those with more influence have achieved their positions only after lengthy legislative service, the value of legislative membership may be calculated in long-range career terms rather than in terms of immediate political power. In some systems experience in the legislature may be a prerequisite for eventual participation in a policy-making process centered in arenas other than the legislature. Thus if political decisions are dominated by executive-centered elites, most of whom have been recruited from the legislative ranks, then serving in these legislatures will be valuable in career terms, even if no immediate political influence comes with such service.

The value of legislative membership also can be calculated in monetary terms. A politician can be attracted to the legislature because the pay is good or simply greater than what he can earn in another occupation. Legislative experience also can bolster a non-political occupation; mediocre lawyers have become rich and successful lawyers with the help of the publicity associated with a legislative career. Sometimes legislators use their positions in ethically questionable ways that result in financial gain. In almost every legislature members have the opportunity to act in ways that will protect their personal economic interests. Some may engage in more distinctly corrupt practices; bribes and favors can be accepted and the public treasury can be coopted by legislators so inclined.

Some politicians value legislative service in ideological terms. The political influence that comes with membership in many legislatures may be seen by the aspiring legislator as an instrument for advancing public policies in which he believes. Someone may want to serve even if he can't influence decisions at all because of a sense of duty toward his people, his country, his party, or his leader. Such ideological incentives can exist quite apart from a desire for political advantage or financial gain.

Finally, a legislative seat may be psychologically rewarding to the extent that its holder feels that it confers a degree of status and public esteem on him. Such an evaluation would depend quite heavily on the politician's status in private life as well as the esteem generally accorded to the legislature and its members in the political system in question.

Active and Vulnerable Legislatures. As noted, members of active legislatures and members of vulnerable legislatures are key individuals in the political elites of their nations; their interactions with executive leaders are crucial in determining the nature of policy outcomes. In the United States and the Philippines legislators have been without binding obligations to party or president and thus have been in a position to bargain for policy concessions or for more direct financial and political rewards. In Chile, Uruguay, Italy, and the French Fourth Republic, the ability of the executive to govern has depended upon fragile and shifting coalitions within the legislature. Because these legislatures could not be constitutionally dissolved and new elections ordered, executives had to make continuous policy concessions to legislators in order to maintain their majorities. Thus, seats in these legislatures are of immediate political value to those who occupy them.

These seats also have long-run career value. The legislators with the most influence often are professional politicians who have served for some time. Legislative membership is also desirable for those whose ambitions are directed toward the achievement of executive power. In the presidential systems in these two categories—the Philippines, Chile, and the United States—the Congress has been the main source of candidates for president and vice-president. More specifically, the smaller upper house of each legislature has been the arena within which prospective presidential candidates have sought to display their talents. Because these senators are fewer in numbers than members of the lower house and because they are elected from larger constituencies, it is relatively easy for them to establish national reputations.

American politicians such as Humphrey, McGovern, Nixon, Goldwater, Johnson, and Kennedy all used the Senate as a springboard to recent presidential and vice-presidential nominations. Similarly, Chile's last three elected presidents—Allende, Frei, and Allesandri—were senators immediately before becoming president, as were most of their election opponents. In the Philippines every president except one has come from the Senate as have the major losing candidates. (Stauffer, 1970:345). Moreover, in most instances these men served in the lower house of the Congress prior to their election to the Senate, thereby completing the picture of a legislative-centered recruitment pattern for the presidency in each of these three systems. In the parliamentary systems located in these categories legislative membership has obvious career value since cabinet members and the prime minister are drawn from the ranks of senior parliamentarians.

The political value of membership in these legislatures is further indicated by the fact that few members leave voluntarily to accept other political positions. In the United States some members of the president's cabinet have been recruited directly from the Congress, but almost always these people have come from the less prestigious House of Representatives, and even then rarely from among the members with the most seniority. In Chile from 1933 to 1969 only eight senators resigned to accept other positions; the three who resigned after 1945 did so to accept the presidency of the Republic. From 1930 to 1965 twenty-three members resigned from the Chamber of Deputies to take other political positions; five did so to fill vacancies in the Senate (Agor, 1971a:26).

The financial value of seats in active and vulnerable legislatures appears to be quite high. American legislators are more generously compensated than any other parliamentarians, while Philippine congressmen clearly lead the nonwestern world. In fact, if the gross national product is used to normalize salary and allowance figures to make them comparable across nations, Philippine legislators would then rank as the best paid in the world (Stauffer, 1975:24). The highest legislative salaries in Europe are paid to Italian deputies (Loewenberg, 1967:50); these salaries are higher than those of other party or union workers and, in addition, a generous pension plan is provided for those who manage to get elected at least twice (Kogan, 1962: 95–96).

Many members of these legislatures come from prosperous families, and they do not become less prosperous as a result of legislative service. Stauffer (1975:26) reports that 50.9 percent of the members of the Philippine House of Representatives and 71 percent of the senators are from families characterized by "extensive wealth." Matthews's (1954) data show that American legislators tend to have their origins in the well-educated, prestigiously employed, successful, and affluent upper and upper-middle classes. Those politicians who are not especially well off when they enter the legislature often do better during their legislative careers. In Costa Rica a study of the incomes of Assembly members showed that 88 percent made more money after their election than they did before, while only 8 percent lost income as a result of their entrance into the legislature

(Baker, 1973:123). And one study of the French Third Republic concluded that members of the National Assembly during that seventy-year period tended to become financially successful in private affairs as a result of their tenure in the legislature (Dogan, 1961:70).

Ideology is of varying importance in these systems. In the United States, the Philippines, and Uruguay, ideology rarely has been a crucial factor. Political parties in these countries are broadly based coalitions formed to win office; even though many will seek the legislature to "do good" more are interested in doing well. Pragmatism rather than ideology guides their actions. In Chile, Italy, and France, ideology is probably more important. The income and influence of Marxist deputies, for example, is tightly regulated by the party, so ideological commitment must provide the basic incentive to serve.

There seems to be very little that distinguishes the value of a seat in an active legislature from a seat in a vulnerable legislature. Seats in both types of legislatures provide immediate political power, long-range career development, and financial and status rewards. As we shall see, these two categories differ substantially in regard to the level of risk associated with a parliamentary career.

In the case of legislatures with a modest degree of policy-making influence, there is a distinction between the value of seats in the more-supported reactive legislatures and the less-supported marginal legislatures, a distinction which stems from the fact that reactive legislatures tend to be party dominated whereas marginal legislatures are characterized by the weakness or absence of parties.

Reactive Legislatures. Because of party dominance, the immediate political value of a seat in a reactive legislature tends to be significantly lower than a seat in either an active or a vulnerable legislature. While the average member of a reactive legislature is not entirely powerless, as the analysis in Chapter 5 demonstrated, still it is clear that opportunities for exercising political power occur irregularly.

Occasional moments of backbench glory aside, these legislative seats are valuable primarily in a career sense. Most reactive systems are led by parliamentarians who hold cabinet positions. In almost all cases the cabinet members have served apprenticeships on the backbenches of their parties before achieving their positions of leadership. A seat in the House of Commons or the Swedish Riksdag is valuable because of the opportunity that it provides for the eventual achievement of political power through elevation to leadership positions in the party, and (if you happen to have a winning party) in the cabinet. Internally, all of these legislatures are dominated by career pand (if you happen to have a winning party) in the cabinet. Internally, all of these legislatures are dominated by career parliamentarians, thereby attesting further to the long-term political value of these positions. In India, for example, veteran Congress party parliamentarians were able to exert a great deal of influence on the policy-making process through the party's Working Committee (Kochanek, 1968:116 ff.).

Even if the political system is entirely controlled by party elites outside parliament, a seat in the legislature may be valuable if the party has determined formally or by custom that legislative experience is a prerequisite for positions of greater political power. During the dominance of Ataturk's Republican People's party in Turkey, all Cabinet members, formal legislative leaders, and top party leaders served apprenticeships in the Grand National Assembly. (Frey, 1965:6). In Mexico it is common for ambitious young politicians to serve in the legislature at an early point in their careers just as recent presidents of that republic have (Scott, 1964:265). From that position, however, the aspirant is expected to move on to bureaucratic and party positions of greater responsibility. This expectation that congressional service will not become a career is enforced by a constitutional provision limiting congressional deputies to only one term in office (Schmitt, 1971:127). The Indian situation is more comparable to the Turkish; members of the cabinet are also members of Parliament, although a long career in the Parliament is not a necessary requisite for ministerial status.

Financially, seats in these legislatures are not as obviously and uniformly lucrative as seats in active and vulnerable legislatures. Loewenberg (1967:53, 110) says that in Germany, the parliamentary salary is "sufficient to be attractive to some," but "it does not compare favorably with business and professional incomes in a prosperous society." And in the Benelux and Scandinavian countries "parliamentary salaries are between one-third and one-half what they are in Germany" (Loewenberg, 1967:50–51).

Writing seventeen years ago, Berrington and Finer (1961:616) painted a rather dismal picture of the British MP's financial situation; they concluded that the MP who had no outside sources of income was "underpaid and underprivileged." Since then, however, three salary revisions, the latest coming in July 1975, have raised parliamentary salaries almost 200 percent over early 1960 levels. It is not yet clear whether or not this will affect a decrease in the number of members pursuing outside occupations, estimated in one study to be 67 percent of the total membership (Barker and Rush, 1970:37). In France, where salaries are currently the second highest in Europe, many members still work at outside professions simultaneously with their mandates, thereby making themselves more comfortable financially (Ehrmann, 1971:144–50). Mexican deputies also seem to fare well. In addition to receiving 33,000 pesos a year for expenses, they receive a salary of 10,000 pesos a month for the entire year, even though the Chamber meets for only four months. By comparison, the average Mexican worker earned just over 7,000 pesos a year in 1965. Finally, most deputies hold other jobs and use their legislative positions to establish contacts that benefit them in these private occupations (de la Garza, 1972:156–58).

It is difficult to generate data more reliable than rumor on the level of corruption in these (or any) legislatures. As a hypothesis, I can suggest that a low level of public support for a legislature may be partially a response to perceived dishonesty among the members of the institution. Put differently, if corruption were visible and rampant—as in the Philippines or Italy—it is difficult to see how support would remain high for very long. If this reasoning is accurate, then we would expect higher levels of corruption among members of marginal legislatures than among members of reactive legislatures.

The psychological value of seats in reactive legislatures should be related to the support dimension. Because membership in a more-supported legislature should carry with it greater status and prestige than membership in a less-supported institution, such an intangible incentive might be significant in a reactive legislature.

There is little data on which to base a proper assessment of ideological motivation. Impressionistically, it seems to vary markedly within this category, and even among legislators from the same parliament. In Europe it would not be surprising to find deputies of rightist and leftist parties who serve in the legislature primarily to discharge ideological obligations. Presumably, as one moves toward the center of the political spectrum, ideological incentives tend to decrease in importance. However, exceptions are apparent; perhaps the only way to describe the attachment of Gaullist deputies to their leader is in terms of ideology. Even the centrist British parties still must contend with a goodly percentage of MPs who view themselves as fighting ideological wars that most others think have long since ended (Piper, 1974). As one party comes to be dominant in its political system as the PRI is in Mexico and as the Congress party was in India, ideological incentives may increase in importance for many members as the more tangible incentives associated with political influence decline in importance. Although it might be interpreted as a stock reply, the most frequently stated reason for seeking a legislative seat given by members of the Legislative Assembly in the Indian State of Rajasthan was "public service"; gaining political power and earning money were the next most-favored responses (Narain and Puri, 1976:317).

Marginal Legislatures. The value of legislative service in marginal legislatures tends to be measured in short-run financial and political terms. As I have said, such legislatures exist in a condition of constant tension with executive elites that only tentatively accept the legitimacy of the institution. Consequently, such legislatures are likely to be short-lived phenomena highly vulnerable to attacks on their constitutional prerogatives and existence. Coups, coercion, and instability foster an atmosphere of high risk in these systems, which encourages politicians to make decisions based on immediate rather than long-run considerations.

One decision might be to stay away from legislative politics and seek entrance into the civil or military bureaucracies that normally run these systems. It follows that among those who decide to run for the legislature are people who refuse to seek or are refused access to these more dominant institutions. They come to the legislature as a less desirable political alternative but one which potentially can provide them with something of value.

A second group of politicians will come to the legislature because they are asked to do so by patrons in either private or public life. In Thailand the supporters of the Government party in the Assembly were often allies of particular cabinet leaders who guaranteed their proteges' nomination and election to the legislature (Mezey, 1975). In Latin America, it is more likely that legislators will represent private patrons—business leaders, landed obligarchs, or the Church. Brazilian parliamentary elections, for example, are generally controlled by the privileged elite, although the degree of control is tightest in the rural areas and somewhat less so in the urban parts of the country (Peterson, 1970:478–81). Legislators in Afghanistan are the representatives of local potentates sent to Kabul to guard the interests of their sponsors (Weinbaum, 1972:68–70).

In all of these situations the legislative seat itself is not of immediate political value. Rather it indicates that its occupant is favorably placed with people of power. One observer of postindependence West Africa concluded that "recruitment to legislatures often became one of the chief rewards for political fidelity, and the Assemblies came increasingly to be composed of local and party chiefs, party workers of long standing loyalty, and notables satisfied to have their influence and worth rewarded with a symbolic, rather than a substantive political role" (Le Vine, 1968:386). It is possible that legislative service under these terms will result in a future promotion. Ethiopian legislators, for example, often received appointments to high administrative positions at the conclusion of their parliamentary careers (Markakis and Beyene, 1967:208).

Added to these two classes of parliamentary aspirants are those who seek the legislature simply because it is of greater value or promise to them than their current private positions. Seligman (1971:27) notes that in developing systems, "political roles confer higher status, higher rewards, and are more abundant than are occupations in the private sectors." Others have suggested that political success leads directly to private success. Wallerstein (1965:17) says that "political posts become a primary source of income, both licit and illicit, and the possibilities of successful private enterprise are early conditioned by political influence." Because political roles in the military and civilian bureaucracies may demand special abilities which are not required for a legislative position, many of those in search of status and financial rewards run for the legislature. The free-for-all nature of the party-less elections held in these nations means that almost anyone has a chance to win.

This type of political environment is more conducive to opportunists than ideologues, and more the element of the status oriented than the policy oriented. Ideological and service incentives count for very little when the value of such legislative seats is calculated. Politicians take what they can get from legislative service, often with little regard for the institution's reputation. For these reasons, such legislatures are characterized by initially low levels of public support that may decrease even further as the country's legislative experience lengthens.

Salaries are often very high by local standards; in Ethiopia, a country with a per capita income of about $60 *a year*, members of the Parliament earned the equivalent of about $250 *a month*—many times the salary of civil servants in the provinces (Markakis and Beyene, 1967:209). In Kenya primary education qualifies a civil servant to earn approximately $600 a year, but an MP makes $6,000–$7,000 a year (Hopkins, 1975a:227). And in Zambia "all members received substantial if not generous salaries, and those were complemented by a variety of postal allowances, committee supplements, tax benefits, and subsistence and travel allowances all of which amounted to between [$6,000–$12,000] annually" (Helgerson, 1970:87).

Salaries also can be supplemented through elicit means. In Thailand stories of legislative corruption abound. One often retold incident occurred during the 1950s when legislators were given farm implements to distribute gratis to their constituents; instead, so the story goes, many sold the tools, pocketing the proceeds. It has been rumored in Bangkok that the government regularly makes licenses and franchises—scarce resources with enormous market value—available to legislators who arc amenable to government leadership.

Ideological incentives are unlikely to be salient in these systems, while status rewards are those that come either from increased wealth or close association with those who are already wealthy and/or powerful.

Minimal Legislatures. Since they are dominated by elites centered in institutions outside the legislature, the value of these legislative seats is defined exclusively in terms of elite expectations toward the legislature. Because elites have no policy-making expectations for these institutions, membership in a minimal legislature will confer very little immediate political influence.

In career terms legislative membership may indicate elite approval for the politician and therefore suggests the possibility of a future promotion to a more influential position. One scholar (Vanneman, 1972:134) has written that the membership of the Supreme Soviet "represents their best sons and daughters—not the most powerful necessarily, but the best, whether they be workers or bureaucrats, socialists or astronauts. It is clearly an elite group." This suggests that a position in the Supreme Soviet may be held in conjunction with another position of influence outside the legislature. At any one time about one-third of the members of the Supreme Soviet are simultaneously party or state officials (Vanneman, 1972:138).

The Tanzanian MPs are also aspirants for higher elite positions and look upon their service in the Bunge as a way of attracting the attention of national party leaders. The removal of incompatability rules which had prevented government officials from sitting in the Bunge has meant that more bureaucrats now are finding their way into the legislature. Members are rewarded with a generous salary— 1,500 £ a year plus 75 shillings in per diem travel and maintenance allowances. These figures should be compared to the annual per capita income in Tanzania—approximately 450 shillings. The salary alone provides "a powerful incentive for members of the Party to seek election" and "is the most tangible reward that can help to bolster the Party's support among the aspiring elite" (Kjekshus, 1974:37).

In the Soviet Union salaries for legislators are much less generous but this is balanced by a strong ideological incentive to serve the party and through it the people and the nation. Such ideological incentives are probably less salient in Tanzania, thus making it necessary that more tangible financial incentives be provided. Periodic proposals to do away entirely with MP salaries or to reduce them to more reasonable levels have never gotten very far among the Tanzanian ruling elite (Kjekshus, 1974:38).

It is clear that legislative seats are valued in different terms from one legislature to another. Immediate influence over political events comes only with membership in active or vulnerable legislatures. In contrast, membership in all legislatures has at least some career value. Membership in most reactive legislatures is an essential first step to national political power. The leaders of West European democracies are primarily senior parliamentarians who have served long apprenticeships in the legislature. The executive leaders of nations with active or vulnerable legislatures tend to be recruited from the ranks of legislators while the legislatures themselves are dominated by their senior members. Membership in marginal legislatures and in minimal legislatures may pay career dividends for those few members who are able to move from these positions to more important party or bureaucratic posts.

Except for certain minimal and reactive legislatures, the financial value of legislative service seems to be consistently high. We may also assume that legislative membership generally offers opportunities of varying legitimacy for increased income from sources outside the legislature.

Public service in all societies is sufficiently honorific to ensure that most of those who enter the legislature gain status by doing so. In developing societies in which high status positions are scarce, legislative service may be evaluated primarily in these terms. The ideological value of a legislative seat varies directly with the strength of the party ideologies in the political system.

One fairly obvious conclusion is that every legislative seat is valuable to someone. No matter what evaluative terms are used, there are always more aspirants than seats. It has never been said that legislative elections were called and no one showed up. The voters may stay home, but aspiring candidates do not. The types of candidates that emerge, and the types that emerge victoriously are determined by the costs and risks associated with contesting for and serving in the legislature. These the politician must set against the subjective value of the seat to determine whether or not he wishes to play the game.

THE COST OF THE LEGISLATURE:
THE PRICE OF WINNING AND LOSING

Certain costs are attached to all forms of political participation. Potential candidates for the legislature must anticipate and weigh the financial, psychological, and physical costs of the contest.

Financial costs will be high in those systems in which candidates are expected to finance their campaigns from their own resources; if the constituency is large and competition is keen, a successful campaign can be very expensive. The financial burden may be mitigated or exacerbated by the wealth and the private occupations of the candidates.

Candidates whose occupations permit them to spend time without financial sacrifice are fortunate. Other candidates must reduce their private activities in order to enter the political arena. This costs them money and, in addition, if the candidate is unsuccessful (and there are always more losers than winners in the political game), his vocation may not be easily resumed. Winning candidates must decide whether to abandon an occupation or attempt to pursue it along with legislative work. Only certain occupations can be reconciled with a political career. Most lawyers and some business executives can pursue their professions and their parliamentary duties simultaneously; others, such as housewives, farmers, and workers will have difficulty doing both things. Many legislators abandon their private occupations and become professional politicians living off their parliamentary salaries exclusively. Should they lose their legislative seats, the economic consequences can be quite severe.

This type of cost can be reduced to the extent that a politician has a *cushion* to fall back on; cushions are "positions to which individuals may retire after they are defeated" (Seligman, 1971:5) These cushions can be private—personal wealth, an occupation easily resumed, or never abandoned—or public—the promise of an appointed govern-ment position or the availability of a compensated party post. The prospective availability of desirable cushions can make a decision to seek membership in the legislature a good deal less costly.

Costs also may be reckoned in psychological terms. In some societies entry into a legislative career may entail a relative loss of status. This is particularly true for people whose personal wealth, family connections, or successful occupations give them a relatively high status position. However, in most instances the process is quite the reverse. Legislative service means a rise in status and is one of the things that makes membership in the legislature valuable. Rather than a possible loss of status from winning, status costs become relevant if a legislator loses his seat in parliament. A defeated legislator may have to "go back to working for a living" and suffer a loss in status and self-esteem, as well as in money. Again, the availability of cushions can reduce this type of cost. If the politician has an alternative position that is financially rewarding and honorific, he can avoid a loss of status on leaving the legislature.

The physical costs of a political career are sometimes less apparent but nonetheless real. Campaigning in all political systems can be a trying affair, drawing excessively on the physical and psychological strength of the candidates. In some political environments campaign-ing can be dangerous as well; candidates have been assassinated, campaign planes and cars have crashed, and some elections have been fought under war conditions. The candidate may also risk per-sonal and physical sanctions from the military or the police, especially in systems where dominant elites do not look fondly upon opposition.

As with financial and status costs, personal costs are also relevant should the parliamentary seat be lost. In some situations this may indicate a politician's broader failure in the political system and may subject him to sanctions from other governmental authorities. This aspect of cost is particularly relativistic; if a legislator or a candidate has always been threatened by others in the system, additional threats resulting from the legislative arena may be less significant to him than to someone who is unaccustomed to such threats. Alternatively, certain politicians may think that such sanctions will not be applied to them, and will ignore this potential cost.

Financial Costs and the Party System. The financial costs to a politician of gaining a seat in parliament depends upon two factors related to the nature of the political party system: the degree of competition for the seat and the degree to which the political party assumes a role in financing political campaigns. Competition either within or between political parties raises the general cost of campaigns for all involved in the election, while the party's role in financing determines the cost of the campaign to the candidates.

The legislative category within which a parliament is placed provides a rough approximation of the political party system with which it coexists. Parties tend to be weak in active, vulnerable, and marginal legislature categories. They tend to be stronger in the reactive category and strongest in the minimal legislature category.

A great deal has been written on what distinguishes strong parties from weak parties (Mezey, 1975; Chambers, 1963; Huntington, 1968). Internally, a strong party has a centralized structure through which it exercises control over nominations to legislative positions and control over the behavior of legislators once they are elected to office. Externally, a strong party will dominate decision making within its political system. A very strong party will be the only party functioning in its political system. Weak parties, in contrast, tend to be highly decentralized internally, with little control over nominations or legislative behavior. Within the political system weak parties have only the most tenuous involvement in decision making, and they compete openly with other party organizations.

Elections tend to be expensive in those legislative systems associated with weak parties. Usually several candidates seek each seat and this competition raises the cost of campaigning. Candidates are responsible for meeting most of these costs because the parties are too weak to raise sufficient funds.

In the United States and the Philippines election costs have been enormous (Milne, 1970; Jewell and Patterson, 1973:148). Candidates traditionally receive little financial support from their parties and therefore legislative seats either go to those who can afford to pursue them or to the candidates who can attract large campaign contributions from private sources. In Costa Rica candidates for the National Assembly are required to make substantial contributions to the campaigns of their parties despite a policy of state subsidies to the parties (Baker, 1973:113–14). In marginal legislative systems candidates running without government support must provide their own funds. Government-sponsored candidates in contrast have access to funds (often public funds) and are able to run more effective campaigns. Even in these cases, however, candidates are often required to contribute to the campaign. Such has been the pattern in Thailand, South Vietnam, and South Korea, to name three Asian examples. In Colombia and Brazil the parties depend heavily on their candidates' contributions. The personal contribution of a candidate for the Colombian Congress may be equivalent to as much as 50 percent of what the candidate will expect to make if elected to office, while in Brazil "candidates will seek the backing of a party but will finance the campaign themselves" (Anglade, 1970:174–75). In Kenya, which has a highly fragmented single-party system, candidates are often expected to distribute money to those who do any kind of work in their campaign. Estimates of money spent by candidates in the 1969 general elections range from $700 to $11,000—enormous sums of money in a very poor nation (Hopkins, 1971a: 12–13).

In the competitive political systems that are included in the reactive legislature category, elections are highly competitive and therefore expensive. However, parties and sometimes the governments of these nations assume a greater burden of campaign financing, thereby reducing the costs of individual candidates. In the United Kingdom campaign funds are raised through the various levels of the party organization. Candidates will make a small contribution, but typically the amount will not exceed that expected of an ordinary member of the constituency party. Both major parties in West Germany finance the campaigns of their candidates for the Bundestag, but part of the funds are raised by taxing the salaries of the party's incumbents in the legislature (Schleth and Pinto-Duschinsky, 1970; Loewenberg, 1967:56). This, of course, is quite different from requiring candidate contributions because it doesn't exclude aspirants for office on the grounds that they cannot contribute. In the Scandanavian countries a comprehensive system of public subsidies for party campaigns has obviated much of the need for candidate contributions or massive party fund-raising enterprises (Andren, 1970).

As the strength of the parties increases, their financial role also increases. In dominant party systems, such as India under the Congress party, or Mexico under the PRI, the parties assume the responsibility of financing electoral campaigns. In Mexico this holds true for the opposition parties as well. In a study of the 1967 election in one Mexican province, Schmitt (1971:128–30) observed that the major opposition party (PAN) nominated lower-middle and middle-class candidates who could not contribute much in the way of money to the campaign when it could have drawn on its more wealthy backers for candidacies.

Election costs are low and none accrue to the candidate in minimal legislatures dominated by highly centralized single parties, such as the Soviet Union. Even in more decentralized systems, such as Tanzania, where competitive elections within the structure of the governing TANU party are permitted, the party has ensured that each candidate will have equal resources with which to contest the election and that personal wealth will not be a factor (McAuslan and Ghai, 1966).

Cost and Occupation. Lawyers and other professionals tend to dominate the membership of most parliaments. This middle- and upper-middle-class bias is only partially related to the financial costs of contesting elections. Even in Britain and Scandinavia, where costs to the candidate are relatively low, few workers find their way into parliament. The available data on the occupational backgrounds of legislators are plentiful but difficult to compare. Every researcher and every official agency, it seems, has its own unique way of collecting, tabulating, and reporting occupational background data. In Table 11.1 data on the membership of twenty-five legislatures are summarized.

The dominance of lawyers and other professionals such as journalists, teachers, and engineers can be explained by the fact that campaigning and serving in parliament must mean time lost from the practice of one's occupation. This presents no real problem for certain types of professionals. Law, for example, may be practiced "on the side" or its practice may be easily resumed upon the termination of a parliamentary career. In fact, lawyers and journalists may advance their careers through the notoriety of parliamentary service. However, for those people "who follow occupations demanding the full-

TABLE 11.1[a]

Occupational Backgrounds of Members of Selected Legislatures (Percentages)

Country (Source)	Lawyers	Other Profess.	Businessmen	Landowners	Politicians Govt. Offs.	Union Rep. Laborer
U.S. Congress[b] (CQ, 1971:129)	56	23	32	9		1
Costa Rica (Baker, 1979:120)		48	7	18	3	
Philippines (House) (Seibert, 1969:203)	66	16		6		
Chile (Chamber) (IPU, 1973:50)	19	36	11	11		15
Italy (IPU, 1968:67)	21	33	1	1	16	27
Uruguay (Senate) (McDonald, 1971:127)	45	55				
Japan (Kuroda, 1970:20)	6	29	24	3	27	10
Sweden (IPU, 1969:69)			30		59	11
Germany (Watson, 1971:189–90)	7	24	13	7	28	16
France (IPU, 1973:58)	7	41	12	6	13	13
Canada (IPU, 1973:45)	24	23	27	7	2	3
Australia (IPU, 1973:31)	13	14	11	18	12	21

Country						
United Kingdom (IPU, 1970:122)	18	28	28	7	2	14
Kenya (Rouyer, 1971:131)	3	33	23		19	8
Iran (Schulz, 1969:79)		16	11	32	38	
Zambia (Helgerson, 1970:80)		22	14		43	
Thailand (Tunsiri, 1971:43)	18	12	46	5	17	
Nigeria (Kurtz, 1971:104)		38	4	1	36	2
Bangladesh (Jahan, 1976:9)	32	34	20	13		
Argentina (IPU, 1973:25)	38	13	10	3		21
Pakistan (Maniruzzaman, 1971:227)	18		19	58		
Soviet Union (Vanneman, 1972:149)	1	31			17	50
Singapore (IPU, 1973:124)	9	43	48			
Poland (IPU, 1969:56)	1	21			45	32

a Figures will total less than 100% because a residual category for occupations not covered has been eliminated.
b Figures for the United States total more than 100% because categories were not reported in a mutually exclusive format.

time and regular exercise of duties, be they manual workers, industrial managers, or salaried professionals" (Guttsman, 1960: 146),
significant occupational sacrifices may be necessitated by a career in
politics. These people may risk the loss of a job or seniority or the
erosion of their skills if they enter politics for any period of time.

These considerations affect workers most severely. As Table 11.1
indicates, workers comprise a small percentage of the membership of
most legislatures. The only exceptions are countries with strong
leftist parties, such as Italy or France, or countries dominated by
communist parties. Fifty of the sixty-five workers elected to the
French National Assembly in 1946 and sixty-one of the seventy
elected in 1956 were Communist party deputies (Hamon, 1961: 549).
Similarly, most of the workers in the Chilean Congress were members
of the marxist coalition. In these cases the party, often through its
union connections, sees to it that workers who serve in the legislature
undergo no financial hardships. In a minimal legislature, such as the
Supreme Soviet, workers and peasants comprise 50 percent of the
membership, although it should be added that many of those so
classified no longer pursue these occupations and are in fact party
officials that the elite prefers to continue to identify as members of the
proletariat.

Occupational considerations also tend to reduce the number of
business people serving in the legislature, although certainly not to
the extent that workers are discouraged. In full-time legislatures
businessmen may find it difficult to keep up with their occupations.
They may lose position if they are away from their firms for any length
of time, and, if they are very successful in business, the fortunes of
their company may be directly affected by their absence.

After intensive study of the Third and Fourth Republics, Dogan
(1961:64) concluded that deputies "cease generally to pursue effectively their original occupations during a legislative session. A man
who makes a career of politics abandons his vocational career."
Hughes (1962:53–64) estimates that 50 percent of the members of the
Swiss Parliament had no outside occupation while Loewenberg
(1967:110) reports that for the 1957–61 Bundestag 47 percent of the
members had no outside occupations.

Other positions on the public payroll are becoming increasingly
reconcilable with parliamentary service. In France, Japan, Sweden,
Germany, and Italy significant percentages of parliamentarians either

serve simultaneously as government officials or are on temporary leave from government posts. Seats in many marginal legislatures are looked upon as simply one other type of government position to be distributed as patronage by those in power. Thus in the seven parliaments elected between 1958 and 1963 in former French Africa, 55.5 percent of the members had had previous experience as government employees (LeVine, 1968:378).

Costs of Losing: Cushions. The cost of losing a seat in the legislature can be mitigated by the existence of a cushion—a position that a candidate can retreat to if he loses. These cushions have both financial and status aspects. Financially, the question is whether the alternative position can continue to support the politician in the style to which he has become accustomed while serving in the legislature. In status terms the question is whether or not the new position is as prestigious and respectable as legislative membership. To the extent that cushions are comparable in financial and status terms to a seat in the legislature, the legislature becomes a less riskier and therefore a more attractive place for the politician to be.

Membership in American legislatures is so politically and financially rewarding that those who leave the Congress are likely to return to private life in better shape financially, and with a higher status than they had before they began their political careers. Many former congressmen stay in Washington, employing their contacts and skills to aid paying clients who feel in need of congressional influence and expertise. Others retire to political cushions prepared and provided by friends. Judgeships, appointive administrative positions, and lucrative business positions are likely resting places for those who must leave the Congress.

Even those who don't make it to the legislature seem to profit from the experience of running and losing. In one study defeated candidates for the Oregon state legislature reported that they suffered no loss in social esteem or in their occupations; in fact, 80 percent of those interviewed thought that their career opportunities had been enhanced by the experience (Kim, 1971:197). Most of the losers in this race and all of the winners reported some reward from the legislative election experience at little cost to them (Kim, 1970:885). Presumably a similar study centered on the Congress, where rewards are potentially greater, would show similar results.

Cushions appear to be a good deal more tenuous in vulnerable legislatures. Studies of French and Italian legislators have shown an increase in the number of professional politicians "for whom the alternative to politics is unemployment" (Sartori, 1961:596). French parliamentarians during the Third Republic seemed to be less eminent, less successful members of their professions when they entered the Chamber of Deputies; consequently most of their efforts were directed toward remaining on the public payroll (Dogan, 1961:70). However, politicians in Uruguay found leaving the Congress to be relatively painless. There, legislative service helped politicians "to build their administrative future through a political base. Likewise well-known intellectuals . . . may serve one or two terms in the Senate or Chamber, adding to . . . their own prestige" (McDonald, 1971:130).

In Western European parliamentary systems I have categorized as reactive, the power of dissolution in the hands of the cabinet has always been conceived as a means of enforcing party discipline, on the theory that members would rather go along with their party leaders than be compelled to face their constituents and, possibly, the loss of their legislative seats. The growing tendency of members of these parliaments toward longer legislative careers may suggest that they have limited alternatives outside parliament. Although the occupation data suggest that many legislators have nominal middle-class professions to which they can return, the resumption of these professions may not provide sufficient funds or status for the former parliamentarian.

The cost of losing a position in a marginal legislature can be very high. A study of candidates defeated in South Korean legislative elections found 59 percent reporting that their defeat had reduced their social esteem, 22 percent reporting impaired social relations, 50 percent indicating a hindrance to their occupations, 44 percent saying that their income had decreased, and 17 percent claiming that their career opportunities had been hindered (Kim, 1971:197). Similarly, one analyst of Kenyan politics suggests that much of the behavior of legislators in Kenya reflects their feelings of job insecurity, a direct consequence of a dearth of nonpolitical alternatives: "Loss of position in Kenya can be fateful. The income gap between high status positions and other positions held by those with about the same education or resources is extremely high" (Hopkins, 1971a:31). In such situations it is not unreasonable to expect that politicians will devote much of their time to protecting their positions or at least attempting to build their resources against the day when they may have to leave public office. Wallerstein (1965:7) observes that in the weak one-party West African systems the elite is composed of "men who literally could not afford to lose political power."

It can be hypothesized that government party legislators are a bit more insulated from these costs than opposition politicians. In these systems the composition of executive-centered elites tends to be more stable than either the composition or the existence of the legislature. It is possible that the government will provide cushions for its legislative supporters if they decide to disband the legislature itself. From a different perspective, the legislature may be a cushion for members of the elite who have been removed from their positions of power. The government may reward them for past service by providing a legislative seat as a sinecure or a form of severance pay.

Politics in these systems is a sometimes hazardous, always unpredictable business. All politicians are inclined to take what they can get. Many spend a great deal of their time in the public service scheming to provide themselves with cushions to be used when that service ends or is interrupted by forces beyond their control. Land, wealth, contacts, and obligations carefully gathered can tide one over periods of instability. For this reason, corruption is endemic in these political systems and the legislature is no exception. Self-preservation is a superior value to institutional integrity.

The cost of losing a seat in a minimal legislature depends on the circumstances under which it is lost. If the member loses his seat through a process of formal rotation, financial and status losses should be negligible. The member of the Supreme Soviet who serves a term as a reward for past performance will return afterwards to his local area with honor and probably higher status. However, should he have been *asked* to leave because of some indiscretion or a falling out with the party elite, the consequences in these systems can be especially severe. Costs in terms of finance, status, and physical well-being may be assessed. In fact, the costs are so well-known and so formidable that they probably have to be imposed very rarely.

The case of minimal legislatures that permit competition within the party is a bit more complicated. Some of the Tanzanian legislators who lost their reelection campaign to members of their own TANU party in the 1965 election clearly suffered severe losses in esteem and money. While some found cushions in government appointments, others returned to their villages in disgrace (Hopkins, 1971b:37–38).

Personal Costs. The personal cost of legislative politics in supported legislatures is not very great. Aside from the normal hazards of physical exhaustion, mental stress, and disrupted home life, politicians in these systems suffer no extraordinary personal costs.

In less-supported legislatures the situation is quite different. Elections in the Philippines have been characterized by violence; candidates and their workers have died in alarming numbers. This turbulence reflects the nature of competitive politics in that country prior to the Marcos coup which frequently took on the aspects of a family vendetta (See Landé, 1964). In marginal legislatures candidates, particularly opposition candidates, may be exposed to sanctions from the police or the armed forces. Legislators and candidates for the legislature have been detained in Thailand, South Vietnam, and South Korea. In military dominated systems coups d'état and the closing of the legislature are always a possibility and actions such as this can involve official sanctions against members of the parliament. Military coups in Ghana and Uganda, for example, made life hazardous for many politicians, including legislators. In Syria, 28 percent of the deputies in the 1954 legislature at one time or another had been imprisoned or exiled as a result of changes in the composition of the ruling elite (Winder, 1963:54). In preliberation South Vietnam just running for the legislature was a dangerous enterprise. Assassinations by guerillas as well as incarceration by the police were both real possibilities.

RISK: THE PROBABILITIES OF WINNING AND LOSING

Costs always are conditioned by an evaluation of the risks. The costs involved in winning legislative membership become less significant as the risk of losing an election decreases. Put simply, most people are willing to bet much more on a sure thing than on a long shot. Similarly, the cost of losing a legislative seat becomes less significant to the extent that tenure in the legislature becomes more certain and predictable. There is no need to worry about what will happen if you lose your seat in the legislature if, for whatever reasons, there is little probability that such an event will come to pass.

The Probability of Winning. The major factor affecting the probability of winning an election is the nature of the party system. Just as parties can ameliorate the costs of competing for office, parties can influence the chances that a particular candidate will win or lose. Consequently this aspect of risk is reduced in stronger party systems and increased in weaker party systems.

In political systems dominated by a single party designation as the party's nominee is tantamount to election because the general election is either noncontested or weakly contested. This is the case in countries dominated by communist political parties. Also, in Mexico candidates of the governing party usually win, except for those few unfortunate enough to be nominated in the occasional constituency where the small opposition parties happen to be strongest. One interesting exception to these generalizations is Tanzania. The single party in that country—TANU—often endorses two or three candidates in a constituency and provides each with equal access to campaign resources. The uncertainty engendered by such a procedure is indicated by the 1965 election results, which saw many incumbents, including ministers, defeated, often by political unknowns.

In competitive party systems, the uncertainty of election results is usually greater than in single party systems, but even then parties can and do lend some predictability to the outcome. Stable institutionalized parties develop allegiances among the voters which contribute to long-term party dominance of particular legislative constituencies. Thus, in the United States and Great Britain, even though almost all legislative seats are contested, only a handful of constituencies are marginal ones in which election outcomes are really uncertain.

In other systems proportional representation provides the party with an additional means of increasing the predictability of election outcomes for its candidates. When a list system is used, the location of a candidate's name at the top of the list can ensure his victory and thereby permit him to make a more rational decision on the costs that he cares to incur. Candidates at the bottom of the list are assured of losing, so they need not commit any resources to the battle. The success or failure of candidates in the middle ranks of the list is determined by the overall size of the party's vote rather than by the efforts or resources expended by individual candidates.

Other proportional representation systems work differently. In Chile, Italy, and Finland, PR is used to divide seats among the political parties. However, voters also indicate their preference for particular candidates and these votes determine to whom the party's seats go. Thus a candidate's personal resources can, in these instances, increase his chances of electoral success (Gil, 1966: 215–19; Kogan, 1962:61–62; Pesonen, 1972:213–15). Finally, the German electoral system provides a combination of a single-member and a proportional representation system. This combination permits the party to assure the election of some candidates by placing their names on both the proportional list and in a single-member district. If a candidate loses his constituency, he may still win in the proportional allotment phases of the election if his name is high enough on his party's list (Loewenberg, 1967:63–83).

In the weak or no-party systems in the marginal category both costs and uncertainty are maximized. When elections are irregular and parties are fluid, long-term allegiances to parties or candidates do not develop. Elections are often contested by numerous candidates, many running as independents, thereby further increasing the uncertainty of the outcome. The result is that the candidates with the most money to spend can significantly increase their probability of victory and this situation can occur in almost any district, not simply in a marginal few.

Such arrangements often work to the advantage of the government party. In Thailand the various government parties that have contested the sporadic elections held in that country invariably return more of their candidates than any other party grouping. By using its access to public funds, its control of the electoral machinery, and the aid of the bureaucracy pluralities are engineered for government candidates in district contests in which there are often as many as six candidates for each available seat (Mezey, 1975). In South Vietnam prior to 1975 campaigning against government candidates was a discouraging process. In the 1959 election Nguyen Tuyet Mai ran for the legislature against a protegé of the infamous Madame Nhu; she describes her experiences in these terms:

I soon learned that it did not pay to run as a real independent in "democratic" Vietnam. Concentrated against my candidacy was the entire administrative structure of Bien Hoa, reinforced by the secret agents of Dr. Tuyen's organization (modestly called the "Service for Social and Political Research of the Presidency") . . . the military authorities stationed in the province, and all the frightened "functionaries" of Bien Hoa for whom Mrs. Nhu's (*i.e.*, the Government candidate's) electoral defeat could mean trouble from higher authorities. (Nguyen, 1962:13)

Candidates who do well without government support are usually people with personal resources to rely on. Sometimes these resources are financial, but not always. In Thailand a candidate can win if his name is well known in the constituency. A school teacher, or the scion of a famous family, or someone who previously served in the legislature and is fondly remembered all can make good candidates. The Government party makes an effort to coopt likely winners into its ranks, but when it fails to do so, these candidates can win on their own.

In other countries the government may not field a slate of legislative candidates. Military governments in Latin America traditionally remain aloof from electoral politics. In Brazil all parties are highly personalized and are led by people of wealth and influence. Those with the greatest of these resources are the likely winners and after the election they reach an appropriate modus vivendi with the bureaucrats who run the country.

Losing. The risk of losing a legislative seat once it is won depends upon the vulnerability of the legislator to electoral defeat and the vulnerability of the legislature to extraconstitutional attacks.

The risk of electoral defeat will increase with the frequency of elections simply because frequent elections mean more opportunities to be defeated. If elections are not only frequent but at irregular intervals, the risk of defeat becomes greater. When elections are predictable, the incumbent can prepare; these preparations plus the advantages that usually accrue to incumbents make the office-holder a likely winner in an election campaign. A surprise election, however, may find an incumbent in a more vulnerable position and thereby neutralize any advantage he might have.

Institutional vulnerability is, of course, directly correlated with the degree to which the legislature is supported. In less-supported legislatures where coups and the abrupt closure of the legislature are likely to occur, a legislative career may be nasty, brutish, and short. In more-supported legislatures these events are unlikely to occur and therefore they are not a factor in the career calculations of aspiring politicians.

In legislative settings where electoral and institutional vulnerability is low, the legislative career will become professionalized. Members will come to the legislature with the expectation of staying. Personnel turnover will be low because few incumbents will leave voluntarilly and few will be defeated. Legislative service will become a career to which the incumbent devotes most of his time and energy, while his commitments to his nonlegislative occupation declines or disappears entirely.

Electoral vulnerability is moderate in active and vulnerable legislatures. Legislators serve long, fixed terms which cannot be shortened by executive action. The constitutions under which these legislatures operate do not provide a means for premature dissolution of the legislature. Although most reactive legislatures can be dissolved by the government, this option has fallen into disuse. The threat of a sudden election was thought to be a way for the government to encourage legislators to support its policies. However, governments have found elections as onerous as have legislators and seem to be unenthusiastic about braving an election when there is a clear option not to do so. Consequently, the electoral vulnerability of these legislators is not significantly increased by the existence of the dissolution power.

When elections are held, the data indicate that the members of active, vulnerable, and reactive legislatures generally stand a much better chance of winning than of losing. American legislators appear to be nearly invincible. Only 6 percent of the incumbent members of the United States House of Representatives who sought reelection between 1956 and 1970 were defeated; 16 percent of the senators running for reelection between 1952 and 1970 lost (Jewell and Patterson, 1973: 122). First-termers seldom account for more than 20 percent of the membership of the House of Representatives; most of the time the figure is closer to 15 percent.

The American case seems somewhat extreme. First-termers accounted for 43 percent of the members elected to the Philippine Congress in 1970 (Dodd, 1973:16), a bit over one-third of the total membership of the Italian Chamber of Deputies during the 1946–58 period (Sartori, 1961:585), and 29 percent of the members of the 1956 French National Assembly (Loewenberg, 1967:88).

For reactive legislatures the data are similar. Sixteen percent of the membership of the 1959 British House of Commons and 26 percent of the 1965 German Bundestag were newcomers (Loewenberg, 1967:88). Hughes (1962:54) estimates that usually about 25 percent of the Swiss National Councillors are first-termers. The turnover rate resulting from elections to the Canadian House of Commons has been estimated at approximately 40 percent (Kornberg, 1970:71). While there is some variation in these figures, they do indicate a fair degree of continuity in the membership of these legislators from one election to the next, which further suggests that the vulnerability of parliamentarians to electoral defeat is not extraordinarily high.

Those systems that formally discourage legislative careerism are exceptions to this generalization. As we have noted, members of the Mexican Congress are constitutionally restricted to serving one term. The Congress party of India has an informal arrangement whereby one-third of its parliamentarians are rotated out of office at each election. Thus, 48 percent of the MPs elected to the Third Lok Sabha (1962–67) had no previous legislative experience (Berry, 1971:82).

When elections are held for seats in marginal legislatures, vulnerability to defeat is very great. Outcomes are unpredictable largely because of the party-less election campaigns and the high number of independent candidacies. In the 1969 election in Afghanistan, for example, 60 percent of the 160 Wolesi Jirgah incumbents who sought reelection were defeated (Weinbaum, 1972:69). In 1965 most of the 250 incumbent members of the Ethiopian Parliament sought reelection, but only 87 were successful (Markakis and Beyene, 1967:211). First-term legislators accounted for 69 percent of the 1960 Libyan Assembly (Winder, 1962:422), 63 percent of the 1969 Thai National Assembly (Tunsiri, 1971), and 60 percent of all Syrian deputies elected between 1919 and 1954 (Winder, 1962:425).

Electoral vulnerability is not a factor in minimal legislatures. In Marxist countries legislators are rotated in and out of the legislature for a variety of reasons. These occurrences are seldom considered as a loss of position. Rather, these members are either being replaced by others to whom the elite wants to give the honor of legislative membership, or they are being moved to other nonlegislative positions of influence.

Institutional vulnerability is a very salient consideration for members of less-supported legislatures. In recent years Philippine, Chilean, and Uruguayan legislators have had their political careers abruptly ended by military coup; some have been imprisoned or exiled. In the case of some less-supported legislatures the threat to a legislative career may lie in constitutional alterations rather than in military action. For example, the coming of the Fifth French Republic saw the departure from office of 406 incumbent members of the National Assembly of the Fourth Republic, including sixty-two who decided not to seek reelection (Ehrmann, 1971:146).

In marginal legislatures the threat of military intervention is omnipresent and such occurrences constitute the major impediment to
legislative careerism. In Thailand elections rarely have been held on
schedule during that country's forty-six years of constitutional government. It has been more common for the life of the parliament to be
ended by a coup d'état rather than by the constitutional requirement
for reelection.

Also in these legislatures many legislative careers are foreshort-
ened by anticipated rather than actual military intervention. Legislators may serve just long enough to attract sufficient attention to
enable them to move out of the legislature to a position of greater
influence and presumably greater stability. The institution's vulnerability to attack by nonlegislative elites will discourage politicians from
planning their careers around the legislature. Risk is high in such
legislative systems and the wise politician makes what he can as
quickly as he can and then leaves for safer havens.

The probability of losing a legislative position once elected to it is
summarized in Figure 11:1 for our five types of legislatures. Electoral
and institutional vulnerability are greatest in marginal legislatures
and, to a slightly lesser extent, in vulnerable legislatures. For members of these legislatures the risk of losing a position is greatest.
Institutional vulnerability is very low in active, reactive, and minimal
legislatures, with modest electoral vulnerability in the first two
categories and little vulnerability in the last.

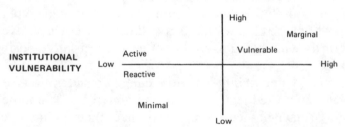

FIGURE 11.1   Comparing Legislatures: Electoral and Institutional Vulnerability

Three concepts have been used to organize the diverse data presented in the foregoing discussion: the subjective *value* of the legislative seat and the *cost* and *risk* involved in attaining and holding that
seat. While we have noted several instances of intracategory varia-

tion, some general assessments can be made which will suggest the nature of parliamentary recruitment in the five types of legislatures that we have defined.

Membership in active legislatures is valuable to politicians for political, career, and financial reasons, while status and ideological considerations are secondary in importance. Seeking legislative membership is very costly to the individual politician and his success in gaining office depends quite heavily on the personal resources that he is willing and able to contribute. Once in office, however, the rewards more than compensate for the cost, while the risk involved in seeking and serving in the legislature is minimal. Thus, membership in these institutions is very attractive.

The risks are somewhat greater in a vulnerable legislature. This risk stems from the possibility of extraconstitutional attacks on legislative prerogatives—events which make parliamentary service much less attractive. In the short run, however, risks appear to be reasonable as attested to by the relatively long and secure tenure of legislators. In fact, some analysts have noted the overdependence of these politicians on parliamentary service as a way to earn a living, a factor that suggests that cushions may not be widely available if one unexpectedly loses position.

Membership in reactive legislatures is valuable primarily because of career considerations. Financial, ideological, and status value are secondary considerations, while little immediate political influence stems from legislative membership. The cost of winning is minimal for legislators, although some must make financial sacrifices to remain in office. Risk is relatively low. Many members enjoy quite lengthy stays in office and extraconstitutional action against them or their highly supported institutions is quite improbable.

Membership in marginal legislatures is valuable primarily in financial terms. The importance of political influence, career, and status considerations varies between and within legislatures, while ideological factors are usually irrelevant. Costs are very high; electoral politics is carried on in an unstructured free-for-all atmosphere in which those with money and the willingness to spend it are advantaged. Risks are also high. Cushions exist for only a few favored legislators, and the sudden end of a legislative career is always a possibility. Much of the legislative behavior in these systems can best be understood in terms of cushion building. These legislatures can be summarized as high risk–high reward systems.

Service in a minimal legislature carries few risks, no costs, and the mostly intangible rewards of status and ideological gratification. Tenure is designed to be short and cushions are generally available as long as the loss of position is part of the normal course of events.

Chapter 12

THE LEGISLATURE AND SYSTEM MAINTENANCE: INTEGRATION, MOBILIZATION, AND LEGITIMIZATION

Ideally a legislature, because of what it is as well as because of what it does, can have an important role to play in promoting the integration of the political system, mobilizing support for regime policies and legitimizing the regime. Because a legislature is a national institution with a membership drawn from the entire country, it has the capacity to bring representatives from various subcultures together in a common political elite. Also, by providing regional, ethnic, or ideological subcultures with representation in the political system, integration at the mass level can be advanced. Representation also should increase the support for specific policies because citizens who feel that they have had a say in the policy-making process should be inclined to acquiesce in or support these policies, even if they do not agree with them. Finally, the incorporation of all elements in society into the political process through legislative representation should render the regime itself legitimate. It can claim the right to govern not simply because it possesses a monopoly of coercive instruments but because the inclusion of its citizens in the policy process leads them to accept and support its right to govern. Also, institutionalized legislatures may embody many of the national symbols of the country and salient legislative activity can confer those symbols upon both the regime and the policies that they enact.

All of these system-maintenance activities of the legislature are *symbolic* in the sense that they rely less on specific legislative action and more on the legislature just "being there." As such they may be capable of dealing with less severe threats to stability, but they may not be very effective in the face of more serious challenges. In those situations legislatures and their members may be capable of engaging in more concrete activities to facilitate system maintenance.

For example, the policies passed by the legislature can be integrative. National identity may be fostered by laws creating a national flag or a national airline or a national railway system. Differences among political subcultures can be compromised during the deliberative phase of policymaking, resulting in policies that bring contesting elements of society more closely together. The public deliberation and passage of regime policy proposals can render those policies legitimate in the hearts and minds of citizens. Legislators may more actively mobilize support for regime policies by going to their constituents, explaining policies to them, and encouraging their compliance. They may act to make these policies more palatable by bringing constituency grievances back to national administrators who in turn can react by altering implementation practices to eliminate sources of grievances. Legislatures can legitimize a regime by meeting regularly and openly and thus symbolizing to the population the existence and operation of a constitutional (i.e., legitimate) political system. By converting popular wishes expressed in parliamentary elections into policy decisions that reflect these wishes, legislatures can increase the legitimacy of regimes that claim to rely upon the will of the people.

The plethora of unstable political systems around the world, most of which have legislatures, suggests that many legislatures are not very effective either as symbolic or active system-maintenance instruments. These legislatures may be unsuccessful for several reasons. Their members may be irresponsible or incompetent, or a legislature simply may not be an appropriate institution for the political system in question. More likely, when legislators are associated with unstable political systems, it may indicate basic weaknesses or cleavages in the political system that are beyond the capacity of legislatures or other political institutions to resolve. Legislatures are essentially creatures of the political system in which they exist and while they can contribute much to that system, they are ordinarily incapable of transforming it—of creating integration out of disintegration, of legitimizing that which has no other claim to legitimacy, or mobilizing support for unpopular and oppressive policies.

Similarly, legislatures associated with stable political systems are not necessarily the sole or immediate cause of such stability. If a system is well integrated and highly legitimate, the legislature's contribution may simply be to refrain from doing anything to disturb that salubrious state of affairs. Alternatively, it may, through symbols or action "maintain" the situation, but only rarely will it have been responsible for having brought political order to a society.

Also legislatures need not be the only structures in society that are capable of performing system-maintenance activities. As was the case with representational activities, it is likely that the more structures in a society that engage in system-maintenance activities, the more successful any one structure will be. If a legislature is the only integrative element in a system subject to strong disintegrative forces, the legislature must surely fail to bring about integration. However, if a strong party system also exists to help cope with disintegrative tendencies, the legislature is more likely to be successful in what it does.

When legislatures are associated with stable, integrated, and legitimate political systems, they themselves are likely to be the objects of support from both mass and elite publics. Thus active, reactive, and minimal legislatures operate in stable political systems to whose maintenance they do not detract and may contribute. When legislatures are associated with unstable political systems, they are likely to be less supported. Thus, vulnerable and marginal legislatures usually operate in systems characterized by instability to which the legislature may contribute or which it may be incapable of doing anything about.

What legislatures actually do in regard to system maintenance is a function both of elite and mass expectations. Incumbent elites will generally expect legislatures to engage in any form of system-maintenance activity that will not pose a short-term threat to their own incumbency. In minimal, marginal, and vulnerable legislatures these expectations will favor symbolic activity as well as more concrete activities aimed at mobilizing support for regime policies; they will oppose activities that threaten their dominance, such as the seeking of policy compromises in legislative arenas over which they exercise little control.

However, these elite expectations may well run counter to mass expectations that, as we have seen, very strongly favor the representational activities of legislators. Clearly it is difficult—perhaps impossible in a severely divided society—for a legislator to reconcile the particularistic concerns of constituents with the general concerns of national elites. Because of the role strain imposed by these conflicting sets of expectations, members of marginal and vulnerable legislatures are likely to be less successful and less active in regard to system maintenance than their counterparts in minimal legislatures where mass expectations have a much less significant effect on legislative activity.

Members of active and reactive legislatures are less likely to confront conflicting mass and elite expectations and are also less likely to have to deal with severe threats to political stability. While elites in these systems would prefer that legislative acts advance their own immediate interests, they generally accept the legitimacy of mass expectations to the contrary. Legislators in these systems then have the luxury of being able to engage in those system-maintenance activities that are acceptable to both mass and elite publics and to avoid those which will evoke the enmity of either side. In any event such activities do not assume an especially high priority because, as we've said, these legislatures function in generally stable political systems.

In the discussion that follows I will pay more attention to the system-maintenance performance of legislatures in unstable than in stable political systems, primarily because that's where most of the research work has been done. Unfortunately, but understandably, researchers have focused on the legislature's attempts to maintain political stability in essentially unstable systems and have generally ignored the question of whether or not legislatures have positively contributed to the stability of already-stable political systems.

INTEGRATION

Jean Grossholtz (1970:94) defines the process and the problem of integration in the following terms:

Integration implies some level of effective commitment to the commonality of all groups or political levels, but it does not require the obliteration of primary identifications of race, religion, family or culture. The process of integration involves the penetration of the primary, occupational or geographic groups by a broader national identification. In essence, integration creates an alternative secular and more adaptive form of association holding out to the individual the option of securing his goals through associations of larger size. . . . The acceptability of the central political institutions and associations depends on the level of security that contending groups feel is provided them and their interests, and on the recognition on the part of the contenders that the interests of other groups are legitimate.

Legislatures are presumed to contribute to integration by virtue of their "peculiar capacity to centralize decision-making while preserving pluralistic and often decentralized power" (Sisson and Snowiss, 1975:13).

Alternative Integrative Structures. Of course, the integrative capacity of the legislature is not entirely "peculiar" to it alone; there are other structural arrangments which are capable of providing for diversity within a common national setting. Federalism is one of the more venerable arrangements and attempts to deal with problems of territorial diversity by dividing political authority between national and local governmental levels, thereby allowing the various regions to maintain control over their own immediate affairs and reserving to the central authority control over those affairs that the various regions agree to be of concern to all.

While federalism has been an effective structural form in the United States, Switzerland, Germany, India, and other countries, it has been somewhat less of a success in countries such as Nigeria and Kenya. Malcolm Jewell (1977:16–20) has suggested two major limitations on the effectiveness of federalism as an integrative mechanism. First, it may emphasize rather than moderate differences. In Nigeria, for example, the federal structure was based on regions, each of which was dominated by a different tribe. This resulted in a party system in which each party drew most its support from one tribe, leading to the exacerbation of tribal and regional differences and the ultimate breakdown of the system in civil war.

Another problem occurs when the geographical areas of the country are heterogeneous. In Malaysia, for example, where most states have substantial minority blocs, the rights of these groups would not be guaranteed simply by delegating authority to the states. The success of federalism in India, in contrast, is a result of the development of relatively homogeneous language states which serve to alleviate the anxieties of the numerous language groups in the nation.

Where federalism has worked recently to facilitate integration, or where integration has been achieved in the absence of a federal system, the party system has been the key variable. In Malaysia the Alliance party has brought integrative pressures to bear on Chinese and Malay groups (Musolf and Springer, 1977:114) and in India the Congress party was at least as important as the federal structure in integrating that society. In Kenya the governing KANU party feared the disintegrative effects of federalism and so abolished the Senate, the "federal" part of the national legislature, and saw to it that legislation was passed that practically eliminated the power of the regional governments. Clearly, Jomo Kenyatta decided that Kenya was to be integrated through his own personal charisma and through KANU and not by a system of regional autonomy which in his view exacerbated tribal differences (Stultz, 1970). Finally, and perhaps most obviously, the degree to which the Soviet Union today represents an integrated society is much less a product of the federal system and much more a product of the integrative capacities of the Communist party.

The examples of India, the Soviet Union, and Malaysia confirms Grossholtz's observation (1970:95) that the legislature "is an expression of the party system," or, put differently, that the integrative activities of the legislature—the things that it does and the things that it can do—are a product of the party system with which it coexists. Thus, legislatures operating without the assistance of an integrative party system will be hard put to bring any degree of integration to a disintegrated society.

Legislative Responses to Integrative Problems. There are various things that legislatures can do to respond to disintegrative forces in society. Symbolic actions involve no clear policy determination; rather they are abstractions designed to placate those who are making demands on the system. As noted in Chapter 9, legislators may respond to constituency demands by simply making a speech in the legislature, and even though that action does not result in a policy that speaks to the demand, it does represent a symbolic act which can in certain circumstances satisfy those who have made the demand. Similarly, legislatures may symbolically represent all groups in society by providing seats in the legislature for everyone and thus an opportunity for everyone to be a part of the national political system.

The legislature has at least two characteristics that make it uniquely able to provide such a response. First, it is a multimember body, the membership of which can be distributed to fit the demographic contours of any nation. Second, it is also an institution that requires no special skills of those who serve in it. If such skills were required, it might be difficult to achieve demographic balance, as the experience of bureaucracies would seem to indicate. In the Pacific Islands (Meller, 1973:5) and in Tanzania (Hopkins, 1971b:75–77) evidence has been found that the composition of the legislature is more representative of the population than the composition of bureaucratic elites, and it is reasonable to believe that the situation would be similar in other nations.

There is evidence that in nations characterized by ethnic conflict, efforts are made that result in the allocating of seats in the legislature in proportion to the distribution of particular groups in the population. Such appears to be the case in such plural societies as Lebanon, Malaysia, Kenya, the Soviet Union, and, to some extent, Yugoslavia and India, as the data in Table 12:1 suggest. In that table a gini coefficient has been computed to assess the fit between the distribution of groups within the population and the distribution of seats within the legislature. If every group were represented in the legislature in exact proportion to its percentage of the national population, the gini coefficient would be zero. Alternatively, if one group monopolized all of the seats in the legislature to the exclusion of all other groups, then the gini coefficient would be 1.0 (Alker, 1965:35–42).

TABLE 12.1

Gini Coefficients Measuring Proportionality of
Minority Representation in Six Legislatures

Country (Source)	Year	Groups	Gini Coefficient
Lebanon (Crowe, 1970:276; Baaklini, 1972:217)	1968–72	Eight religious groups	.10
Malaysia (Jewell, 1977:33)	1964	Three racial groups	.13
Kenya (Rouyer, 1971:177, 179)	1963	Fifteen tribal groups	.17
Soviet Union (Vanneman, 1972:154)	1966	Seventeen nationality groups	.19
Yugoslavia (Cohen, 1977:136)	1969	Ten nationality groups	.24
Rajastan (Sisson and Shrader, 1977:62)	1962–67	Seven caste groups	.43

In all of these societies religious, racial, tribal, national, or class identifications have been a basis for representation in the legislature and for these groups the legislature must at least symbolize their involvement with the nation as a whole. Whether or not such symbolic representation is sufficient to create an integrated society depends on the severity of the cleavages involved. Thus Lebanon, with perhaps the most perfect fit between population distribution and legislative seats at this writing appears to be in the process of disintegrating. In the case of Malaysia, it was after the data demonstrating strong symbolic representation in the legislature was collected that the country was besieged by race riots that led to the suspension of Parliament and a period of martial law. On the other hand, the other four systems included in Table 12:1, although having somewhat higher gini coefficients than Lebanon and Malaysia, have been more stable than those two countries. In the cases of the Soviet Union, Yugoslavia, and Rajasthan, much of the stability is attributable to strong party systems, while in Kenya political stability resided in the charisma of President Jomo Kenyatta.

Electoral Systems, Symbolic Representation, and Integration. Whether or not groups are fairly represented in the legislature, and whether or not such representation has an integrative effect depends to some degree on the electoral system that is employed. Jewell (1977) surveys the effect of five different electoral systems on the integrative capacities of the legislature—separate electorates, reserved seats, single-member districts, multimember districts, and proportional representation. He concludes that separate electorates—a process by which voters are segregated by group—exacerbated ethnic conflict and retarded integration in countries such as Ceylon, colonial India, and Fiji. Legislators·who owed their election to the votes of only one ethnic group became so strongly attached to the interests of that group that they were incapable of empathizing with the views of other groups and thus incapable of developing national policies.

In contrast, the practice of reserving legislative seats for members of certain ethnic groups should encourage integration because it guarantees representation to each ethnic group while at the same time requiring the candidate to appeal to voters from all groups. The legislator, it is argued, thereby becomes dependent on the votes of various groups which in turn should moderate his position on ethnic issues. In India the reserving of seats for Scheduled Caste members, and in Lebanon for religious groups, has meant that candidates for these seats have had to rely on the votes of members of other castes or religions. However, the question remains as to whether the legislator elected by this procedure actually represents the group for which the seat is reserved, or whether that tie is not simply balanced but overwhelmed by the need to create a broad political alliance in order to win elections.

In the case of single-member districts the integrative effect of the electoral system is contingent upon the method used for defining legislative districts. If districts are drawn in such a way as to ensure minority-group representation—as they have been in Ceylon—then groups will be adequately represented. However, if a group is too evenly distributed across the country—as are Indians in Malaysia or black people in the United States—then they will be denied adequate representation by the single-member district system. The integrative effects of the system are questionable. In countries such as Northern Ireland, where minorities are geographically concentrated, the system did nothing to reduce conflict because it ensured that Catholics would have only Catholic candidates to vote for and Protestants only Protestant candidates. On the other hand, the system in the United States has generally produced more heterogeneous districts which have compelled legislative candidates to appeal to a broader spectrum of the society.

Jewell finds that multimember plurality systems in which several legislators run at large in a district with the candidates with the most votes winning the seats reduces minority-group representation by encouraging the dominant group to vote only for their own people. He says that in the United States this system, used in many state and local legislative bodies, has substantially reduced the number of legislators who could be elected directly by black voters and other minority groups.

Proportional representation, in comparison, has had an integrative effect in many countries because it encourages political parties to have representatives of many different groups on their list and thereby make it more attractive to voters from all groups. This has been the case in Belgium, Germany, and Israel. However, if parties decide to weigh their lists heavily in favor of a particular group in society, the integrative effects of this electoral system could be reduced.

Representation and Compromise. The limitations of this type of analysis should be obvious. Not very much of the integration of the United States or the disintegration of Northern Ireland can be attributed to single-member district systems. Reserved seat systems have accompanied relative political stability in India and complete chaos in Lebanon. Proportional representation has had an integrative impact in Germany and Italy and a disintegrative impact in postindependence Indonesia. Clearly much more is involved than how members are elected to the legislature and, in many more countries, contesting groups demand much more than simply symbolic representation in the legislature. Presumably the reason why groups want to be represented in the legislature is so that their interests will be reflected and protected in the policy-making process. If all groups are represented in the legislature, it becomes an arena in which differences among groups can be compromised.

The extent to which this actually occurs is questionable, however, because the legislator must deal with the problem of reconciling the needs of his constituents with the needs of other groups and the needs of the nation as a whole. If, for example, resources are scarce and the "needs of the nation" suggest an allocation that would clearly disadvantage certain areas or groups, what is the legislator who represents these potential "losers" to do: facilitate integration by voting for the nation, or contribute to disintegration by defending his constituents? Doing the former does violence to the representational expectations of those who elect him, the consequences of which we discussed in detail in Chapter 9, but doing the latter alienates the legislator from his colleagues in the emerging "national elite" and violates the expectations of central executive elites.

In Yugoslavia, for example, meetings of the Chamber of Nationalities have seldom resulted in the compromising of regional conflicts or in the mobilization of a consensus behind a policy, but have simply provided occasions for "the raw articulation of republican and provincial interests" (Cohen, 1977:148). When legislators seek to act differently (in a more "integrative manner"), the consequences may be severe. Thus, one Croatian representative was subjected to the ignominity of being removed from office by his constituency because he had assumed a "federal" perspective on several matters in dispute between his republic and the authorities in Belgrade, and because he had criticized Croat leaders for not doing more to oppose the development of republican nationalism (Cohen, 1977:142).

In many systems compromises cannot be reached in the legislature because the groups represented view the situation as a zero-sum game. In Belgium, for example, the Parliament has not been very successful in resolving the serious linguistic conflict between Flemings and Walloons; one of the reasons for this is that the issue "does not lend itself easily to compromise. Given the either/or quality of the conflict, it has been difficult to placate the competing groups by granting incremental benefits or by extracting incremental costs" (Obler, 1973b:12). Similarly, in Lebanon, despite a political system designed explicitly for power-sharing among the major religious groups in the country, compromises have been difficult to reach as legislators have had to view themselves as representatives of their own religious communities. In one sense this is a product of the constitutional arrangement which, instead of fostering integration, can be viewed from another perspective as legitimizing the existence of these groups, encouraging group identity, and discouraging a national identification.

On the other hand, in political systems where disintegrative conflict is much less intense, the legislature may be more successful in providing an arena for conflict management. Thus, in Colombia, the legislature "has served as a key political institution in the territorial and political integration of the country, providing a forum where regional politicians interact and relate to political party and governmental activity" (Hoskin, 1975:154). And in Malaysia, where ethnic divisions are very severe and highly salient, a recent study concludes that the Parliament in that country is providing an arena for identifying issues that "penetrate communal boundaries" and "is playing an important role in fashioning political debates and implementing development strategies which may help transcend the limits of communal politics" (Musolf and Springer, 1977:133).

In sum, it can be said that the most that the legislature can do in the face of severe disintegrative pressures is to respond symbolically by affording all groups adequate representation, and that this response is likely to be quite inadequate if that is all that the political system is prepared to do. If, however, such responses are coupled with a strong integrative party system, as is the case in Malaysia, and, perhaps, a federal structure, as is the case in Switzerland, then symbolic representation in the legislature may be useful. Symbolic representation alone can probably deal effectively with only minor disintegrative pressures.

INCREASING SUPPORT FOR POLICIES

One problem confronting all political systems is that of making their policies palatable to their citizens. Government policies can always be imposed by force but it is generally agreed that policies are more likely to be successful if people obey them not simply because they have to but because they think they are right. Achieving this degree of support for policies is not always easy, especially in societies undergoing rapid socioeconomic changes. The short-run results of development programs can range from inconvenience to severe dislocations for sizable segments of the population and, because the presumably long-run benefits of these programs are not immediately apparent, it is difficult to mobilize support for them. Even in societies which are not changing very rapidly there is still the problem of explaining new government policies to those who are immediately affected by them and of encouraging their support for what has to be done.

Legislative activities designed to mobilize support, like those aimed at encouraging integration, can be either symbolic or concrete. One example of the former is the so-called cathartic, or safety-valve functions of legislatures.

The Safety Valve. It has been frequently observed that legislative debates can have the effect of allowing dissident elements whose policy positions are not adopted to "blow off steam" in the domesticated confines of the legislature. The presumed effect of this is to "cleanse" the losing side of its frustrations and thereby increase their degree of acceptance for what is ultimately decided. Packenham (1970:530) used these terms in describing the cathartic activities of the Brazilian Congress:

they reduced tension, provided reassurance, and generally enhanced satisfaction with or acquiescence in the policies and programs of the ruling government. In this sense, the Congress was a safety-valve or way of letting off steam in a political system where nobody got all he wanted and/or where the government was not willing to let everyone have what he wanted.

Similarly, in Costa Rica

Heated debate on political issues is reported to satisfy the psychic-aggressive needs of groups within the Costa Rican parties and at all levels of society. . . . The cathartic function of heated political debates was accompanied by an educational function in that the public experienced situations where an air of serenity prevailed among the actors in the Assembly once the debate was over. The lesson imparted was that political opponents need not be deadly enemies and that heated debate or discussion of a political nature need not preclude collaboration and civility. (Baker, 1973:247–48)

Although these activities have been reported for only a few legislatures, it is reasonable to suspect that it is carried out by almost all of them. Vitriolic debates take place as a matter of course in legislatures, and while not specifically designed to increase support for the policies that emerge from the legislature, nonetheless they have that effect because losing groups feel that they have had their say through their representatives.

The Platform. Closely related to this safety-valve function is the capacity of the legislature to provide the government with both a platform and an audience for expounding its programs. In Mexico, for example, the president

uses his annual report to Congress to describe the achievements of his regime. The media give a tremendous amount of coverage to this speech, and it is a principal vehicle for the President to describe the success of his programs and explain future objectives. Following the President's speech, the Chamber President responds to the national executive and his response contains little more than adulatory praise for everything contained in the President's address. (de la Garza, 1972:123–24)

One assessment of the Lebanese Chamber of Deputies concludes that the

Chamber's strength derives from the president's concern for the balancing and managing of support for his regime. In so doing, he must give constant attention to the Chamber, the members of which are there because they have demonstrated their strength. The president needs to satisfy at least their minimal demands or he will be faced with a stalemate. (Crowe, 1970:300)

Finally, one analysis of the legislatures of the Central African Republic, Chad, Congo-Brazzaville, and Gabon, suggests that

The chief function of the Assembly, then, is to provide an organized and recognized body of loyal supporters of the regime who can claim to represent a national synthesis of particular interests and who therefore provide both a semblance of parliamentary approval for the policy and program of the regime and practical support as a team of local political agents. (Quoted in Packenham, 1970:539)

The Intermediary. This last point suggests a more active role for the legislator in mobilizing support for government policies, a role that involves some of the constituency activities of legislators that we dealt with in Chapter 9. More specifically, it draws upon the legislator's role as an intermediary between his constituency and the central government. The support-building impact of these activities is based on the assumption that legislators can bring the problems and the views of the periphery to the attention of the central government, which will then respond either by designing policies that fit the needs of the periphery or by altering the manner in which existing policies are being implemented so as to make them more acceptable to those who have to live under them. In addition, elites also expect the legislator to "penetrate" the periphery on the government's behalf—to articulate its position to the constituency and thereby attempt to mediate between the demands of the local areas and needs and capacities of the center. This last expectation is, of course, a source of conflict for many legislators who find it difficult to act simultaneously as a representative of the government and the constituency.

In marginal legislatures such as Afghanistan and Kenya, legislators clearly choose to be the advocate of the constituency. In Afghanistan Weinbaum (1977:116) estimates that between 40 and 50 percent of the Wolesi Jirgah membership can be classified as "agents" who act as full-time intermediaries on behalf of their constituents or local elites in their interactions with the central administration. In Kenya a sample of MPs ranked various linkage activities that they performed on behalf of their constituents as the activities which occupy most of their time, but ranked the job of explaining government policies to constituents as something to which they devoted very little of their time (Barkan and Okumu, 1974:11). These attitudes clearly reflected the expectations of their constituents, only 8.3 percent of whom ranked "explaining government policies to constituents" as the most important activity to which Kenyan MPs should devote their time, compared to the 34 percent who opted for telling the government what the people in the district want, and the 29 percent who selected "obtain projects and benefits for the district" (Barkan, 1975:22).

As these data suggest and as other studies also have indicated (Hakes, 1970:111–12) Kenyan MPs are not very enthusiastic about acting as the government's agents in the constituency despite the expectations of government officials and of President Jomo Kenyatta, who said in 1965 that "Members of Parliament have a most important duty in the rural areas to urge the people to follow the advice of technicians. . . . We must all work together to capture their imagination, and to see that they are interested and trained" (Stultz, 1970:322). Although Kenyatta's views may have changed somewhat since that statement was made, a more recent analysis still concludes that many MPs do not even attempt to defend government policies despite the expectation of government officials that they should (Hopkins, 1975b:39).

In Malaysia the nature of the legislator's activities as an intermediary is influenced by their partisan affiliation. Government party members emphasize the importance of explaining government policies in their constituencies while Opposition legislators are more oriented toward the role of representing their districts before the government (Musolf and Springer, 1977:126–28).

In minimal legislatures elite expectations about the legislator's role as an intermediary overwhelm any contrary mass expectations. Thus, 33 percent of a sample of members of the Tanzanian Bunge selected explaining government policies to their constituency as the most important aspect of their job, compared with 16 percent who selected promoting the constituency (Hopkins, 1971b:167). These perceptions are clearly reinforced by the sanctions that TANU does not hesitate to apply to those legislators who are perceived to be acting independently in their constituencies (Barkan, 1975:24–25). Similarly, in Singapore, MPs were assumed to have the responsibility of explaining an unpleasant government policy to their constituents and thus "increase the support input of the ruling party to permit the leadership to ignore as far as it can afford, the pressures from the ground and continue to pursue its established priorities" (Chee, 1976:439).

Finally, it should be mentioned that activities designed to mobilize support for government policies are not peculiar to marginal and minimal legislatures. While it has not been looked at very carefully by scholars, there is some evidence that members of other types of legislatures choose this activity as part of their job. For example, a member of the United States House of Representatives has been quoted as saying that he was constantly questioned by

state and local authorities, officials of private organizations, and individuals on how the programs work. . . . Many local leaders may not understand the purposes of the legislation or see its relevance to their communities. The Congressman or Senator, by organizing community conferences, mailing materials and in other ways, can supply important information, interpretation, justification and leadership in his constituency. . . . These activities of explaining, justifying, interpreting, interceding, all help, normally, to build acceptance for government policy, an essential process in democratic governments. (Quoted in Beer, 1966:45–46)

It is important to note that the congressman's statement indicates that the mobilization activity in which he was engaged was in response to *mass* expectations—"state and local authorities, officials of private organizations, and individuals"—and not a response to elite expectations. This suggests that legislators in the course of carrying out their responsibilities to their constituents—something which I've said they do primarily because of mass expectations reinforced by electoral sanctions—also, perhaps unintentionally, increase the level of support for public policies. If legislators provide an accessible route for constituency complaints about the manner in which policies are implemented and enforced, and if they are also capable of providing redress when that is warranted, such activities cannot help but raise support for policies above the level that would obtain were such channels absent or nonfunctioning.

LEGITIMIZATION

By legitimization I mean maintaining or increasing the level of diffuse support for the regime or, put differently, increasing the support that accrues to the regime apart from the extent to which its specific policies are supported.

The capacity of a legislature to legitimize a regime depends upon the fact that it is an elected body and therefore its actions can be advertised as decisions of the people. In all political systems, from western democracies to workers' democracies, political decisions—no matter who makes them—are justified as embodying both the will and the interests of the people. It is reasonable to assume that elites engage in this type of hyperbole because "popular" decisions have a higher claim to legitimacy than decisions that cannot be spoken of in these terms. The argument is, quite simply, that if people think they are making the decisions in the political system, either directly or through their representatives, they will be disposed toward thinking of the political system as legitimate. Thus, different types of political leaders are prepared to tolerate a legislature and to accept the costs that go with such an investment because the legislature constitutes a democratic symbol that pays sizable dividends in terms of domestic and even international legitimacy.

The Legislature as a Symbol Only. The legitimization explanation for the existence of a legislature is most frequently invoked during discussions of minimal legislatures because the casual observer can see no other reason why such institutions should exist. While other reasons do exist (as readers of this book are by now aware), the legitimization argument should not be discarded.

In the Soviet Union the Supreme Soviet is still said to institutionalize and reflect the concept of Socialist Democracy (Vanneman, 1972:231), and an analysis of the 1971 parliamentary elections in Czechoslovakia concludes that the events "seemed clearly to legitimize the regime, since they appeared at best to be a public display of personal reaffirmation of the policies and the leadership of the Communist Party and the National Front. At a minimum, they seemed to signify the cessation of hostility toward the regime" (Dinka and Skidmore, 1973:402).

Legitimization activities have also been suggested as a major function for some marginal legislators. Packenham (1970:528) writes that Brazilian legislators "even where their debate and activities had little or no consequences for elite decision-making [were] enhancing the power of the president insofar as congressional activity legitimized his role and thus provided him with a less costly means for exercising his power." Similarly, the Thai legislature has been described as providing the government "with the appearance if not the reality of democracy" and therefore legitimizing the role of the executive-centered elites who actually run the country (Mezey, 1972:691).

Finally, legitimization also has been suggested as a function of active and reactive legislatures. In western Europe, "parliament projects some of the most salient political symbols of European politics; the building in which the members meet, the costumes of its officers, the pageantry of its great occasions, its daily ceremony, its ritual of speech are, for most citizens, the embodiment of politics . . ." (Loewenberg, 1971a:183). In the United States "the constitutional and traditional base of the legislature and orderly procedures that it follows make legislative action appear legitimate; it has the quality of rectitude. It is regarded by the public as right and proper" (Jewell and Patterson, 1973:11).

What these diverse examples suggest is that legislatures, wherever they are found, symbolize—by their existence, by their procedures, or through the processes by which their members are elected—popular participation in the political arena which endows them with a legitimacy that other institutions find difficult to achieve on their own.

Legislative Saliency and Legitimacy. It has also been argued that the legitimizing impact of the legislature is related to its salience. Gerhard Loewenberg (1971a:190) has hypothesized that "the continuity and salience of parliament affect the durability of public support for the regime, which in turn affects regime stability." Packenham (1970:527–28) in his discussion of the legitimizing impact of the Brazilian Congress suggests that this effect was contingent upon the legislature "meeting regularly and uninterruptedly" and upon the activities of the legislature being "widely reported in the press."

Loewenberg uses data from a reactive legislature (the United Kingdom) and a vulnerable legislature (the Reichstag of Weimar Germany) to test his hypothesis. He takes the number of sittings of the legislature and the membership turnover rate as indices of regime stability, with a decline in sittings and an increase in turnover indicators of instability. In comparing the data for both countries for the 1924–35 period, Loewenberg found that in Germany the annual average number of days on which Parliament met declined through the period while it remained relatively stable in Britain; also, the percent of legislators without previous parliamentary experience tended to increase from election to election in Germany while remaining relatively constant in Britain (Loewenberg, 1971a:195). While causation is, of course, difficult to establish in an analysis such as this, events seem to support Loewenberg's hypothesis. The decline in legitimacy of German political institutions during this period and their eventual breakdown stands in marked contrast to the continued legitimacy and persistence of British institutions during this same period.

Further support for the Loewenberg hypothesis comes from an analysis of seven African countries. In three countries in which military coups occurred (Ghana, Nigeria, Uganda) the annual number of parliamentary meetings tended to decline in the period preceeding the coup, while in four countries in which coups had not taken place (Tanzania, Malawi, Kenya, Zambia) the annual number of meetings either remained constant or increased (Hakes, 1973:14–24). The change in the frequency of parliamentary meetings, and not the absolute number of parliamentary meetings was associated with regime instability.

Another indicator of legislative saliency is media coverage. In Mexico, for instance, a content analysis of three newspapers during the period from 1940 to 1968 showed that activities related to the legislature were usually carried on page one, and that coverage of the Congress had steadily increased since 1940 in each of the three cases (de la Garza, 1972:117). Again, a causal connection is difficult to establish, but it is apparent that during this period the Mexican political system has been perhaps the most stable in Latin America.

Legitimacy and Electoral Conversion Functions. In some countries, the legitimacy that people accord to the system depends on more than just the symbols of democracy that the legislature embodies; there is, in addition, the idea that elections to the parliament are somehow tied to policy outputs or policy commitments. Loewenberg (1971a:187) suggests that the performance of electoral conversion functions by parliament affects the level of public support for the regime, which in turn affects regime stability. Beer (1966:44) has written in similar terms when he suggests that the electoral process is an occasion for a set of commitments between politicians and the public about the future course of public policy which in turn lays a "foundation of consent and acceptance for relevant Government programs in the future."

To test this hypothesis, Loewenberg uses the presence of antiregime parties as an indicator of the difficulties that the legislature will have in performing electoral conversion functions, arguing that the ability to produce policies that are responsive to popular needs depends on the ability of the government to command a legislative majority. Thus, during the 1928–35 period, there was a sharp rise in the percent of the total vote won by antiregime parties in Germany and no increase at all in Great Britain (Loewenberg, 1971a:193), a situation which presumably impeded the electoral conversion activities of the Reichstag compared to the performance of the House of Commons. Hakes (1973:31), in his test of the same hypothesis, looks to a decline in the percentage of contested legislative seats as an indirect indicator of a failure to perform electoral conversion functions and finds that the decline was greatest in the three countries where coups occurred and lower in the four noncoup countries.

Does the Legislature Legitimize? Of the three system-maintenance activities with which we've been concerned in this chapter, legitimization is perhaps the most difficult to analyze. On the one hand, the connection between legitimacy and legislative activity seems so obvious that it should be easily demonstrable. But despite the valiant efforts of Loewenberg and Hakes, legislative performance has been associated but not causally connected with regime legitimacy.

Furthermore, in the short run at least, legislatures may depend upon elites for their legitimacy more than elites depend upon legislatures. Astiz (1974:18) argues that contrary to Packenham's analysis, the Brazilian Congress draws its legitimacy from the regime. Sisson and Snowiss (1975:24–25) suggest that this is the case in every new nation where legislatures did not exist prior to independence or where they were forced upon partisan elites by departing colonial powers as part of the price of independence.

It can be said that a supported legislature positively contributes to the legitimacy of a regime and that a nonsupported legislature *may* contribute. It is difficult to believe that marginal and vulnerable legislatures that can and have disappeared overnight are the major source of legitimacy for the executive-centered elites who run these political systems. In the case of some of these legislatures, in fact, the elites acquire some legitimacy by doing away with the legislature, as Stauffer (1975) notes in connection with the Marcos coup against the Philippine Congress, or as the support for deGaulle's efforts to reduce the influence of the French National Assembly indicates (Patterson, et al., 1973:309–10). In those countries in which the legislature is more representative of upper-class voters than the lower classes, and quite resistant to reforms that may run counter to the interests of economic elites (Packenham, 1970:578; Astiz, 1973a:122), it is difficult to perceive the legislature as a symbol of popular rule and as a legitimizing agent for the entire regime.

CONCLUSION

At the outset of this volume I suggested that the legislature was a remarkably flexible institution capable of a variety of functions in any given political system. It was this flexibility, I argued, which inhibited comparative analysis of legislatures because it so often seemed that legislatures in different countries shared little more in common than a generic title, the meaning of which was not even agreed upon by those who researched the area.

In that first chapter I speculated that the great variation in legislative activity from one nation to the next was attributable to the dominance of different expectations concerning the legislature in different countries. I posited three sets of expectations, or three legislative models, each of which incorporated a different ordering of legislative activities. A policy-making model assumed that the legislature would occupy a central role in the policy-making process and that its performance of other activities would derive from that policy role. In countries where a representation model of the legislature was subscribed to, the policy-making activities of the legislature would be less salient and instead the activities that involve responding to the demands of constituents and interest groups would be viewed as the primary legislative task. Finally, a system maintenance model would emphasize the role of the legislature in fostering the legitimacy and stability of the political system, and these activities would take precedence over the policy-making and representational activities of the legislature.

Once depositing this perspective in the first chapter, I set out to discover exactly what it was that the various legislatures around the world actually did, detouring for one chapter to deal with a methodological problem. Simply put, the problem was how to bring some order to the vast array of information that had been gathered on so many legislatures. The answer was to construct a typology that would permit me, for purposes of comparative analysis, to merge data on similar legislatures. The five-fold typology, which by now should be permanently emblazoned on the reader's memory, was based upon the salience of the legislature's policy-making role and the support accruing to the legislature from mass and elite publics. Armed with this tool, I plunged into the substantive topics of legislative behavior—policy making, constituency and interest group relations, and system-maintenance activities—emerging at this point, some ten chapters later, with the requirement imposed both by compassion for the reader and by the diminishing stamina of the author to bring this treatise to a close.

How best to do this? Rather than simply summarizing what has been said at such length before, I thought that it might be nice, even appropriate, to return to the first chapter and resurrect the three legislative models upon which we speculated, and see whether or not they can add to our understanding of the body of data that we have presented on the five legislative types.

ACTIVE LEGISLATURES

The performance of the active legislature approximates the policy-making model. These few legislatures, operating through strong committee systems, involve themselves at every phase of the policy-making process and stand as at least the equal of executive-centered elites, to whose expectations the performance of the active legislature generally conforms. While the expectations of mass publics are probably more congruent with the representation model, the secure and supported policy-making prerogatives of the active legislature provide its members with the capacities and resources to deal with the particularized demands of mass publics as well as the more generalized demands of interest groups. The apparent capability of the active legislature combined with its accessibility assures it of a very heavy load of both types of demands, and the high level of support accruing to the legislature attests to its general success in dealing with its demand load. Pursuant to the specifications of the policy-making model, the system-maintenance activities of the active legislature are implicit rather than explicit and flow directly from the legislature's policy activism. The model assumes that the political system is rendered legitimate and conflict is successfully managed when public policies are the product of open deliberation among representatives of the people. While the relative stability of the two countries that have active legislatures cannot be wholly attributed to legislative performance, it is reasonable to say that the legislature at least contributes to that level of stability and certainly does not detract from it.

VULNERABLE LEGISLATURES

In their self-perceptions and activities members of vulnerable legislatures aspire to the policy-making model. Like active legislatures, these institutions are also very much involved in all phases of the policy-making process and are assisted in this involvement by strong committee systems. They too are the objects of a heavy volume of particularized and generalized demands from individuals and interest groups oriented toward the representation model, and their policy-making prerogatives assist them substantially in responding to these demands. The difference between the active and vulnerable legislature stems from the fact that the expectations of executive-centered elites concerning the legislature are incongruent with the specifications of the policy-making model and are more congruent with the outlines of the system-maintenance model. The executive seeks a legislature which will be supportive of its personnel and policies and views with some hostility legislative policy-making or representation activities that do not contribute to this support. The tension between legislative perceptions and behavior on the one hand and executive expectations on the other leads to a low level of support for the legislature, less successful legislative performance in response to demands, and little in the way of implicit and explicit system maintenance activities on the part of the vulnerable legislature. That these legislatures have an uncertain life expectancy is attested to by the fate of the Congresses of the Philippines, Chile, Uruguay, the French Fourth Republic, and the Weimar Republic. Their inability to deal successfully with political demands is indicated by their lack of mass support and by the fact that when these institutions have been abolished by executive elites, no mass mourning or resistance has marked their passing. Finally, the adversary relationship between executive-centered elites and legislators means that legislative activity seldom mobilizes support for the regime or otherwise contributes to the stability of the political system.

THE REACTIVE LEGISLATURE

The performance of the reactive legislature replicates the representation model posited in Chapter 1. Its members, the executive-centered elites, and mass publics agree that these legislatures are not to be considered the center of the national policy-making process. Rather the reactive legislature involves itself in policy making by seeking to influence the shape of policy on behalf of those whom they represent. Because systems with reactive legislatures are dominated by relatively strong party systems, any exercise of legislative influence in the initiation and deliberation of policy is most likely to take place in partisan arenas rather than in autonomous committee arenas. Oversight activities are likely to be the province of the opposition parties and therefore are more likely to take place in plenary than in partisan arenas because the potential for effective oversight rests heavily upon the capacity of the legislature to bring governmental inefficiency or malfeasance to public light. In their individual capacities members of reactive legislatures concentrate on dealing with a substantial but manageable load of particularized constituency requests. They are assisted in these activities by their party organizations and also by cooperative bureaucrats who view these activities as legitimate. Their success in dealing with their demand load is attested to by the relatively high level of support accruing to these institutions. These legislatures must deal less frequently with the generalized demands of interest groups who, sensitive to the relative capabilities of various political actors and institutions, direct most of their efforts towards influencing executive-centered elites. Political systems with reactive legislatures are usually stable and while it is difficult to demonstrate an empirical connection between legislative activity and this degree of stability, it is possible to make a compelling argument to that effect. The argument would go something like this: reactive legislatures, aggressively representing mass publics, encourage policy makers to be responsive to mass demands and thereby increase the level of support for the policies that ultimately emerge and, in addition, render the regime that produces those policies legitimate. Furthermore, in such systems the legislature comes to symbolize the involvement of people with their polities; the institution's continuous functioning and the regular appearance of the government at its sessions to justify and defend their actions contribute to the maintenance of the political system.

MARGINAL LEGISLATURES

Marginal legislatures are characterized by a lack of congruence between the behavior of legislators and the expectations of both mass publics and executive-centered elites. In addition, role consensus among the legislators themselves seems to be absent. Some aspire to the policy-making model for their institutions despite its inappropriateness given the apparent strength of executive-centered elites. Most behave in a manner congruent with the more realistic representation model, while some subscribe to the system-maintenance model which is the one preferred by executive-centered elites. However, mass publics in marginal legislature countries, like those elsewhere, hold to a representation model of the legislature. This dissensus results in an absence of support for the legislature either from mass or from elite publics. These legislatures are the objects of a very heavy demand volume despite their limited capacities because they are the most accessible and usually the only accessible institution in their countries. But their members do not deal very effectively with this demand load because many of them do not perceive their role in these terms and those who do, although they devote a great deal of effort to the task, are stymied both by the sheer volume of requests and by the attitudes of uncooperative executive elites without whose assistance these demands cannot be met. These elites view the legislature as an inconvenience at best whose only possible redeeming value might be as a legitimizer of their power. However, the legislature's own lack of support from mass publics, combined with the magnitude of the tasks involved in legitimizing an unpopular regime that in all likelihood is beset by strong disintegrative pressures, means that the legislature fails to perform even these system-maintenance activities. Given these "failures" there is no reason for executive-centered elites to support the legislature. Thus, coups or other extraconstitutional actions directed against marginal legislatures are quite common and these institutions disappear, reappear, and disappear once again on a more or less regular basis.

MINIMAL LEGISLATURES

The behavior of members of minimal legislatures conforms to the requirements of the system-maintenance model. Legislators and executive-centered elites agree that the major activities that legislators are expected to undertake are those that are designed to increase support for regime policies and to legitimize the regime in the eyes of its citizens. The control of executive-centered elites is reinforced by their dominance of legislative recruitment as well as their ability to invoke sanctions that may well extend beyond the political careers of the legislators. Mass publics in minimal legislature systems expect some representation from their legislators but are aware that such activities take place within the strictures imposed by the expectations of executive-centered elites. For their part, elites realize that if the legislature is to be effective in its system-maintenance activities, some allowances for legislative-representation activities must be made, allowances which may on occasion take the form of minimal policy adjustments in response to the demands of constituents as conveyed through legislators. The important point is that all of this takes place at the discretion and under the control of the executive-centered elites to whose expectations all legislative activities must ultimately conform. The demands of mass publics are dealt with in the context of these elite expectations, and while these demands are not always met, and while the level of mass support for the legislature may not be exceptionally high, it is not their support that counts for the legislature but rather the support of executive-centered elites. Because legislators do not really have the option of deviating substantially from elite expectations, elite support for the legislature is a given.

THE LEGISLATIVE MODEL

The premise of the discussion to this point and indeed throughout this book has been that one single legislative model is not descriptive of the variety of institutions that call themselves legislatures nor of those institutions that fall within an even more rigorous definition of legislatures such as the one that we have been using. The title of this section should not suggest that having come this far I now intend to change premises. What I do intend to do in this last section of this last chapter is to suggest that one particular legislative model will be the locus toward which the legislatures of the world are likely to gravitate now and in the near future.

The story of the policy-making model is the story of the American Congress. The failure of this model to take root anywhere else in the world save Costa Rica suggests, but of course does not prove, that this type of legislature is one more of those idiosyncratically American phenomena (the two-party system is another) that prospers here and will likely continue to do so, but for reasons that we do not entirely understand. Were it not that the American Congress is one of the most visible and widely researched legislatures in the world, and the legislature to which Americans implicitly or explicitly compare others, and were it not for the fact that this book is being written primarily for an American audience, one would feel justified in ignoring, or at least paying less attention to both this "peculiar" institution and the policy-making model that describes it.

The system-maintenance model will continue to be most appropriate for understanding those political systems dominated by the expectations of strong and relatively homogeneous political elites that are able through the strength of either their arms or their ideology to dominate the political perceptions and political actions of most of their citizens. Such elites will continue to perceive their political institutions primarily in terms of system-maintenance activities. Whether or not one believes that the number of such political systems is going to increase depends upon whether or not one believes that authoritarian or totalitarian systems are in the ascendancy. Evidence for such beliefs depends upon where you look. The recent history of Portugal and Spain provide substance for the argument that such systems are tenuous, heavily dependent upon single personalities, and therefore on the way out. The history of the Soviet Union is evidence to the contrary.

The acute reader will notice that I've saved the representation model for the last and will therefore assume that this is my future legislative model. It is indeed, and these in brief are my reasons:

First, it seems clear that such a model is at one with the expectations of mass publics throughout the world and I continue to believe in the democratic ethic that suggests that for a political system to remain viable over the long run, it must roughly coincide with the expectations of its citizens. Obviously, citizen desires for representation may be less salient than their desire to eat and to live and to enjoy life, but I would argue that the capacity of a government to provide these opportunities for its citizens is directly related to its responsiveness, which in turn is closely related to its representative nature.

Second, the representation model does not make the assumptions about the legislature's policy-making potential that are embodied in the policy-making model. While devotees of the American Congress may continue to argue that any legislature can and should become the focus of its nation's policy-making process, more will I think agree with Mill (and with me) that to govern is the function of the executive, and that the legislature's proper function is to represent the views of citizens, influence the policy-makers, and reserve for itself the formal, final say on policy as the ultimate means of assuring policy responsiveness.

Third, the representation model is one with which elites who seek policy-making control can live, and it is a model that legislators can live with because under it they continue to be active participants in the political process. Assuming that legislators are willing to concede policy-making dominance to executive-centered elites, and assuming that these elites are willing to accept the constraints upon this dominance imposed by legislators pursuing representational activities, the representation model seems the one most likely to evoke something approximating an expectational consensus from executive-centered elites, from legislators, and from mass publics, and therefore the model most likely to remain stable in a world in which any degree of stability is difficult to come by.

One last point: legislatures are products of their political environment. To be sure, they can influence the contours of that environment, but in the main their structure, prerogatives, and procedures are responsive to the expectations of others. Thus, changes in legislative types—from vulnerable to reactive, or from marginal to minimal—result from changes in expectations, which in turn result from changes in the political culture of a nation. Some change of this nature may be evoked by legislative performance, but substantial changes in people's expectations about their political institutions are, I think, evoked primarily by more cosmic events such as the development of a dominant consensual ideology, the crystallization of a strong party system, the emergence of a charismatic leader, a revolution, or a civil war. The argument of the preceeding paragraphs then is simply this: when as a result of these environmental changes a political system reaches some degree of stability, the legislature to be incorporated in the scheme of things is more likely to be a representation model than a policy-making or system-maintenance model.

REFERENCES

ADAMS, J. C., and P. BARILE (1966) The Government of Republican Italy. 2nd ed. Boston: Houghton Mifflin.

AGOR, W. H. (1970) "The Senate in the Chilean Political System." In Legislatures in Developmental Perspective, ed. A. Kornberg and L. Musolf. Durham, N.C.: Duke Univ. Press.

———. (1971a) The Chilean Senate. Austin: Univ. of Tex. Press.

——— (1971b) "The Decisional Role of the Senate in the Chilean Political System." In Latin American Legislatures: Their Role and Influence, ed. W. H. Agor. New York: Praeger.

AHMAD, M. (1970) Government and Politics in Pakistan. Karachi: Space Printers.

AHRENBERG, K. L. (1960) "The Political Power of Economic-Labor-Market Organizations: A Dilemma of Finnish Democracy." In Interest Groups on Four Continents, ed. H. W. Ehrmann. Pittsburgh, Pa.: Univ. of Pittsburgh Press.

ALKER, H. R. (1965) Mathematics and Politics. New York: Macmillan.

ALMOND, G., and G. B. POWELL (1966) Comparative Politics. Boston: Little, Brown.

———, and S. VERBA (1963) The Civic Culture. Princeton, N.J.: Princeton Univ. Press.

ANDREN, N. (1970) "Partisan Motivations and Concern for System Legitimacy in the Scandanavian Deliberations on Public Subsidies." In Comparative Political Finance, ed. A. J. Heidenheimer. Lexington, Mass.: D. C. Heath.

ANDREWS, W. G. (1975) "Constitutional Dictatorship in Gaullist France: A Study in Constitutional Theory." Prepared for delivery at the Annual Meeting of the American Political Science Association, San Francisco, Calif., Sept. 2–5, 1975.

ANGLADE, C. (1970) "Party Finance Models and the Classification of Latin American Parties." In Comparative Political Finance, ed. A. J. Heidenheimer. Lexington, Mass.: D. C. Heath.

ASTIZ, C. A. (1969) Pressure Groups and Power Elites in Peruvian Politics. Ithaca, N.Y.: Cornell Univ. Press.

———(1973a) "Role, Recruitment and Background of Brazilian Legislators and Congressional Staff Members." Prepared for delivery at the World Congress of the International Political Science Association, Montreal, Aug. 1973.

———(1973b) "The Decay of Latin American Legislatures." In Legislatures in Comparative Perspective, ed. A. Kornberg. New York: David McKay.

———(1974) "The Current Role of the Brazilian Congress." Prepared for delivery at the Seminar on Legislative Development, Rio de Janeiro, Aug. 12–15, 1974.

BAAKLINI, A. I. (1972) "Legislatures and Political Development: Lebanon, 1840–1970." Ph.D. dissertation, State Univ. of New York–Albany.

———, and J. J. HEAPHEY (1976) "Legislative Institution Building in Brazil, Costa Rica, and Lebanon." Sage Professional Papers in Administrative and Policy

Studies, Vol. 3, Series No. 03–027. Beverly Hills, Calif., and London: Sage Publications.

BAERWALD, J. J. (1974) Japan's Parliament: An Introduction. London: Cambridge Univ. Press.

BAILEY, F. G. (1960) "Traditional Society and Representation: A Case Study of Orissa." Archives Europeenes de Sociologie 1, no. 1:121–41.

BAKER, C. E. (1971) "The Costa Rican Legislative Assembly: A Preliminary Evaluation of the Decisional Function." In Latin American Legislatures: Their Role and Influence, ed. W. H. Agor. New York: Praeger.

———(1973) "Costa Rican Legislative Behavior in Perspective." Ph.D. dissertation, Univ. of Fla., Gainesville.

BARKAN, J. D. (1975) "Bringing Home the Pork: Legislator Behavior, Rural Development, and Political Change in East Africa." Prepared for delivery at the Conference on Legislatures and Development, Carmel, Calif., Aug. 11–15, 1975.

———, and J. J. OKUMU (1974) "Political Linkage in Kenya: Citizens, Local Elites, and Legislators." Prepared for delivery at the Annual Meeting of the American Political Science Association, Chicago, Ill., Sept. 1974.

BARKER, A., and M. RUSH (1970) The British Member of Parliament and His Information. Toronto: Univ. of Toronto Press.

BEER, S. H. (1966) "The British Legislature and the Problem of Mobilizing Consent." In Lawmakers in a Changing World, ed. Elke Franke. Englewood Cliffs, N.J.: Prentice-Hall.

BERRINGTON, H. B., and S. E. FINER (1961) "The British House of Commons." International Social Science Journal 13, no. 4: 600–619.

BERRY, W. M. (1971) "The Radical Uses of Parliament: The Dyanamics of Legislative Change in India, 1962–1967." Ph.D. dissertation, Duke Univ., Durham, N.C.

BHARADVAJA, B. (1972–73) "Lok Sabha Committee on Subordinate Legislation, 1953–1971." Indian Political Science Review 7 (Oct.–March):8–22.

BHATNAGAR, S., and L. M. DOGRA (1973) "Legislator's Welfare Role: A Study of the Role Perceptions of Himachal MLAs." Journal of Constitutional and Parliamentary Studies 7 (Apr.-June): 134–45.

BILL, J. A. (1971) "Politics of Legislative Monarchy: The Iranian Majlis." In Comparative Legislative Systems, ed. H. Hirsch and M. D. Hancock. New York: Free Press. Pp. 343–59.

BLONDEL, J. (1973) Comparative Legislatures. Englewood Cliffs, N.J.: Prentice-Hall.

———, et al. (1969–70) "Comparative Legislative Behaviour." Government and Opposition 5 (Winter): 67–85.

BOYD-CARPENTER, J. (1971) "Development of the Select Committee in the British Parliament." The Parliamentarian 52 (Apr.): 101–4.

BOYER, W. W. (1964) Bureaucracy on Trial. Indianapolis, Ind.: Bobbs-Merrill.

BOYNTON, G. R., and G. LOEWENBERG (1974) "The Development of Public Support for Parliament in Germany, 1951–59." The British Journal of Political Science 3 (Apr.): 169–89.

———, S. C. PATTERSON, and R. D. HEDLUND (1968) "The Structure of Public Support for Legislative Institutions." Midwest Journal of Political Science 12 (May): 163–73.

BRACHER, K. D. (1968) "The Crisis of Modern Parliament." In Comparative Politics: Notes and Readings, ed. R. C. Macridis and B. E. Brown. 3rd ed. Homewood, Ill.: Dorsey Press.

BROMHEAD, P. (1957) "Some Notes on the Standing Committees of the French National Assembly." Political Studies 5 (June): 140–57.

BROWN, B. E. (1963) "Pressure Politics in the Fifth Republic." Journal of Politics 25 (Aug.): 509–25.

BROWN, R. M. (1971) "Indian State Legislative Behavior: The Uttar Pradesh Legislative Assembly, 1952–1968." Ph.D. dissertation, The American University, Washington, D.C.

BUTT, R. (1969) The Power of Parliament. London: Constable.

CAYROL, R., J. L. PARODI, and C. YSMAL (1976). "French Deputies and the Political System." Legislative Studies Quarterly 1 (Feb.): 67–99.

CHAMBERLAIN, L. (1946) The President, Congress and Legislation. New York: Columbia Univ. Press.

CHAMBERS, W. N. (1963) Political Parties in a New Nation: The American Experience, 1776–1809. New York: Oxford Univ. Press.

CHEE, C. H. (1976) "The Role of Parliamentary Politicians in Singapore." Legislative Studies Quarterly 1 (Aug.): 423–41.

CHU, C. H. (1974) Minority Representation in the Malaysian Legislature. Ph.D. dissertation, Univ. of Ky., Lexington.

CHUBB, B. (1963) "Going About Persecuting Civil Servants: The Role of the Irish Parliamentary Representative." Political Studies 11 (Oct.): 272–86.

CLAPP, C. L. (1964) The Congressman. Garden City, N.Y.: Doubleday.

CLARKE, H. D., R. G. PRICE, and R. KRAUSE (1975) "Constituency Service Among Canadian Provincial Legislators: Basic Findings and a Test of Three Hypotheses." Canadian Journal of Political Science 8 (Dec.): 520–42.

COHEN, L. J. (1977) "Conflict Management and Political Institutionalization in Socialist Yugoslavia: A Case Study of the Parliamentary System." In Legislatures in Plural Societies, ed. A. F. Eldridge. Durham, N.C.: Duke Univ. Press.

CONGRESSIONAL QUARTERLY (1971) Weekly Report, Jan. 15, 1971. Washington, D.C.: Congressional Quarterly, Inc.

COTTA, M. (1974) "A Structural-Functional Framework for the Analysis of Unicameral and Bicameral Parliaments." European Journal of Political Research, 2 (Sept.): 201–24.

CRANE, W. (1961–62) "The Errand-Running Function of Austrian Legislators." Parliamentary Affairs 15 (Winter): 160–69.

———, and M. W. WATTS (1968) State Legislative Systems. Englewood Cliffs, N.J.: Prentice-Hall.

CRICK, B. (1968) The Reform of Parliament. London: Weidenfeld and Nicolson.

———(1970) "Parliament in the British Political System." In Legislatures in Developmental Perspective, ed. A. Kornberg and L. D. Musolf. Durham, N.C.: Duke Univ. Press.

CROWE, R. E. (1970) "Parliament in the Lebanese Political System." In Legislatures in Developmental Perspective, ed. A. Kornberg and L. D. Musolf. Durham, N.C.: Duke University Press.

CZUDNOWSKI, M. M. (1970) "Legislative Recruitment Under Proportional Representation in Israel: A Model and a Case Study." Midwest Journal of Political Science 14 (May): 216–48.

DARLING, F. C. (1960) "Marshal Sarit and Absolutist Rule in Thailand." Pacific Affairs 33 (Dec.): 347–60.

DAVIDSON, R. H. (1969) The Role of the Congressman. New York: Pegasus.

———(1970a) "Congress in the American Political System." In Legislatures in Developmental Perspective, ed. A. Kornberg and L. Musolf. Durham, N.C.: Duke Univ. Press.

———(1970b) "Public Prescriptions for the Job of Congressman." Midwest Journal of Political Science 14 (Nov.):648–66.

———(1976) "Breaking Up Those Cozy Triangles: An Impossible Dream?" Prepared for delivery at the Symposium on Legislative Reform and Public Policy, Univ. of Neb., Lincoln, March 11–12, 1976.

DE GRAZIA, A. (1967) "Toward a New Model of Congress." In The First Branch of Government, ed. A. de Grazia. Garden City, N.Y.: Doubleday.

DE LA GARZA, R. O. (1972) The Mexican Chamber of Deputies and the Mexican Political System. Ph.D. dissertation, Univ. of Ariz., Tucson.

DENNIS, J. (1970) "Support for the Institution of Elections by the Mass Public." American Political Science Review 64 (Sept.): 819–35.

DEXTER, L. A. (1969) How Organizations Are Represented in Washington. Indianapolis, Ind.: Bobbs-Merrill.

DICKSON, A. D. R. (1975) "MP's Readoption Conflicts: Their Causes and Consequences." Political Studies 23 (March): 62–70.

DINKA, F., and M. J. SKIDMORE (1973) "The Function of Communist One-Party Elections: The Case of Czechoslovakia, 1971." Political Science Quarterly 88 (Sept.): 395–422.

DI PALMA, G. (1977) Surviving Without Governing: The Italian Parties in Parliament. Berkeley: Univ. of Calif. Press.

DIX, R. H. (1967) Colombia: The Political Dimensions of Change. New Haven, Conn.: Yale Univ. Press.

DJORDJEVIC, J. (1960) "Interest Groups and the Political System of Yugoslavia." In Interest Groups on Four Continents, ed. H.W. Ehrmann. Pittsburgh, Pa.: Univ. of Pittsburgh Press.

DODD, J. W. (1973) "The Concept of Institutionalization: Questions and Comments—A Case Study of the Philippine House of Representatives." Unpublished manuscript, Department of Political Science, Univ. of Tenn., Knoxville.

DOGAN, M. (1961) "Political Ascent in a Class Society: French Deputies, 1870–1958." In Political Decision-Makers, ed. D. Marvick. Glencoe, Ill.: Free Press.

DOWSE, R. E. (1972) "The M. P. and His Surgery." In the Backbencher and Parliament, ed. D. Leonard and V. Herman. London: St. Martin's.

DUFF, E. A. (1971) "The Role of Congress in the Colombian Political System." In Latin American Legislatures: Their Role and Influence, ed. W. H. Agor. New York: Praeger.

DUVERGER, M. (1954) Political Parties: Their Organization and Activity in the Modern State. New York: Wiley.

EASTON, D. (1965) A Systems Analysis of Political Life. New York: Wiley.

———(1975) "A Re-Assessment of the Concept of Political Support." British Journal of Political Science 5 (Oct.): 435–57.

EDELMAN, M., and S. ZELNIKER (1973) "Information Utilization in the Knesset: The Question of Legislative Autonomy." Prepared for delivery at the Ninth World Congress of the International Political Science Association, Montreal, Aug. 1973.

EDINGER, L. (1968) Politics in Germany. Boston: Little, Brown.

EHRMANN, H. W. (1961) "French Bureaucracy and Organized Interests." Administrative Science Quarterly 5 (March): 534–55.

———(1971) Politics in France. 2nd ed. Boston: Little, Brown.

ELDER, N. C. (1970) Government in Sweden. New York: Pergamon.

ELLWOOD, J. W., and J. A. THURBER (1976) "Some Implications of the Congressional Budget and Impoundment Act for the Senate." Paper prepared for delivery at the 1976 Annual Meeting of the American Political Science Association, Chicago, Ill., Sept. 1976.

FENNELL, L. C. (1971) "Congress in the Argentine Political System: An Apprai-sal." In Latin American Legislatures: Their Role and Influence. New York: Praeger.

FENNO, R. F. (1966) The Power of the Purse. Boston: Little, Brown.

——(1969) "The House of Representatives and Federal Aid to Education." In New Perspectives on the House of Representatives, ed. R. L. Peabody and N. W. Polsby. 2nd ed. Chicago: Rand McNally.

——(1973) Congressmen in Committees. Boston: Little, Brown.

FEREJOHN, J. A. (1974) Pork Barrel Politics: Rivers and Harbors Legislation, 1947–1968. Stanford, Calif.: Stanford Univ. Press.

FINER, S. E. (1960) "Interest Groups and the Political Process in Great Britain." In Interest Groups on Four Continents, ed. H. W. Ehrmann. Pittsburgh, Pa.: Univ. of Pittsburgh.

FIORINA, M. P. (1977) Congress: Keystone of the Washington Establishment. New Haven, Conn.: Yale Univ. Press.

FRANZICH, S. E. (1971) A Comparative Study of Legislative Roles and Behavior. Ph.D. dissertation, Univ. of Minn., Minneapolis.

FREEMAN, J. L. (1955) The Political Process: Executive Bureau–Legislative Committee Relations. Garden City, N.Y.: Doubleday.

FREY, F. W. (1965) The Turkish Political Elite. Cambridge, Mass.: M.I.T. Press.

GALLI, G., and A. PRANDI (1970) Patterns of Political Participation in Italy. New Haven, Conn.: Yale Univ. Press.

GALLOWAY, G. (1954) Congress at the Crossroads. New York: Thomas Y. Crowell.

GIL, F. G. (1966) The Political System of Chile. Boston: Houghton Mifflin.

GOGUEL, F. (1971) "Parliament Under the Fifth French Republic: Difficulties in Adapting to a New Role." In Modern Parliaments: Change or Decline?, ed. G. Loewenberg. Chicago: Aldine-Atherton.

GOODMAN, A. E. (1975) "Correlates of Legislative Constituency Service in South Vietnam." In Legislative Systems in Developing Countries, ed. G. R. Boynton and C. L. Kim. Durham, N.C.: Duke Univ. Press.

GOODWIN, G. (1970) The Little Legislatures: Committees of Congress. Amherst, Mass.: Univ. of Mass. Press.

GORDON, M. R. (1971) "Civil Servants, Politicians, and Parties: Shortcomings in the British Policy Process." Comparative Politics 4 (Oct.): 29–58.

GREEN, M. J. (1975) Who Runs Congress? 2nd ed. New York: Bantam Books.

GROSSHOLTZ, J. (1964) The Philippines. Boston: Little, Brown.

——(1969) "Integrative Factors in the Malaysian and Philippine Legislatures." Paper prepared for delivery at the 65th Annual Meeting of the American Political Science Association, New York, Sept. 1969.

——(1970) "Integrative Factors in the Malaysian and Philippine Legislatures." Comparative Politics 3 (Oct.): 93–114.

GRUMM, J. G. (1973) "A Paradigm for the Comparative Analysis of Legislative System." Sage Research Papers in the Social Sciences (Comparative Legislative Studies Series, No. 90–006). Beverly Hills, Calif., and London: Sage Publications.

GUTTSMAN, W. L. (1960) "Social Stratification and Political Elite." The British Journal of Sociology 11 (June): 137–50.

HAKES, J. E. (1970) "The Parliamentary Party of the Kenya African National Union: Cleavage and Cohesion in the Ruling Party of a New Nation." Ph.D. dissertation, Duke Univ., Durham, N.C.

————(1973) "Weak Parliaments and Military Coups in Africa: A Study in Regime Instability." Sage Research Papers in the Social Sciences, Comparative Legislative Studies Series No. 90–004. Beverly Hills, Calif.: Sage Publications.

————, and J. HELGERSON (1973) "Bargaining and Parliamentary Behavior in Africa: A Comparative Study of Zambia and Kenya." In Legislatures in Comparative Perspective, ed. A. Kornberg. New York: David McKay.

HAMMOND, S. (1974) Personal Staffs of Members of the United States House of Representatives. Ph.D. dissertation, The Johns Hopkins Univ., Baltimore, Md.

HAMON, L. (1961) "Members of the French Parliament." International Social Science Journal 13, no. 4: 545–66.

HARGROVE, E. C. (1974) The Power of the Modern Presidency. New York: Knopf.

HARRISON, A. H., and J. DOUGLAS (1972) India's Democracy. New York: Norton.

HARRISON, M. (1958) "The Composition of Committees in the French National Assembly." Parliamentary Affairs 11 (Spring): 172–79.

HART, H. C. (1971) "Parliament and Nation-Building: England and India." In Modern Parliaments: Change or Decline?, ed. G. Loewenberg. Chicago: Aldine-Atherton.

HECKSCHER, G. (1960) "Interest Groups in Sweden: Their Political Role." In Interest Groups on Four Continents, ed. H. W. Ehrmann. Pittsburgh, Pa.: Univ. of Pittsburgh Press.

HELGERSON, J. L. (1970) Institutional Adaptation to Rapid Political Change: A Study of the Legislature in Zambia from 1959 to 1969. Ph.D. dissertation, Duke Univ., Durham, N.C.

HENNIS, W. (1971) "Reform of the Bundestag: The Case for General Debate." In Modern Parliaments: Change or Decline?, ed. G. Loewenberg. Chicago: Aldine-Atherton.

HERMAN, V. (1972) "Backbench and Opposition Amendments to Government Legislation." In The Backbencher and Parliament, ed. D. Leonard and V. Herman. London: Macmillan.

HINCKLEY, B. (1976) "Seniority 1975: Old Theories Confront New Facts." British Journal of Political Science 6 (Oct.): 383–99.

HIRSCH-WEBER, W. (1960) "Some Remarks on Interest Groups in the German Federal Republic." In Interest Groups on Four Continents, ed. H. W. Ehrmann. Pittsburgh, Pa.: Univ. of Pittsburgh Press.

HOPKINS, R. (1970) "The Role of the M.P. in Tanzania." American Political Science Review 64 (Sept.): 754–71.

————(1971a) "The Kenyan Legislature: Political Functions and Citizen Perceptions." Prepared for delivery at the Shambaugh Conference on Legislatures in Developing Countries, Iowa City, Nov. 1971.

————(1971b) Political Roles in a New State: Tanzania's First Decade. New Haven, Conn.: Yale Univ. Press.

————(1975a) "The Kenyan Legislature: Political Functions and Citizen Perceptions." In Legislative Systems in Developing Countries. Durham, N.C.: Duke Univ. Press.

————(1975b) "The Influence of the Legislature on Development Strategy: The Case of Kenya and Tanzania." Prepared for delivery at the Conference on Legislatures and Development, Carmel, Calif., Aug. 1975.

HOSKIN, G. W. (1971) "Dimensions of Representation in the Colombian National Legislature." In Latin American Legislatures: Their Role and Influence, ed. W. H. Agor. New York: Praeger.

————(1975) "Dimensions of Conflict in the Colombian National Legislature." In

Legislative Systems in Developing Countries, ed. G. R. Boynton and C. L. Kim. Durham, N.C.: Duke Univ. Press.

——— (1976) "The Colombian Congress and the National Front: An Unanticipated Consequence." Prepared for delivery at the 1976 Triennial World Congress of the International Political Science Association, Edinburgh, Aug. 1976.

HOUGH, J. F. (1975) "The Legislature in the Soviet Union." Prepared for delivery at the Conference on Legislatures in Contemporary Societies, Albany, N.Y., Jan. 20–24, 1975.

HUGHES, C. (1962) The Parliament of Switzerland. London: Cassell.

HUGHES, S. W. (1971) "Governmental Decision-Making in Chile: The Relative Decisional Positions of the Executive and the Legislature." Ph.D. dissertation, Univ. of N. C., Chapel Hill.

———, and K. J. MIJESKI (1973) Legislative-Executive Policy-Making: The Case of Chile and Costa Rica. Sage Research Papers in the Social Sciences (Comparative Legislative Studies Series No. 90–007). Beverly Hills, Calif., and London: Sage Publications.

HUITT, R. K. (1961) "Democratic Party Leadership in the Senate." American Political Science Review 55 (June): 333–44.

HUNTINGTON, S. P. (1968) Political Order in Changing Societies. New Haven, Conn.: Yale Univ. Press.

HYDEN, C., and C. LEYS (1972) "Elections and Politics in Single-Party Systems: The Case of Kenya and Tanzania." British Journal of Political Science 2 (Oct.): 389–420.

HYSON, S. R. V. (1974) "The Role of the Backbencher—An Analysis of Private Members' Bills in the Canadian House of Commons." Parliamentary Affairs 28 (Summer): 262–72.

INTER-PARLIAMENTARY UNION (1968, 1969, 1970, 1973) Chronicle of Parliamentary Elections, Vols. 2, 3, 4, 7. Geneva: International Center for Parliamentary Documentation.

JABER, K.A. (1975a) "The Role and Function of the Legislature of the Hashemite Kingdom of Jordan: An Appraisal." Paper prepared for delivery at the Conference on Legislatures in Contemporary Society, Albany, N.Y., Jan. 1975.

——— (1975b) "The Parliament of the Hashemite Kingdom of Jordan: Its Role in Social and Economic Development." Prepared for delivery at the Conference on Legislatures and Development, Carmel, Calif., Aug. 1975.

JACKSON, R. J. (1971) "The Dynamics of the Congressional Committee System in the Philippines." Unpublished paper.

———, and M. M. ATKINSON (1974) The Canadian Legislative System. Toronto: Macmillan of Canada.

JAHAN, R. (1976) "Members of Parliament in Bangladesh." Legislative Studies Quarterly 1 (Aug.): 355–70.

JAIN, R. B. (1975) "Innovations and Reforms in Indian Parliament." Prepared for delivery at the Second International Conference on Legislatures in Contemporary Societies, Albany, N.Y., Jan. 20–24, 1975.

JAMES, D. B. (1974) The Contemporary Presidency. 2nd ed. New York: Pegasus.

JAMES, J. A. (1972) "Legislatorial Decision-Making in Kenya." Prepared for delivery at the Annual Meeting of the African Studies Association, Philadelphia, Nov. 1972.

——— (1975) "The Impact of Legislatures on Educational Policy Formation in the Developing Nations." Prepared for delivery at the Conference on Legislatures and Development, Carmel, Calif., Aug. 1975.

JENNINGS, I. (1969) Parliament. 2nd ed. London: Cambridge Univ. Press.
JEWELL, M. E. (1970) "Attitudinal Determinants of Legislative Behavior: The Utility of Role Analysis." In Legislatures in Developmental Perspective, ed. A. Kornberg and L. D. Musolf. Durham, N.C.: Duke Univ. Press.
——— (1977) "Legislative Representation and National Integration." In Legislatures in Plural Societies, ed. A. Eldridge. Durham, N.C.: Duke Univ. Press.
———, and C. L. KIM (1976a) "Sources of Support for Legislative Institutions: Kenya, Korea, and Turkey." Paper prepared for delivery at the annual meeting of the Southern Political Science Association, Atlanta, Ga., Nov. 1976.
———, and C. L. KIM (1976b) "Sources of Support for the Legislature in a Developing Nation." Comparative Political Studies 8 (Jan.): 461–89.
———, and S. C. PATTERSON (1973) The Legislative Process in the United States. 2nd ed. New York: Random House.
JOHNSON, N. (1963) "Questions in the Bundestag." Parliamentary Affairs 16 (Winter): 22–34.
JONES, C. O. (1969) "The Agriculture Committee and the Problem of Representation." In New Perspectives on the House of Representatives, ed. R. L. Peabody and N. W. Polsby. 2nd ed. Chicago: Rand McNally.
JUVILER, P. H. (1960) "Functions of a Deputy in the Supreme Soviet of the USSR, 1938–1959." Ph.D. dissertation, Columbia Univ., New York, N.Y.
KATZNELSON, I., and M. KESSELMAN (1975) The Politics of Power. New York: Harcourt Brace, Jovanovich.
KELLEY, R. L. (1971) "The Role of the Venezuelan Senate." In Latin American Legislatures: Their Role and Influence, ed. W. H. Agor. New York: Praeger.
——— (1973) "The Venezuelan Senate: A Legislative Body in the Context of Development." Ph.D. dissertation, Univ. of N.M., Albuquerque.
KIM, C. L. (1970) "Political Attitudes of Defeated Candidates in an American State Election." American Political Science Review 64 (Sept.): 879–87.
——— (1971) "Toward a Theory of Individual and Systemic Effects of Political Status Loss." Journal of Developing Areas 5 (Jan.): 193–206.
——— (1973) "Consensus on Legislative Roles Among Japanese Prefectural Assemblymen." In Legislatures in Comparative Perspective, ed. A. Kornberg. New York: David McKay.
———, and G. LOEWENBERG (1976) "The Cultural Roots of a New Legislature: Public Perceptions of the Korean National Assembly." Legislative Studies Quarterly 1 (Aug.): 371–88.
———, and S. T. PAI (1976) "The Patterns of Constituency Work Among Members of a New Legislature: The Case of the Korean National Assembly." Paper prepared for delivery at the 10th World Congress of the International Political Science Association, Edinburgh, Aug. 1976.
———, and B. K. WOO (1975) "Political Representation in the Korean National Assembly." In Legislative Systems in Developing Countries, ed. G. R. Boynton and C. L. Kim. Durham, N.C.: Duke Univ. Press.
KIM, Y. C. (1975) "The Committee System in the Japanese Diet: Recruitment, Orientations, and Behavior." In Legislative Systems in Developing Countries, ed. G. R. Boynton and C. L. Kim. Durham, N.C.: Duke Univ. Press.
KING, A. (1975) "Executives." In Handbook of Political Science, Vol. 5, ed. F. I. Greenstein and N. W. Polsby. Reading, Mass.: Addison-Wesley.
——— (1976) "Modes of Executive-Legislative Relations: Great Britain, France, and West Germany." Legislative Studies Quarterly 1 (Feb.): 37–65.
KINGDON, H. W. (1973) Congressmen's Voting Decisions. New York: Harper and Row.

KJEKSHUS, H. (1974) "Parliament in a One-Party State—the Bunge of Tanzania, 1965–1970." The Journal of Modern African Studies 12 (May): 19–43.

KLINE, H. F. (1977) "Committee Membership Turnover in the Colombian National Congress, 1958–1974." Legislative Studies Quarterly 2 (Feb.): 29–43.

KNEZO, G. J., and W. J. OLESZEK (1976) "Legislative Oversight and Program Evaluation." The Bureaucrat 5 (Apr.): 37–51.

KOCHANEK, S. A. (1968) The Congress Party of India. Princeton, N.J.: Princeton Univ. Press.

KOESTER (1968) "Standing Committees in the British House of Commons." Parliamentarian 49 (Apr.): 64–72.

KOGAN, N. (1962) The Government of Italy. New York: Crowell.

KORNBERG, A. (1967) Canadian Legislative Behavior. New York: Holt, Rinehart and Winston.

———(1970) "Parliament in Canadian Society." In Legislatures in Developmental Perspective, ed. A. Kornberg and L. Musolf. Durham, N.C.: Duke Univ. Press.

———(1975) "Observations on Informal Participation in the Canadian House of Commons." Prepared for delivery at the Conference on the Role of Parliamentary Politicians in Asia, Penang, Malaysia, March 1975.

———, and W. Mishler (1976) Influence in Parliament: Canada. Durham, N.C.: Duke Univ. Press.

KRUSIUS-AHRENBERG, L. (1960) "The Political Power of Economic and Labor-Market Organization: A Dilemma of Finnish Democracy." In Interest Groups on Four Continents, ed. H. W. Ehrmann. Pittsburgh, Pa.: Univ. of Pittsburgh Press.

KURODA, Y. (1970) "Patterns of Recruitment: Japanese Diet, 1946–1963." Prepared for delivery at the meeting of the American Political Science Association, Los Angeles, Calif.

———(1975) "The Japanese Diet and Socio-Economic Development: Organized Business, Bureaucracy, and the Ruling Party." Prepared for delivery at the Second International Conference on Legislatures in Contemporary Societies, Albany, N.Y., Jan. 20–24, 1975.

KURTZ, D. M. (1971) "The Nigerian Legislative Elite, 1954–1965: Integration and Disintegration." Ph.D. dissertation, Tulane Univ. New Orleans, La.

LANDE, C. H. (1964) Leaders, Factions and Parties: The Structure of Philippine Society. New Haven, Conn.: Yale Univ. Southeast Asia Studies Monograph Series, No. 6.

LAPALOMBARA, J. (1964) Interest Groups in Italian Politics. Princeton, N.J.: Princeton Univ. Press.

LAVAU, G. (1960) "Political Pressures by Interest Groups in France." In Interest Groups on Four Continents, ed. H. W. Ehrmann. Pittsburgh, Pa.: Univ. of Pittsburgh Press.

LEES, J. D. (1977) "Legislatures and Oversight: A Review Article on a Neglected Area of Research." Legislative Studies Quarterly 2 (May): 193–208.

LEHNEN, R. G. (1976) American Institutions, Political Opinion, and Public Policy. Hinsdale, Ill.: Dryden Press.

LEITES, N. (1959) On the Game of Politics in France. Stanford, Calif.: Stanford University Press.

LEONARD, D. (1972) "Private Members' Bills Since 1959." In the Backbencher and Parliament, ed. D. Leonard and V. Herman. London: St. Martin's.

———, and V. HERMAN (1972) The Backbencher and Parliament. London: St. Martin's.

LE VINE, V. T. (1968) "Political Elite Recruitment and Political Structure in French Speaking Africa." Cahiers d'Etudes Africaines 8, no. 3:369–89.

LINZ, J. J. (1975) "Legislatures in Organic Statist-Authoritarian Regimes—The Case of Spain." Prepared for delivery at the Conference on Legislatures and Society, Carmel, Calif., Aug. 1975.

LOEWENBERG, G. (1967) Parliament in the German Political System. Ithaca, N.Y.: Cornell Univ. Press.

———(1971a) "The Influence of Parliamentary Behavior on Regime Stability: Some Conceptual Clarifications." Comparative Politics 3 (Jan.): 177–200.

———(1971b) "The Role of Parliaments in Modern Political Systems." Intro. to Modern Parliaments: Change or Decline?, ed. G. Loewenberg. Chicago: Aldine-Atherton.

———(1972) "Comparative Legislative Research." In Comparative Legislative Behavior: Frontiers of Research, ed. S. C. Patterson and J. C. Wahlke. New York: Wiley.

———(1973) "The Institutionalization of Parliament and Public Orientation to the Political System." In Legislatures in Comparative Perspective, ed. A. Kornberg. New York: David McKay.

———, and C. L. KIM (1976) "The Representative Orientations of Legislators and Legislatures in Five Countries." Prepared for delivery at the Annual Meeting of the American Political Science Association, Chicago, Ill., Sept. 1976.

LOWI, T. (1969) The End of Liberalism: Ideology, Policy, and the Crisis of Public Authority. New York: Norton.

LYNSKEY, J. J. (1966) "The Role of the British Backbencher in the Modification of Government Policy: The Issues Involved, the Channels Used, and the Tactics Employed." Ph.D. dissertation, University of Minnesota, Minneapolis.

———(1970) "The Role of the British Backbenchers in the Modification of Government Policy." Western Political Quarterly 23 (June):333–47.

———(1973–74) "Backbench Tactics and Parliamentary Party Structure." Parliamentary Affairs 27 (Winter): 28–37.

MACARTNEY, W. J. A. (1969) "The Parliaments of Botswana, Lesotho, and Swaziland." Parliamentarian 50 (Apr.): 92–101.

McAUSLAN, J. P. W. B., and Y. P. GHAI (1966) "Constitutional Innovation and Political Stability in Tanzania: A Preliminary Assessment." Journal of Modern African Studies 4 (Dec.): 479–515.

McCOY, T. L. (1971) "Congress, the President, and Political Instability in Peru." In Latin American Legislatures: Their Role and Influence, ed. W. H. Agor. New York: Praeger.

McDONALD, R. H. (1971) "Legislative Politics in Uruguay: A Preliminary Statement." In Latin American Legislatures: Their Role and Influence, ed. W. H. Agor. New York: Praeger.

MAHESHEWARI, S. R. (1968) "Informal Consultative Committees of Parliament." Journal of Constitutional and Parliamentary Studies 2:1: 27–53.

———(1976) "Constituency Linkage of National Legislators in India." Legislative Studies Quarterly 1 (Aug.): 331–54.

MALLORY, J. R. (1963) "The Uses of Legislative Committees." Canadian Public Administration 6 (March):1–12.

———(1971) The Structure of Canadian Government. Toronto: Macmillan of Canada.

MANIRUZZAMAN, T. (1971) "Crises in Political Development and the Collapse of the Ayub Regime in Pakistan." Journal of Developing Areas 5 (Jan.): 221–37.

MANLEY, J. F. (1970) The Politics of Finance: The House Committee on Ways and Means. Boston: Little, Brown.

MARKAKIS, J., and A. BEYENE (1967) "Representative Institutions in Ethiopia." Journal of Modern African Studies 5 (Sept.): 193–220.

MATTHEWS, D. R. (1954) The Social Backgrounds of Political Decision-Makers. New York: Random House.

MAYHEW, D. E. (1974) Congress: The Electoral Connection. New Haven, Conn.: Yale University Press.

MELLER, N. (1966) "The Identification and Classification of Legislatures." Philippine Journal of Public Administration 10 (Oct.): 308–19.

————(1973) "The Pacific Legislature—Spearhead for Political Change." Prepared for delivery at the 2nd Annual Meeting of the Association for Social Anthropology in Oceania, Orcas Island, Washington, March 21–23, 1973.

MEZEY, M. L. (1972) "The Functions of a Minimal Legislature: Role Perceptions of Thai Legislators." Western Political Quarterly 25 (Dec.): 686–701.

————(1973) "The 1971 Coup in Thailand: Understanding Why the Legislature Fails." Asian Survey 13 (March): 306–17.

————(1975) "Legislative Development and Political Parties: The Case of Thailand." In Legislative Systems in Developing Countries, ed. C. L. Kim and G. R. Boynton. Durham, N.C.: Duke University Press.

————(1976) "Constituency Demands and Legislative Support: An Experiment." Legislative Studies Quarterly 1 (Feb.): 101–28.

————(1977) "Support for the Legislature: Clearing Away the Underbrush." Prepared for delivery at the Annual Meeting of the American Political Science Association, Washington, D.C., Sept. 1977.

————, and S. G. MEZEY (1974) "Student Attitudes Toward the Legislature: A Cross-National, Multi-Institutional Approach." Prepared for delivery at the Annual Meeting of the American Political Science Association, Chicago, Ill., Aug. 1974.

MILBRATH, L. W. (1963) The Washington Lobbyists. Chicago: Rand McNally.

MILL, J. S. (1958) Considerations on Representative Government. New York: The Liberal Arts Press.

MILNE, R. S. (1970) "Philippine and Malaysian Fund-Raising and Expenditure Practices in the Southeast Asian Context." In Comparative Political Finance, ed. A. J. Heidenheimer. Lexington, Mass.: D. C. Heath.

MITCHELL, A. (1966) Government by Party. London: Whitcombe and Tombs.

MODELSKI, I. B. (1973) "Seym Committees in the Polish Political System." Ph.D. dissertation, Wayne State University, Detroit, Mich.

MOE, R. C., and S. C. TEEL (1971) "Congress as Policy-Maker: A Necessary Reappraisal." In Congress and the President: Allies and Adversaries, ed. R. C. Moe. Pacific Palisades, Calif.: Goodyear.

MOHAPATRA, M. K. (1971) Intervenors and Non-Intervenors: A Study of Legislators' Administrative Role Orientations in an Indian State. Ph.D. dissertation, Univ. of Ky., Lexington.

MORELL, D. (1972) "Legislative Intervention in Thailand's Development Process: A Case Study." Asian Survey 12 (Aug.):627–46.

————(1975) "Thailand's Legislature and Economic Development Decisions." Prepared for delivery at the Conference on Legislatures and Development, Carmel, Calif., Aug. 1975.

MOREY, R. D. (1971) "Representational Role Perceptions in the Japanese Diet: The Wahlke-Eulau Framework Reexamined." Prepared for delivery at the Annual

Meeting of the American Political Science Association, Chicago, Ill., Sept. 1971.

MULLER, E. N. (1970) "The Representation of Citizens by Political Authorities: Consequences for Regime Support." American Political Science Review 64 (Dec.): 1149–66.

MURPHY, J. T. (1968) "Partisanship and the House Public Works Committee." Prepared for delivery at the Annual Meeting of the American Political Science Association, Washington, D.C., Sept. 1968.

MUSOLF, L. D., and J. F. SPRINGER (1975) "The Parliament of Malaysia and Economic Development: Policymaking and the MP." Prepared for delivery at the Conference on Legislatures and Development, Carmel, Calif., Aug. 1975.

———(1977) "Legislatures and Divided Societies: The Malaysian Parliament and Multi-Ethnicity." Legislative Studies Quarterly 2 (May): 113–36.

NARAIN, I., and S. L. PURI (1976) "Legislators in an Indian State: A Study of Role Images and Pattern of Constituency Linkages." Legislative Studies Quarterly 1 (Aug.): 315–30.

NEEDLER, M. (1968) Latin American Politics in Perspective. Rev. ed. New York: Van Nostrand.

NELSON, D. N. (1975) "Citizen Participation in Romania: The People's Council Deputy." Prepared for delivery at the Annual Meeting of the American Political Science Association, San Francisco, Calif., Sept. 2–5, 1975.

NEUSTADT, R. (1960) Presidential Power: The Politics of Leadership. New York: Wiley.

NGUYEN, T. M. (1962) "Electioneering: Vietnamese Style." Asian Survey 2 (Nov.): 11–18.

NORTON, P. (1976) "Dissent in Committee: Intra-Party Dissent in Commons Standing Committees, 1959–1974." The Parliamentarian 57 (Jan.): 15–25.

NOUSIANINEN, J. (1971) The Finnish Political System. Cambridge, Mass.: Harvard Univ. Press.

OBLER, J. (1973a) "The Role of National Party Leaders in the Selection of Parliamentary Candidates: The Belgian Case." Comparative Politics 5 (Jan.): 157–84.

———(1973b) "The Regulation of Linguistic Conflict in Brussels." Prepared for delivery at the Annual Meeting of the American Political Science Association, New Orleans, La., Sept. 4–8, 1973.

OCAYA-LAKIDI, D. (1975) "The Uganda Parliament and Land Reform." A paper prepared for delivery at the Conference on Legislatures in Contemporary Society, Albany, N.Y., Jan. 1975.

OGUL, M. S. (1976) Congress Oversees the Bureaucracy: Studies in Legislative Supervision. Pittsburgh, Pa.: Univ. of Pittsburgh Press.

OLSON, K. G. (1967) "The Service Function of the United States Congress." In Congress: The First Branch of Government, ed. A. de Grazia. Garden City, N.Y.: Doubleday.

ORFIELD, G. (1975) Congressional Power: Congress and Social Change. New York: Harcourt Brace, Jovanovich.

ORNSTEIN, N. H., and D. W. ROHDE (1976) "Shifting Forces, Changing Rules, and Political Outcomes: The Impact of Congressional Change on Four House Committees." Prepared for delivery at the Symposium on Legislative Reform and Public Policy, Univ. of Neb., Lincoln, March 11–12, 1976.

PACKENHAM, R. A. (1970) "Legislatures and Political Development." In Legislatures in Developmental Perspective, ed. A. Kornberg and L. Musolf. Durham, N.C.: Duke Univ. Press.

———(1971) "Functions of the Brazilian National Congress." In Latin American Legislatures: Their Role and Influence, ed. W. H. Agor. New York:Praeger.

PALMER, A. (1972) "The Select Committee on Science and Technology." In the Backbencher and Parliament, ed. D. Leonard and V. Herman. London: St. Martin's.

PARKER, G. R. (1973) "Political Beliefs about the Structure of Government: Congress and the Presidency." Prepared for delivery at the annual meeting of the American Political Science Association, New Orleans, La., Sept. 1973.

PASQUET, D. (1967) "An Essay on the Origins of the House of Commons." In Origins of the English Parliament, ed. P. Spufford. London: Longmans.

PATTERSON, S. C., and G. R. BOYNTON (1974) "Citizens, Leaders, and Legislators: Perspectives on Support for the American Legislature." Sage Research Papers in the Social Sciences (Comparative Legislative Studies Series, No. 90–014). Beverly Hills, Calif., and London: Sage Publications.

———, G. R. BOYNTON, and R. D. HEDLUND (1969) "Perceptions and Expectations of the Legislature and Support for It." American Journal of Sociology 75 (July): 62–76.

———, J. C. WAHLKE, and G. R. BOYNTON (1973) "Dimensions of Support for Legislative Systems." In Legislatures in Comparative Perspective, ed. A. Kornberg. New York: David McKay.

PAYNE, J. L. (1971) "The Colombian Congress." In Comparative Legislative Systems, ed. H. Hirsch and M. D. Hancock. New York: Free Press.

PEMPEL, T. J. (1974) "The Bureaucratization of Policy-Making in Postwar Japan." American Journal of Political Science 18 (Nov.): 647–63.

PESONEN, P. (1972) "Political Parties in the Finnish Eduskunta." In Comparative Legislative Behavior: Frontiers of Research, ed. S. C. Patterson and J. C. Wahlke. New York: Wiley.

PETERSON, P. (1970) "Brazil." In Political Systems of Latin America, ed. M. Needler. New York: Van Nostrand.

PICKLES, D. (1972) The Government and Politics of France. London: Methuen.

PIPER, J. R. (1974) "Backbench Rebellion, Party Government and Consensus Politics: The Case of the Parliamentary Labour Party, 1966–1970." Parliamentary Affairs 27 (Autumn): 384–96.

POLE, J. R. (1966) Political Representation in England and the Origins of the American Republic. Berkeley: Univ. of Calif. Press.

POLSBY, N. W. (1971) Congress and the Presidency. 2nd ed. Englewood Cliffs, N.J.: Prentice-Hall.

———(1975) "Legislatures." In Handbook of Political Science, vol. 5, ed. F. I. Greenstein and N. W. Polsby. Reading, Mass.: Addison-Wesley.

PRESTHUS, R. (1971) "Interest Groups in the Canadian Parliament: Activities, Interactions, Legitimacy, and Influence." Canadian Journal of Political Science 4 (Dec.): 444–60.

PUTNAM, R. D. (1972) "The Political Attitudes of Senior Civil Servants in Western Europe: A Preliminary Report." Prepared for delivery at the Annual Meeting of the American Political Science Association, Washington, D.C., Sept. 1972.

PYE, L. W. (1958) "The Non-Western Political Process." Journal of Politics 20 (Aug.): 468–86.

PYNE, P. (1973) "The Role of Congress in the Ecuadorian Political System and Its Contribution to the Overthrow of President Velasco Ibarra in 1961." Occasional Paper No. 7 of the Institute of Latin-American Studies, Univ. of Glasgow, Scotland.

RASHIDUZZAMAN, M. (1969–70). "The National Assembly of Pakistan Under the 1962 Constitution." Pacific Affairs 42 (Winter): 481–93.

RIGGS, F. W. (1973) "Legislative Structures: Some Thoughts on Elected National

Assemblies." In Legislatures in Comparative Perspective, ed. A. Kornberg. New York: David McKay.

RIPLEY, R. B. (1967) Party Leaders in the House of Representatives. Washington, D.C.: The Brookings Institution.

———, and G. A. FRANKLIN (1976) Congress, The Bureaucracy, and Public Policy. Homewood, Ill.: Dorsey.

ROSE, J. (1972) "Questions in the House." In The Backbencher and Parliament, ed. D. Leonard and V. Herman. London: St. Martin's.

ROSE, R. (1974) Politics in England. 2nd ed. Boston: Little, Brown.

ROURKE, F. E. (1969) Bureaucracy, Politics, and Public Policy. Boston: Little, Brown.

ROUYER, A. R. (1971) Political Recruitment in Kenya: The Legislative Elite, 1957–1968. Ph.D. dissertation, Tulane Univ., New Orleans, La.

RUECKERT, G., and W. CRANE (1962) "CDU Deviancy in the German Bundestag." Journal of Politics 24 (Aug.): 477–88.

SAIDI, W. (1976) "Zambia: Parliament and the Party." The Parliamentarian 57 (Jan.): 26–29.

SALOMA, J. S. (1969) Congress and the New Politics. Boston: Little, Brown.

SARTORI, G. (1961) "Parliamentarians in Italy." International Social Science Journal 13, no. 4: 583–99.

———(1975) "Will Democracy Kill Democracy? Decision-Making by Majorities and by Committees." Government and Opposition 10 (Spring): 131–58.

SAYEED, K. B. (1967) The Political System of Pakistan. Lahore: Oxford Univ. Press.

SCHER, S. (1963) "Conditions for Legislative Control." Journal of Politics 25 (Aug.): 526–40.

SCHLESINGER, J. A. (1966) Ambition and Politics: Political Careers in the United States. Chicago: Rand McNally.

SCHLETH, U., and M. PINTO-DUSCHINSKY (1970) "Why Public Subsidies Have Become the Major Sources of Party Funds in West Germany, but Not in Great Britain." In Comparative Political Finance, ed. A. J. Heidenheimer. Lexington, Mass.: D. C. Heath.

SCHMITT, K. M. (1971) "Congressional Campaigning in Mexico: A View from the Provinces." In Comparative Legislative Behavior, ed. H. Hirsch and M. D. Hancock. New York: Free Press.

SCHMITTER, P. C. (1971) Interest Conflict and Political Change in Brazil. Stanford, Calif.: Stanford Univ. Press.

SCHULZ, A. T. (1969) Recruitment and Behavior of Iranian Legislators: The Influence of Social Backgrounds. Ph.D. dissertation, Yale Univ., New Haven, Conn.

SCHWARZ, J. E., and L. E. SHAW (1976) The United States Congress in Comparative Perspective. Hinsdale, Ill.: Dryden Press.

SCOTT, A., and M. HUNT (1966) Congress and Lobbies: Image and Reality. Chapel Hill: Univ. of N.C. Press.

SCOTT, R. (1964) Mexican Government in Transition. Urbana: Univ. of Ill. Press.

SEIBERT, R. F. (1969) "Changes in the Socio-Economic Composition of the Philippine House of Representatives (1946–1965) as Indicators of Political Development." Ph.D. dissertation, Tulane Univ., New Orleans, La.

SELIGMAN, L. G. (1971) "Political Recruitment and Political Risk in Developing Systems." Prepared for delivery at the Shambaugh Conference on Legislatures in Developing Countries, Iowa City, Nov. 1971.

———(1975) "Political Risk and Legislative Behavior in Non-Western Countries." In Legislative Systems in Developing Countries, ed. G. R. Boynton and C. L. Kim. Durham, N.C.: Duke Univ. Press.

SHAKDHER, S. L. (1967) "Administrative Accountability to Parliament in India." The Parliamentarian (July): 133–40.

SHAW, M. (1978) "Committees in Legislatures." In Comparative Committees, ed. J. Lees and M. Shaw. Durham, N.C.: Duke Univ. Press.

SHEE, P. K. (1971) "The People's Action Party of Singapore 1954–1970: A Study in Survivalism of a Single-Dominant Party." Ph.D. dissertation, Indiana Univ., Bloomington.

SINGHVI, L. M. (1970) "Parliament in the Indian Political System." In Legislatures in Developmental Perspective, ed. A. Kornberg and L. Musolf. Durham, N.C.: Duke Univ. Press.

SISSON, R. (1973) "Comparative Legislative Institutionalization: A Theoretical Exploration." In Legislatures in Comparative Perspective, ed. A Kornberg. New York: David McKay.

———, and L. L. SHRADER (1977) "Social Representation and Political Integration in an Indian State: The Legislative Dimension." In Legislatures in Plural Societies, ed. A. Eldridge. Durham, N.C.: Duke Univ. Press.

———, and L. M. SNOWISS (1975) "Legislative Viability and Political Development." Prepared for delivery at the Conference on Legislatures and Development, Carmel, Calif., Aug. 1975.

STAUFFER, R. B. (1970) "Congress in the Philippine Political System." In Legislatures in Developmental Perspective, ed. A Kornberg and L. Musolf. Durham, N.C.: Duke Univ. Press.

———(1975) "The Philippine Congress: Causes of Structural Change." Sage Research Papers in the Social Sciences (Comparative Legislative Studies Series, No. 90–024). Beverly Hills, Calif., and London: Sage Publications.

STORING, J. A. (1963) Norwegian Democracy. Boston: Houghton Mifflin.

STULTZ, N. W. (1969) "Parliament in a Tutelary Democracy: A Recent Case in Kenya." Journal of Politics 31 (Feb.): 95–118.

———(1970) "The National Assembly in the Politics of Kenya." In Legislatures in Developmental Perspective, ed. A. Kornberg and L. Musolf. Durham, N.C.: Duke Univ. Press.

STYSKAL, R. A. (1967) "Strategies of Influence Among Members of Three Voluntary Associations in the Philippines." Ph.D. dissertation, Univ. of Ore., Eugene.

———(1975) "Some Aspects of Group Representation in the Philippine Congress." In Legislative Systems in Developing Countries, ed. G. R. Boynton and C. L. Kim. Durham, N.C.: Duke Univ. Press.

TACHERON, D. G., and M. D. UDALL (1966) The Job of the Congressman. Indianapolis, Ind.: Bobbs-Merrill

TSUNEISHI, W. M. (1966) Japanese Political Style. New York: Harper and Row.

TUNSIRI, V. (1971) "The Social Background and the Legislative Recruitment of the Thai Members of Parliament and Their Political Consequences." Ph.D. dissertation, Ind. Univ., Bloomington.

VALENZUELA, A., and A. WILDE (1975) "The Congress and Chilean Democracy." Prepared for delivery at the Conference on Legislatures and Development, Carmel, Calif., Aug. 1975.

VANNEMAN, J. P. (1972) "The Supreme Soviet of the U.S.S.R.: Politics and the Legislative Process in the Soviet System." Ph.D. dissertation, Pa. State Univ., University Park, Pa.

VERNER, J. G. (1969) "Correlates of Participation in the Guatemalan National Congress." Ph.D. dissertation, Univ. of Kansas, Lawrence.

———(1971) "The Guatemalan National Congress: An Elite Analysis." In Latin American Legislatures: Their Role and Influence, ed. W. H. Agor. New York: Praeger.

VON NORDHEIM, M., and TAYLOR, R. W. (1976) "The Significance of Lobbyist-Legislator Interactions in German State Parliaments." Legislative Studies Quarterly 1 (Nov.): 511–32.

WAHLKE, J. C. (1971) "Policy Demands and System Support: The Role of the Represented." British Journal of Political Science 1 (July): 271–90.

———, H. EULAU, W. BUCHANAN, and W. FERGUSON (1962) The Legislative System. New York: Wiley.

WALKER, J. W. (1952) "Question Time in Canada." Parliamentary Affairs 5 (Autumn):461–68.

WALLERSTEIN, I. (1965) "Elites in French-Speaking West Africa: The Social Basis of Ideas." Journal of Modern African Studies 3 (May): 1–34.

WATSON, G. G. (1971) Recruitment and Representation: A Study of the Social Background and Political Career Patterns of Members of the West German Bundestag, 1949–1969. Ph.D. dissertation, Univ. of Fla., Gainesville.

WEINBAUM, M. G. (1971) "Toward a Classification of Legislative Systems: Its Application and Implications for Developing Nations." Prepared for delivery at the Shambaugh Conferences on Legislatures in Developing Countries, Iowa City, Nov. 1971.

———(1972) "Afghanistan: Non-Party Parliamentary Democracy." Journal of Developing Areas 7 (Oct.): 57–74.

———(1975) "Classification and Change in Legislative Systems: With Particular Application to Iran, Turkey, and Afghanistan." In Legislative Systems in Developing Countries, ed. G. R. Boynton and C. L. Kim. Durham, N.C.: Duke Univ. Press.

———(1977) "The Legislator as Intermediary: Integration of the Center and Periphery in Afghanistan." In Legislatures in Plural Societies, ed. A. F. Eldridge. Durham, N.C.: Duke Univ. Press.

WEINER, M. (1962) The Politics of Scarcity. Chicago: Univ. of Chicago Press.

WHEARE, K. C. (1963) Legislatures. London: Oxford Univ. Press.

WHEELER, R. S. (1970) The Politics of Pakistan. Ithaca, N.Y.: Cornell Univ. Press.

WILDAVSKY, A. (1964) The Politics of the Budgetary Process. Boston: Little, Brown.

WILLIAMS, P. M. (1964) Crisis and Compromise: Politics in the Fourth Republic. Hamden, Conn.: Archon Books.

———(1968) The French Parliament: Politics in the Fifth Republic. New York: Praeger.

WILSON, F. L., and R. WISTE, (1976) "Party Cohesion in the French National Assembly." Legislative Studies Quarterly 1 (Nov.): 467–90.

WINDER, R. B. (1962) "Syrian Deputies and Cabinet Ministers, 1919–1959, Part I." Middle East Journal 16 (Autumn): 407–29.

———(1963) "Syrian Deputies and Cabinet Ministers, 1919–1959, Part II." Middle East Journal 17 (Winter-Spring): 35–54.

ZARISKI, R. (1972) Italy: The Politics of Uneven Development. Hinsdale, Ill.: Dryden Press.

ZEIGLER, H. (1971) "The Effects of Lobbying: A Comparative Assessment." In Comparative Legislative Systems, ed. H. Hirsch and M. D. Hancock. New York: Free Press.

INDEX